Francis Frith's

Wiltshire Living Memories

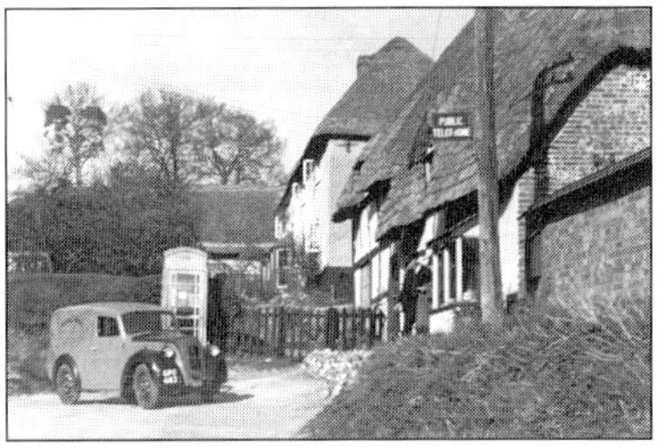

Photographic Memories

Francis Frith's

Wiltshire Living Memories

Tony Cornish

FRITH BOOK Co

First published in the United Kingdom in 2000 by
Frith Book Company Ltd

Hardback Edition 2000
ISBN 1-85937-245-7

Reprinted in Hardback 2001
ISBN 1-85937-245-7

Paperback Edition 2001
ISBN 1-85937-396-8

British Library Cataloguing in Publication Data

Francis Frith's Wiltshire Living Memories
Tony Cornish

Frith Book Company Ltd
Frith's Barn, Teffont,
Salisbury, Wiltshire SP3 5QP
Tel: +44 (0) 1722 716 376
Email: info@francisfrith.co.uk
www.francisfrith.co.uk

Printed and bound in Great Britain

As with any historical database the Frith archive is constantly being corrected and improved and the publishers would welcome information on omissions or inaccuracies

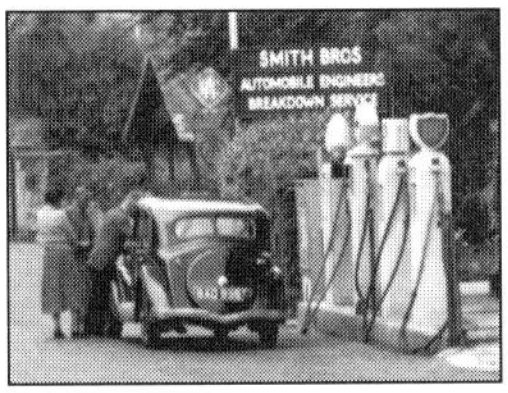

Contents

Francis Frith: *Victorian Pioneer*

FRANCIS FRITH, Victorian founder of the world-famous photographic archive, was a complex and multi-talented man. A devout Quaker and a highly successful Victorian businessman, he was both philosophic by nature and pioneering in outlook.

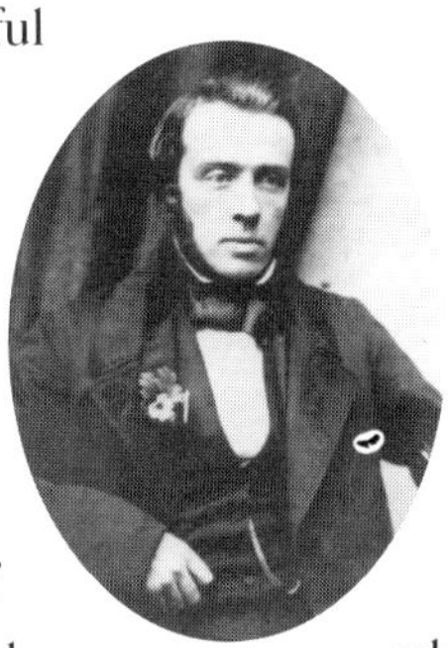

By 1855 Francis Frith had already established a wholesale grocery business in Liverpool, and sold it for the astonishing sum of £200,000, which is the equivalent today of over £15,000,000. Now a multi-millionaire, he was able to indulge his passion for travel. As a child he had pored over travel books written by early explorers, and his fancy and imagination had been stirred by family holidays to the sublime mountain regions of Wales and Scotland. 'What a land of spirit-stirring and enriching scenes and places!' he had written. He was to return to these scenes of grandeur in later years to 'recapture the thousands of vivid and tender memories', but with a different purpose. Now in his thirties, and captivated by the new science of photography, Frith set out on a series of pioneering journeys to the Nile regions that occupied him from 1856 until 1860.

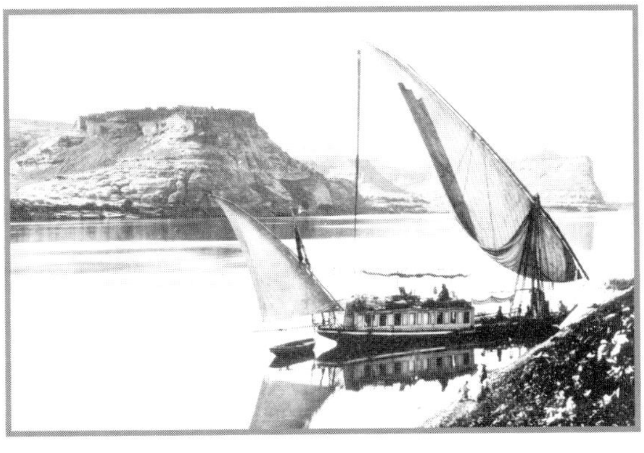

Intrigue and Adventure

He took with him on his travels a specially-designed wicker carriage that acted as both dark-room and sleeping chamber. These far-flung journeys were packed with intrigue and adventure. In his life story, written when he was sixty-three, Frith tells of being held captive by bandits, and of fighting 'an awful midnight battle to the very point of surrender with a deadly pack of hungry, wild dogs'. Sporting flowing Arab costume, Frith arrived at Akaba by camel seventy years before Lawrence, where he encountered 'desert princes and rival sheikhs, blazing with jewel-hilted swords'.

During these extraordinary adventures he was assiduously exploring the desert regions bordering the Nile and patiently recording the antiquities and peoples with his camera. He was the first photographer to venture beyond the sixth cataract. Africa was still the mysterious 'Dark Continent', and Stanley and Livingstone's historic meeting was a decade into the future. The conditions for picture taking confound belief. He laboured for hours in his wicker dark-room in the sweltering heat of the desert, while the volatile chemicals fizzed dangerously in their trays. Often he was forced to work in remote tombs and caves where conditions were cooler. Back in London he exhibited his photographs and was 'rapturously cheered' by members of the Royal Society. His reputation as a photographer was made overnight. An eminent modern historian has likened their impact on the population of the time to that on our own generation of the first photographs taken on the surface of the moon.

Venture of a Life-Time

Characteristically, Frith quickly spotted the opportunity to create a new business as a specialist publisher of photographs. He lived in an era of immense and sometimes violent change. For the poor in the early part of Victoria's reign work was a drudge and the hours long, and people had precious little free time to enjoy themselves. Most had no transport other than a cart or gig at their disposal, and had not travelled far beyond the boundaries of their own town or village. However, by the 1870s, the railways had threaded their way across the country, and Bank Holidays and half-day Saturdays had been made obligatory by Act of Parliament. All of a sudden the ordinary working man and his family were able to enjoy days out and see a little more of the world.

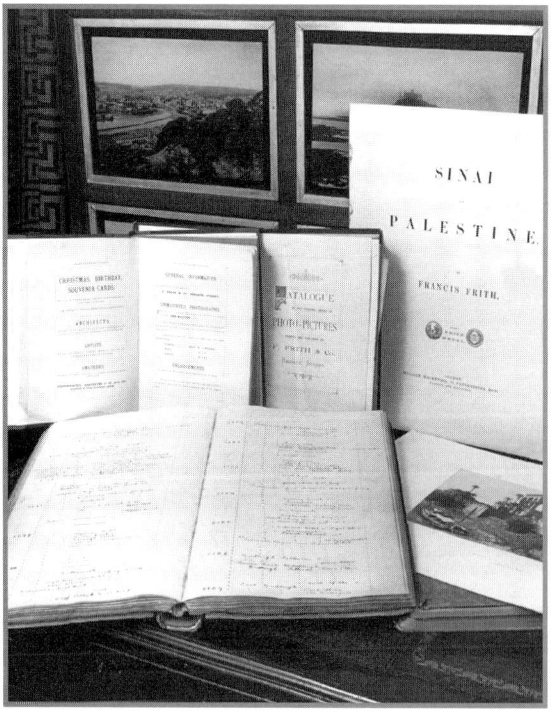

With characteristic business acumen, Francis Frith foresaw that these new tourists would enjoy having souvenirs to commemorate their days out. In 1860 he married Mary Ann Rosling and set out with the intention of photographing every city, town and village in Britain. For the next thirty years he travelled the country by train and by pony and trap, producing fine photographs of seaside resorts and beauty spots that were keenly bought by millions of Victorians. These prints were painstakingly pasted into family albums and pored over during the dark nights of winter, rekindling precious memories of summer excursions.

The Rise of Frith & Co

Frith's studio was soon supplying retail shops all over the country. To meet the demand he gathered about him a small team of photographers, and published the work of independent artist-photographers of the calibre of Roger Fenton and Francis Bedford. In order to gain some understanding of the scale of Frith's business one only has to look at the catalogue issued by Frith & Co in 1886: it runs to some 670 pages, listing not only many thousands of views of the British Isles but also many photographs of most European countries, and China, Japan, the USA and

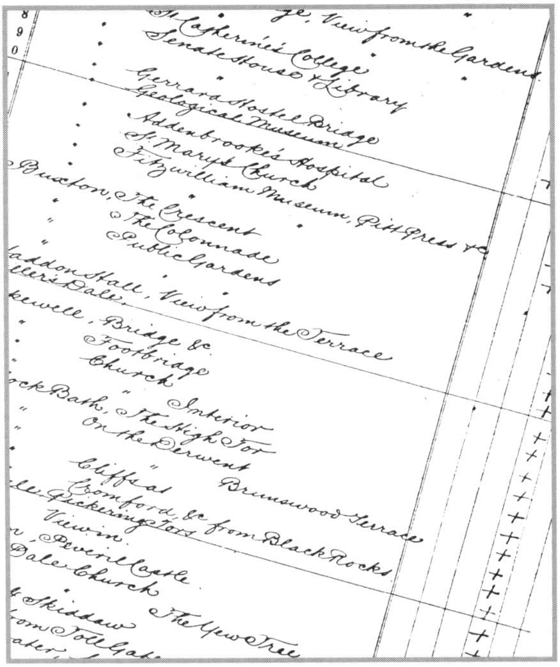

Canada – note the sample page shown above from the hand-written *Frith & Co* ledgers detailing pictures taken. By 1890 Frith had created the greatest specialist photographic publishing company in the world, with over 2,000 outlets – more than the combined number that Boots and WH Smith have today! The picture on the right shows the *Frith & Co* display board at Ingleton in the Yorkshire Dales. Beautifully constructed with mahogany frame and gilt inserts, it could display up to a dozen local scenes.

Postcard Bonanza

The ever-popular holiday postcard we know today took many years to develop. In 1870 the Post Office issued the first plain cards, with a pre-printed stamp on one face. In 1894 they allowed other publishers' cards to be sent through the mail with an attached adhesive halfpenny stamp. Demand grew rapidly, and in 1895 a new size of postcard was permitted called the court card, but there was little room for illustration. In 1899, a year after Frith's death, a new card measuring 5.5 x 3.5 inches became the standard format, but it was not until 1902 that the divided back came into being, with address and message on one face and a full-size illustration on the other. *Frith & Co* were in the vanguard of postcard development, and Frith's sons Eustace and Cyril continued their father's monumental task, expanding the number of views offered to the public and recording more and more places in Britain, as the coasts and countryside were opened up to mass travel.

Francis Frith died in 1898 at his villa in Cannes, his great project still growing. The archive he created continued in business for another seventy years. By 1970 it contained over a third of a million pictures of 7,000 cities, towns and villages. The massive photographic record Frith has left to us stands as a living monument to a special and very remarkable man.

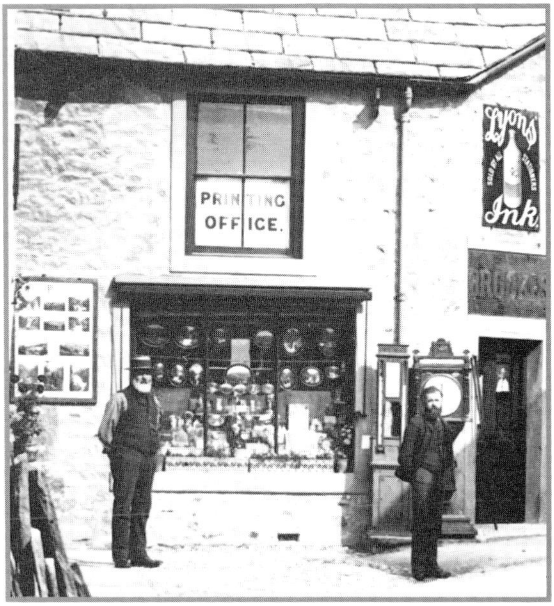

Frith's Archive: *A Unique Legacy*

FRANCIS FRITH'S legacy to us today is of immense significance and value, for the magnificent archive of evocative photographs he created provides a unique record of change in 7,000 cities, towns and villages throughout Britain over a century and more. Frith and his fellow studio photographers revisited locations many times down the years to update their views, compiling for us an enthralling and colourful pageant of British life and character.

We tend to think of Frith's sepia views of Britain as nostalgic, for most of us use them to conjure up memories of places in our own lives with which we have family associations. It often makes us forget that to Francis Frith they were records of daily life as it was actually being lived in the cities, towns and villages of his day. The Victorian age was one of great and often bewildering change for ordinary people, and though the pictures evoke an impression of slower times, life was as busy and hectic as it is today.

We are fortunate that Frith was a photographer of the people, dedicated to recording the minutiae of everyday life. For it is this sheer wealth of visual data, the painstaking chronicle of changes in dress, transport, street layouts, buildings, housing, engineering and landscape that captivates us so much today. His remarkable images offer us a powerful link with the past and with the lives of our ancestors.

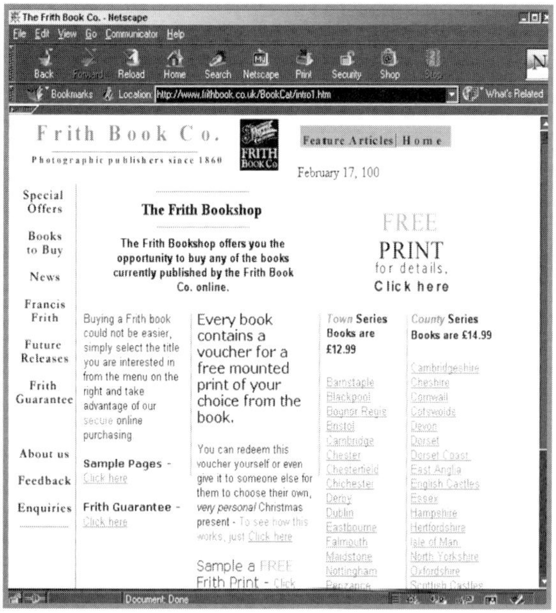

See Frith at www. frithbook.co.uk

Today's Technology

Computers have now made it possible for Frith's many thousands of images to be accessed almost instantly. In the Frith archive today, each photograph is carefully 'digitised' then stored on a CD Rom. Frith archivists can locate a single photograph amongst thousands within seconds. Views can be catalogued and sorted under a variety of categories of place and content to the immediate benefit of researchers.

Inexpensive reference prints can be created for them at the touch of a mouse button, and a wide range of books and other printed materials assembled and published for a wider, more general readership - in the next twelve months over a hundred Frith local history titles will be published! The day-to-day workings of the archive are very different from how they were in Francis Frith's time: imagine the herculean task of sorting through eleven tons of glass negatives as Frith had to do to locate a particular sequence of pictures! Yet the archive still prides itself on maintaining the same high standards of excellence laid down by Francis Frith, including the painstaking cataloguing and indexing of every view.

It is curious to reflect on how the internet now allows researchers in America and elsewhere greater instant access to the archive than Frith himself ever enjoyed. Many thousands of individual views can be called up on screen within seconds on one of the Frith internet sites, enabling people living continents away to revisit the streets of their ancestral home town, or view places in Britain where they have enjoyed holidays. Many overseas researchers welcome the chance to view special theme selections, such as transport, sports, costume and ancient monuments.

We are certain that Francis Frith would have heartily approved of these modern developments in imaging techniques, for he himself was always working at the very limits of Victorian photographic technology.

The Value of the Archive Today

Because of the benefits brought by the computer, Frith's images are increasingly studied by social historians, by researchers into genealogy and ancestory, by architects, town planners, and by teachers and schoolchildren involved in local history projects.

In addition, the archive offers every one of us an opportunity to examine the places where we and our families have lived and worked down the years. Highly successful in Frith's own era, the archive is now, a century and more on, entering a new phase of popularity.

The Past in Tune with the Future

Historians consider the Francis Frith Collection to be of prime national importance. It is the only archive of its kind remaining in private ownership and has been valued at a million pounds. However, this figure is now rapidly increasing as digital technology enables more and more people around the world to enjoy its benefits.

Francis Frith's archive is now housed in an historic timber barn in the beautiful village of Teffont in Wiltshire. Its founder would not recognize the archive office as it is today. In place of the many thousands of dusty boxes containing glass plate negatives and an all-pervading odour of photographic chemicals, there are now ranks of computer screens. He would be amazed to watch his images travelling round the world at unimaginable speeds through network and internet lines.

The archive's future is both bright and exciting. Francis Frith, with his unshakeable belief in making photographs available to the greatest number of people, would undoubtedly approve of what is being done today with his lifetime's work. His photographs, depicting our shared past, are now bringing pleasure and enlightenment to millions around the world a century and more after his death.

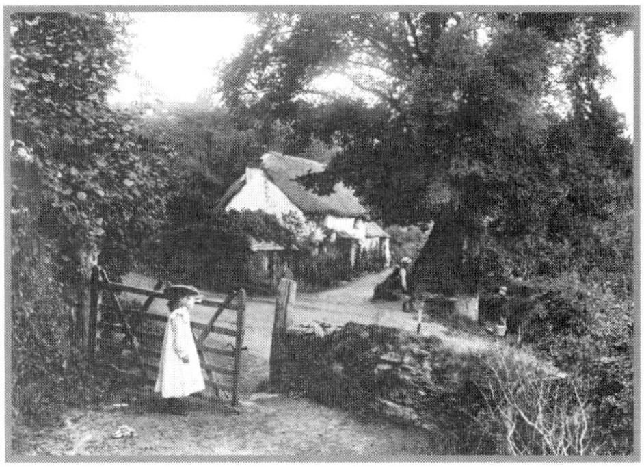

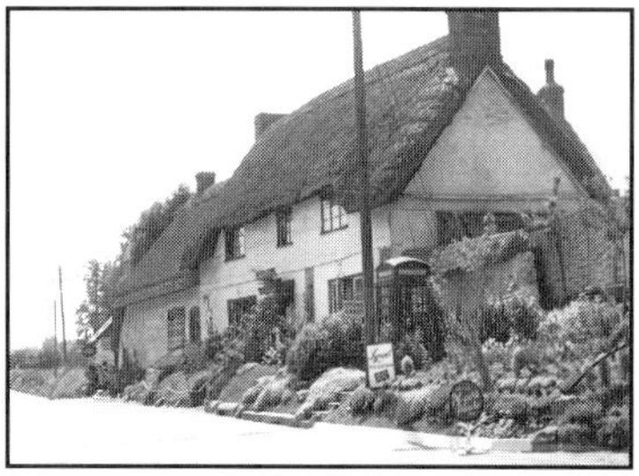

Wiltshire Living Memories
An Introduction

WILTSHIRE IS A county of contrasts. It ranges from the commercial bustle of Swindon on the M4 corridor to sleepy, thatched, archetypal English villages such as Castle Combe. Some of the towns, such as Bradford-on-Avon and Marlborough, are unique in character and manage to combine development with retention of their sense of place. It is a beautiful county, with so many surprises around so many corners. Wiltshire has undeniable antiquity as well as character. Most of the villages are listed in the Domesday Book, many feature in Anglo-Saxon records, and some can trace their roots back to the Roman period or even into the Iron Age. A surprising number have historical connections and credentials that would make many council tourism officers in other parts of the country shed tears of envy.

Wiltshire is also the source of much folklore. Even common expressions such as 'as different as chalk from cheese' find their roots here: this one refers to the difference between the county's chalk uplands and the fertile, lush dairy country.

Wiltshire is littered with the hard evidence of bygone inhabitants. The oldest, most obvious and perhaps most dramatic examples are the standing stones at Stonehenge and Avebury, and the dramatic Silbury Hill is as intriguing a site as any. The reasons for their creation remain mysterious, but perhaps this is part of their appeal. It is

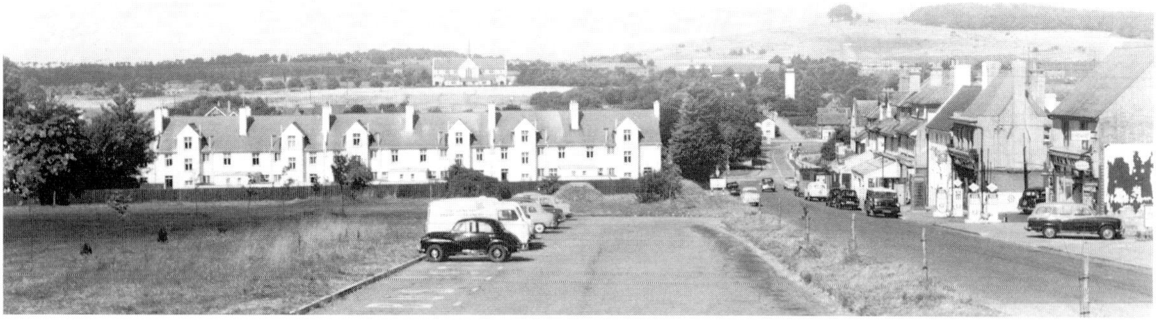

thought that some of the downland barrows are even older than these ancient monuments. Following the prehistoric era, the Romans were here in force. Vespasian conquered the area for Rome, and Roman settlements sprang up at Cunetio (Mildenhall), Sorbiodunum (Old Sarum) and Verlucio (Sandy Lane). Roman roads criss-crossed the present day county. One famous tale is of the hoard of Roman coins found in a lead coffin: the happy finder destroyed the most valuable treasure on his way to the coins - the coffin. Roman buildings have been excavated in many parts of the county; they reveal excellent evidence of the lives and times of these particular invaders.

It seems that Wiltshire has been a battle ground from time immemorial. Stories abound of battles between King Arthur and the Saxon invaders. It is thought that Mount Badon, the scene of one of his greatest victories, is sited in Wiltshire near Badbury. The Gewissas invaded from the south; they fought both the Britons and other Saxon tribes before the matter was settled by Cynric's victory at Old Sarum - his West Saxons held sway from then on. The ancient kingdom of Wessex was established; it battled its way into wider territories, mostly at the expense of neighbouring tribes. In their turn, the Anglo-Saxons had to do their share of fighting off hostile invaders, including Nordic tribes and other Saxon tribes such as the Mercians. In 877 King Alfred narrowly escaped capture by the Danes while celebrating Christmas in Chippenham. The arrival of the Normans after Harold's defeat in 1066 meant many changes. Malmesbury Abbey is perhaps one of the greatest Norman churches in England.

The English Civil war also yields its feast of history. Highworth has a battle-scarred church tower, which is said to have been damaged by Fairfax's cannon when the town was besieged. The county was the scene of a number of engagements. In 1643, Roundway Down near Devizes was the scene of the Royalist victory under Lord Wilmot. The good citizens of Marlborough, which had sided with Parliament, tried, rather unsuccessfully, to beat off an assault of Royalist cavalry. They had to flee from the burning town.

The two World Wars have left their mark in the form of memorials dotted throughout the county. Even the smallest of villages seems to have surrendered many young men to the cause - in places so small, their loss must have been even more keenly felt.

Industry has also changed over many years. In medieval times and before, the economy was essentially agricultural. The forests stretched over far more of the county than they ever would again, and forest villages extracted their livings from them. Being land-locked, the county had no sea-port to facilitate trade, but Wiltshire does

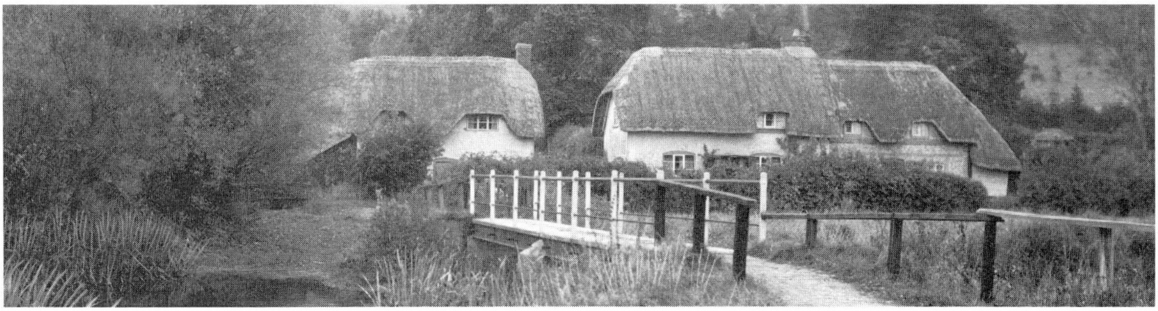

straddle trade routes to and from major conurbations such as London. Early entrepreneurs quickly recognised the possible benefits of interrupting the flow of pigs from South Wales to London while the animals were early into their journey - and so much fatter! The meat-curing business in Calne sprang up from this; it once employed many people. Much of the county's industry was centred around the weaving of broadcloth and other types of fabric. Wiltshire's textile industry has now declined, but the county once had an enviable reputation for quality. There were even types of cloth named after their place of origin, such as the distinctive red and white 'Castlecombe'. The arrival of the railway yards around Swindon in the 19th century produced a population explosion there, and a dramatic shift away from the rural economy that had largely prevailed until then. The yards have gone now, but the M4 corridor contains many thriving modern businesses.

Considering that the county seems to have more than its fair share of beautiful locations, the film industry was sure not to keep away for long. Castle Combe was subject to a Hollywood invasion which seemed at one point to threaten the village's future. 'The Story of Dr Dolittle' was filmed here, and parts of the By Brook were turned into a fishing village (complete with seven boats) and plastic cobbles were laid. Rex Harrison and Anthony Newley were in the village every day. At least the villagers had the chance to be extras at 50s per day, meals and clothes included.

Wiltshire is a county of 1344 square miles, and the 1991 census listed its population as 573,000. At the beginning of the 20th century, the population was 273,869. Although some parts of the county have grown considerably in population, many of the rural parts remain much as they ever were.

Alongside the tales of Roman treasure troves, King Arthur, King Alfred, stone henges and great battles, it would be impossible not to give some mention to the 'normal' Wiltshire folk and how they got their nickname of 'moonrakers'. On the night of a full moon, some Bishops Cannings men were busily smuggling illicit kegs of brandy in a wagon load of hay when they heard the sound of approaching excise men. Quick as they could, they extracted the kegs and threw them into a nearby pond. The excise men were put off, but not fooled - they left, but doubled back to discover the smugglers attempting to recover the submerged kegs with hay rakes. When asked what they were doing, the smugglers indicated the clear reflection of the moon and uttered something like 'Zomebody 'ave lost thic thur cheese and we'm a-rakin for un in thic thur pond'. The excise men smiled at the simpletons and left. The moonrakers smiled at the simpletons and did the same - with the brandy.

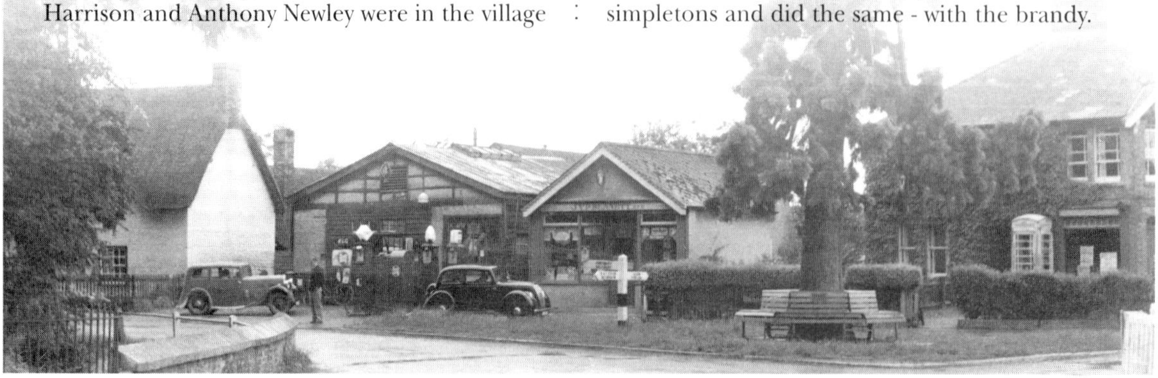

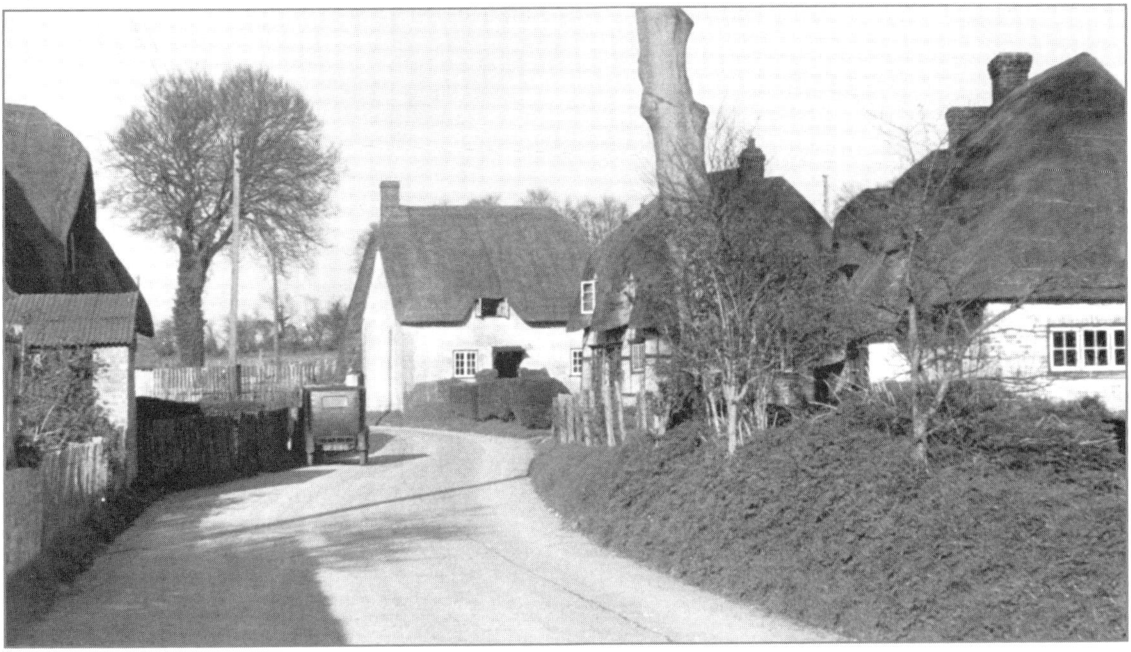

Ablington, The Village c1950 A330003
The large tree has disappeared, but the village remains much as seen here except for the corrugated porch on the right; this has been replaced, mercifully, by a thatched one. The name of the village derives from the Saxon tun (settlement) of Ealdbeald. The village was Alboldintone in the Domesday Book.

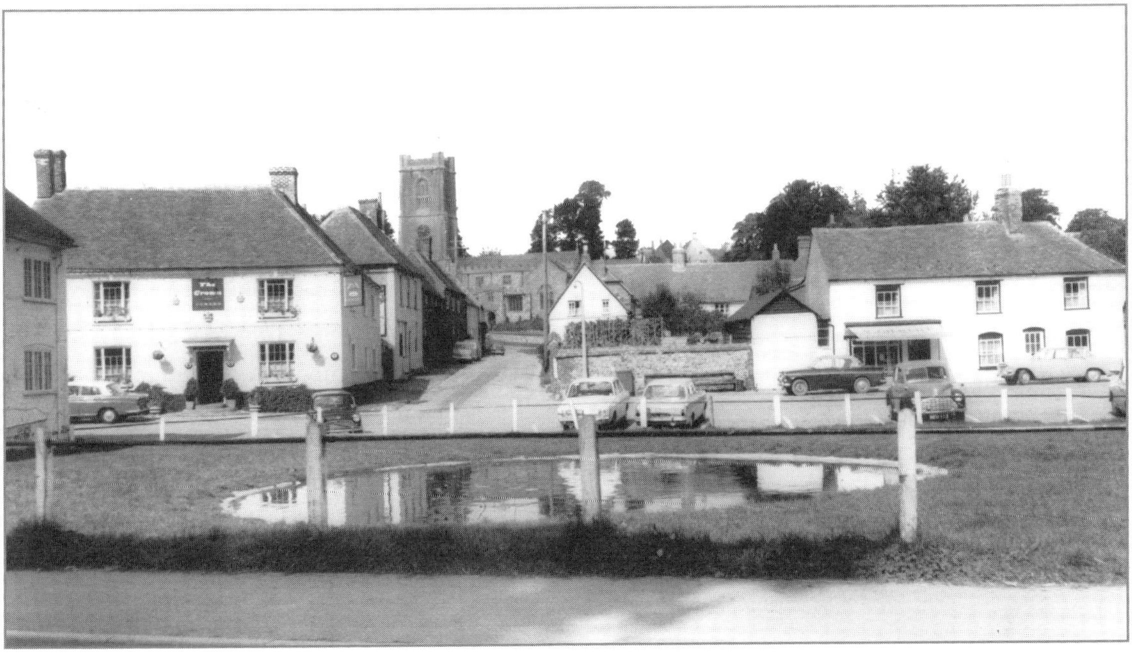

Aldbourne, The Village c1965 A101012
The village name comes from the Saxon burna (stream) of Ealda; it was Aldeborne in the Domesday Book. The church tower in the centre is St Michael's; the church is famed for having the largest Norman doorway of any Wiltshire parish church.

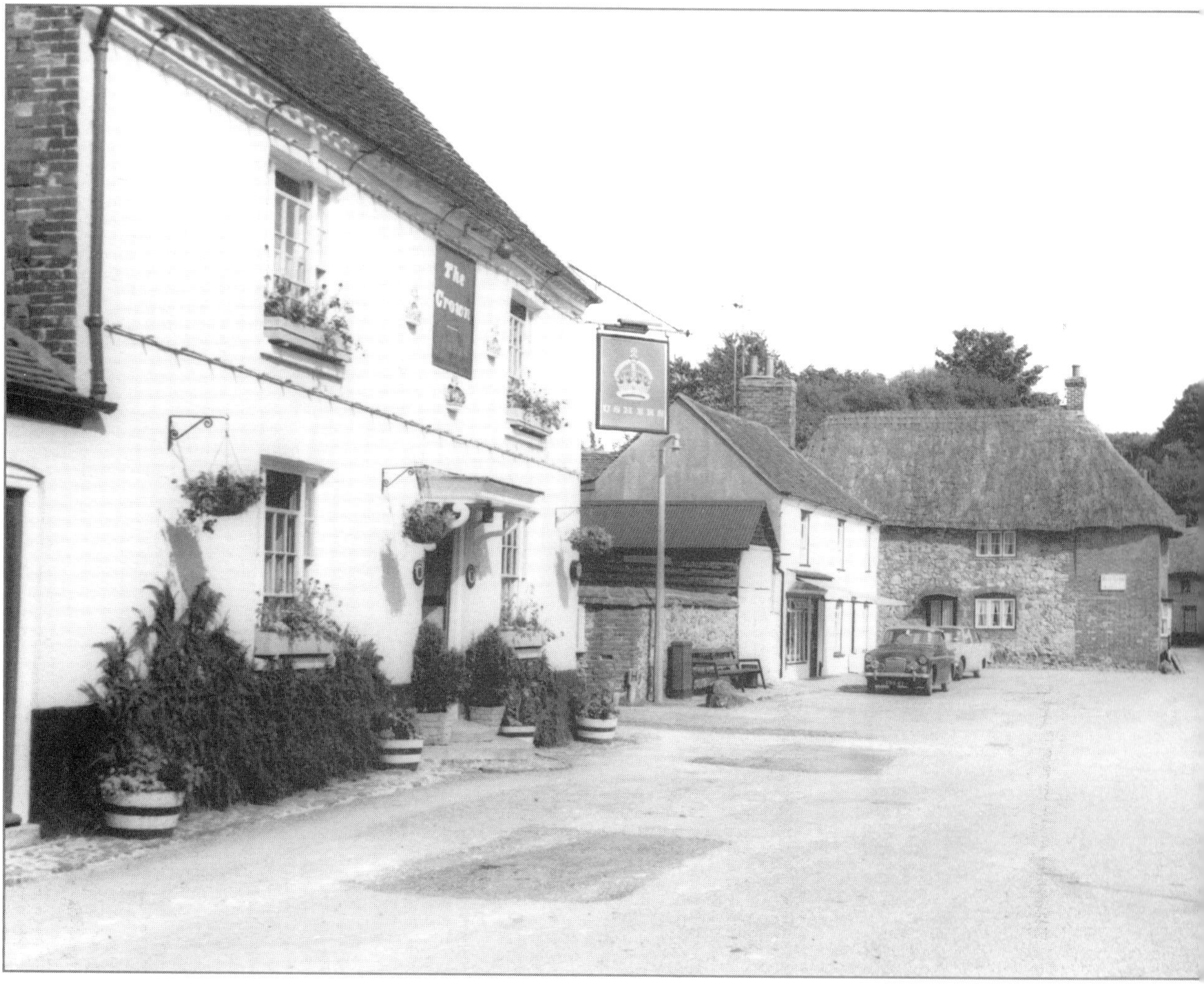

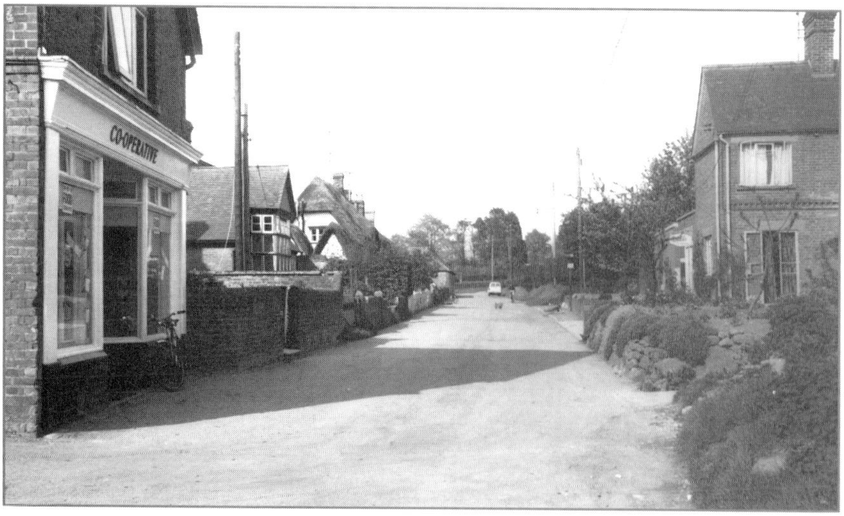

All Cannings
The Street c1965

A142001

The village is situated in a peaceful spot off the Patney Road. It has more recently won Best Kept Village awards for 1985, 1988 and 1993. Note the Co-operative store on the left.

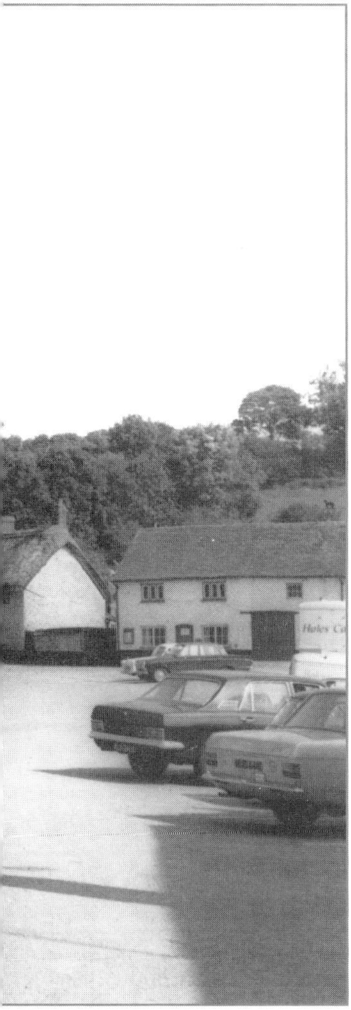

Aldbourne
The Village c1965
A101017

The village was famous for its bell-making industry, which made bells for many Wiltshire churches and beyond. Here we can see the Crown, an Ushers pub, and the Blue Bear beyond.

All Cannings
The Village c1965
A142009

The church tower, to the left and beyond the washing line, is that of All Saints; it can be seen from some distance around. The church has some Norman features, but is essentially 14th-century, with a 15th-century tower and transepts.

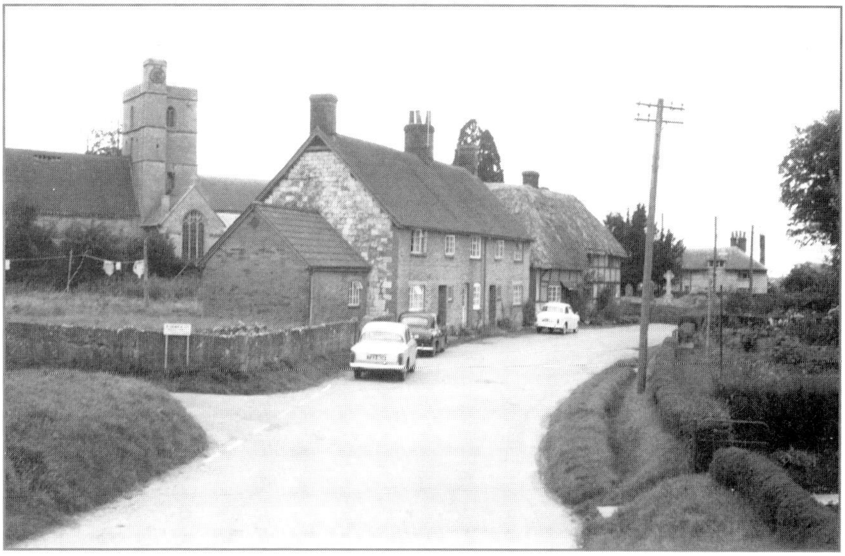

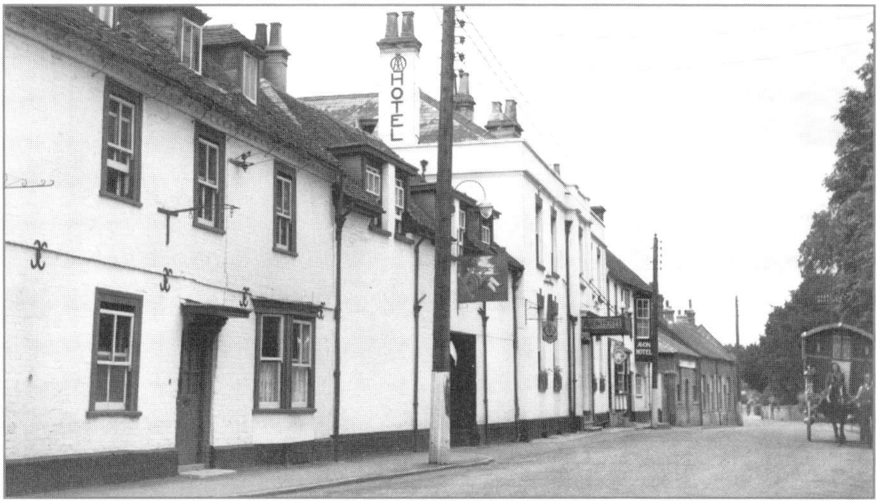

Amesbury
Church Street c1950
A143026

The village's name comes from the Saxon burg (fort) and possibly Ambre, a personal name. Some historians have connected the name with Ambrosius, the Dark Age Welsh hero; Arthur's Guinevere is reputed to have retired to a monastery here. Note the Avon Hotel on the left, and the charming gypsy caravan on the right.

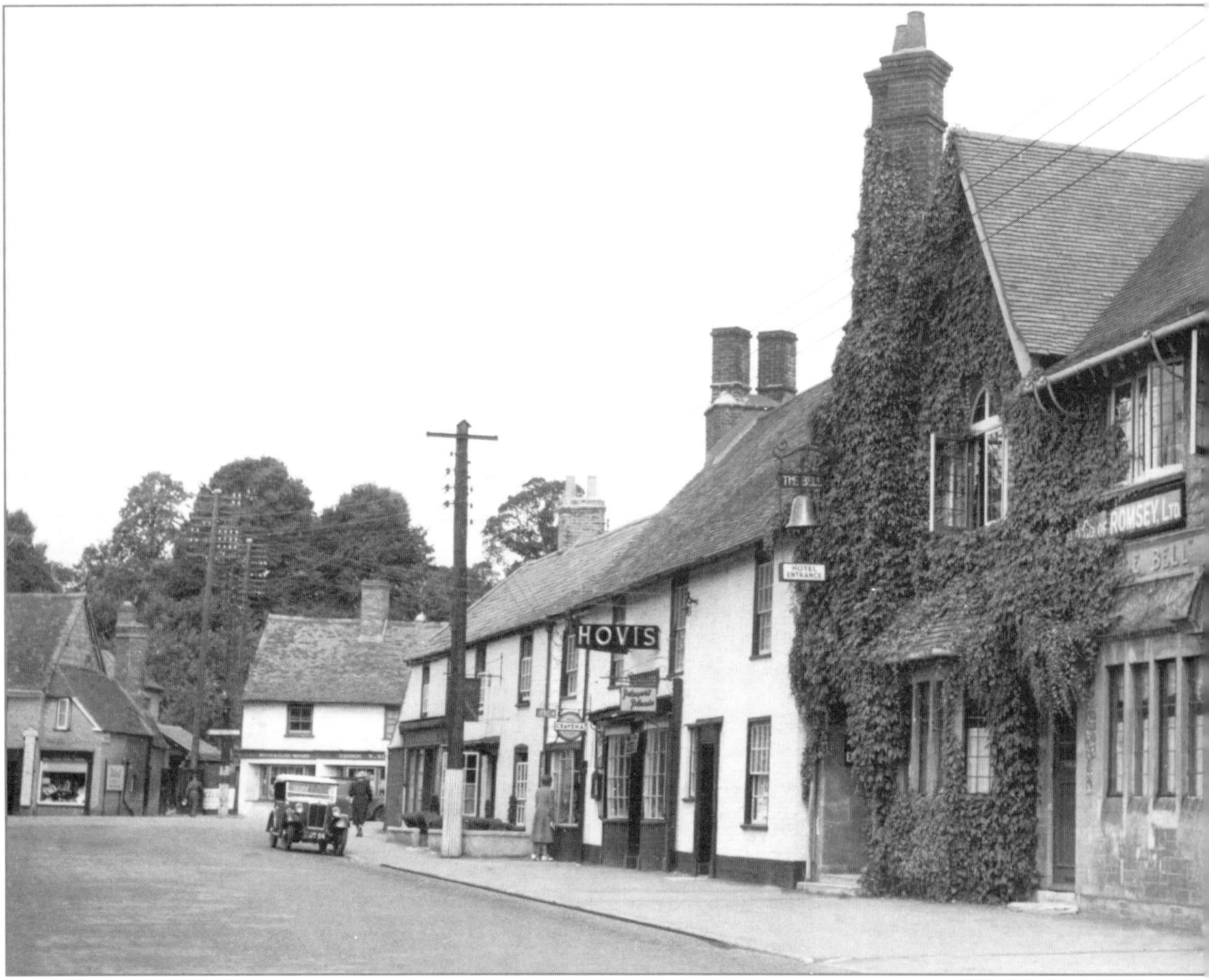

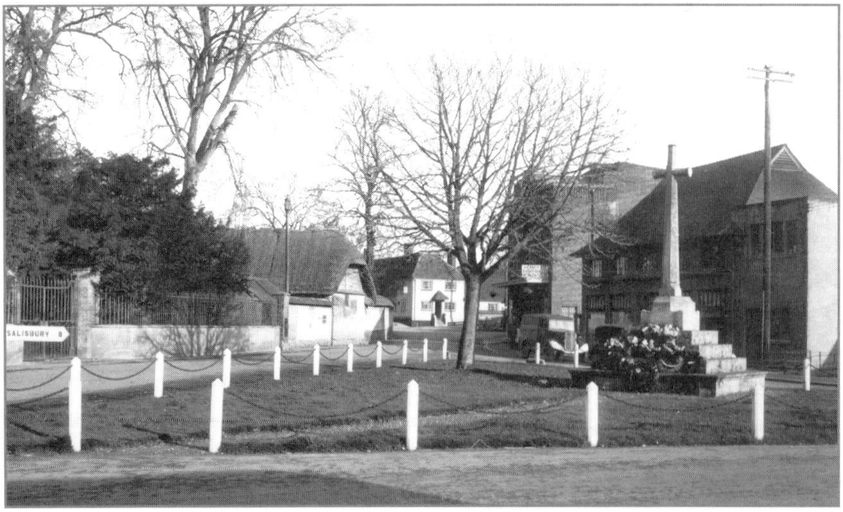

Amesbury
The War Memorial
c1950 A143015

Amesbury is primarily an agriculturally-based community, but its c6,000 inhabitants also depend on the nearby defence establishments and Salisbury to make their living.

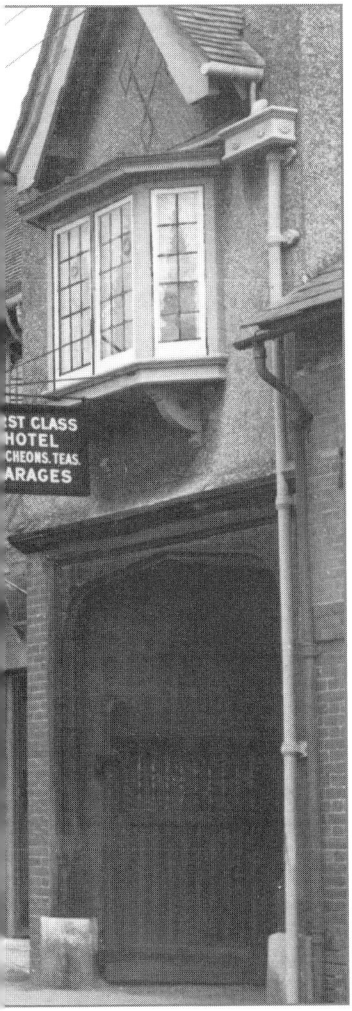

Amesbury, Salisbury Street c1950 A143022

The village lies equi-distant from Stonehenge and Woodhenge, with a legendary connection to King Arthur. It is said that it is here that Arthur said to Guinevere after she fled the court: 'But hither shall I never come again. See thee no more. Farewell'. Note the Bell Hotel, a 'First Class Hotel' no less, on the right, and the Hovis sign over the shop in the centre.

Ashton Keynes, Church Walk with Mill House and the River Thames c1955

A144305

This is a lovely village with the River Thames flowing through it. Many houses only connect to the roads by way of footbridges. King Alfred gave the manor to his daughter Aelfgifu. The name comes from the Saxon aesc (ash tree) and tun (settlement). The Keynes is from Henry Kaignel, who was named as owner of the village in 1242.

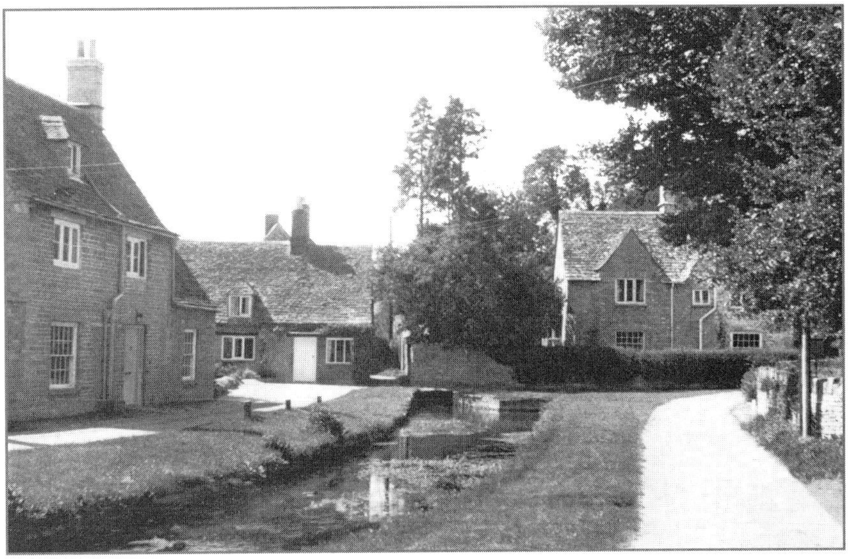

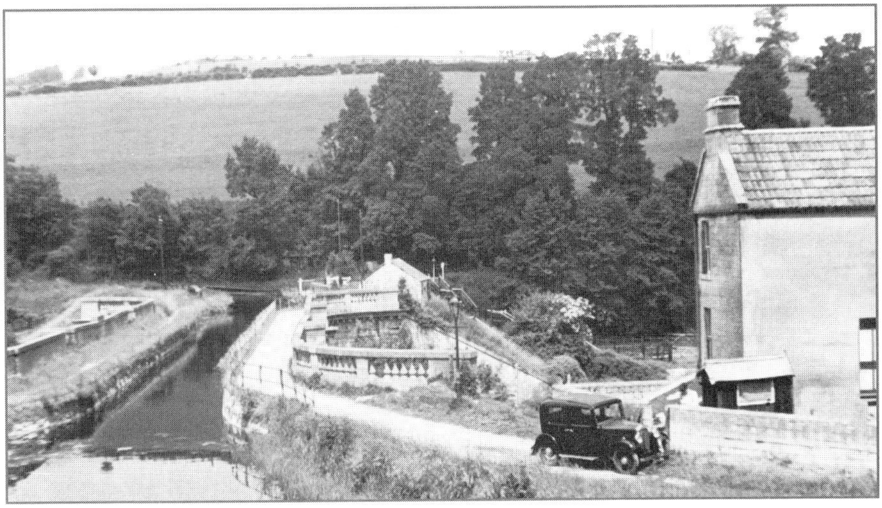

Avoncliff The Aqueduct c1950

A329012

Part of the Kennet and Avon Canal on its way to Bath, this 57-mile-long feat of engineering joins the Rivers Kennet and Avon. Designed and engineered by John Rennie, it was completed in 1810.

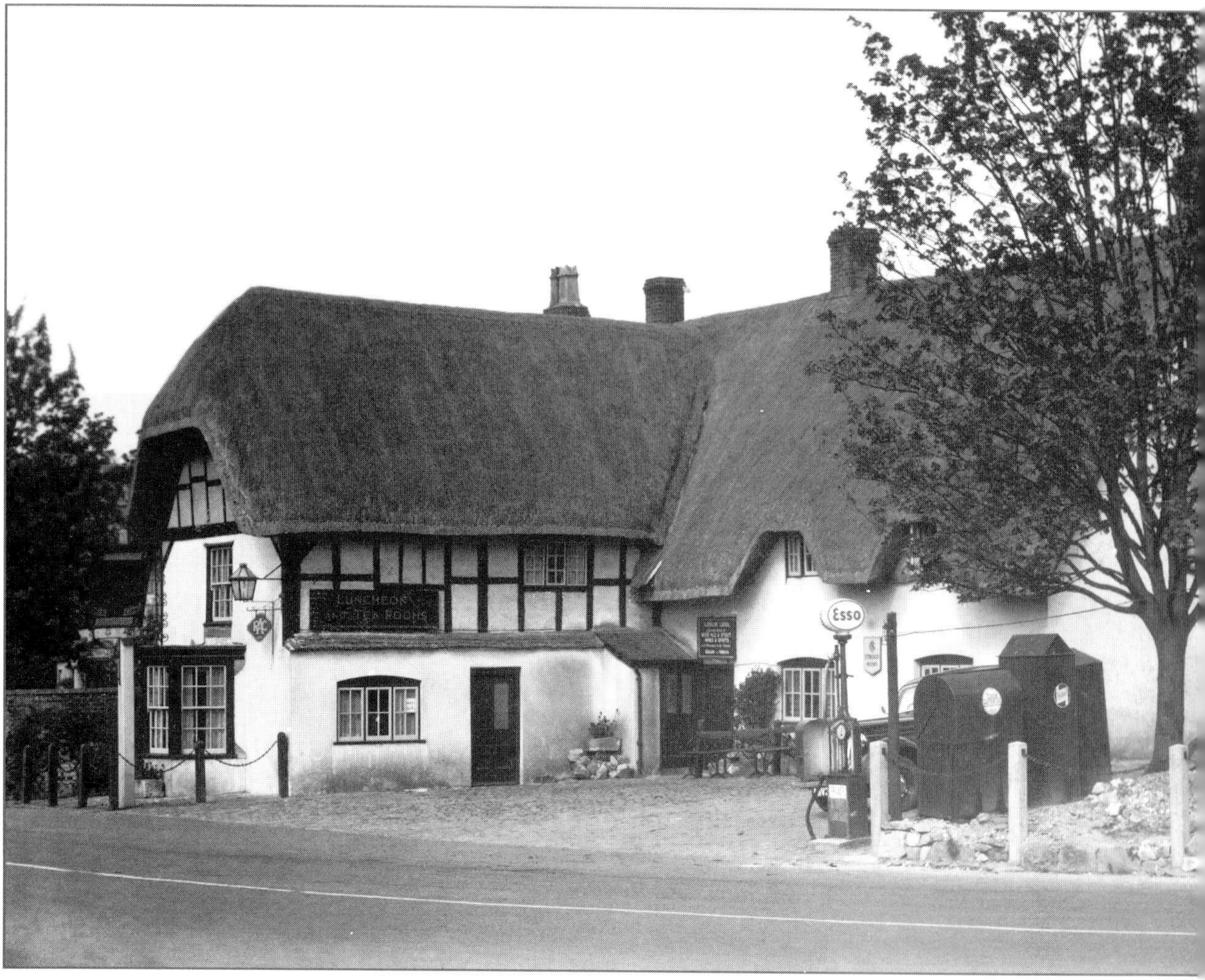

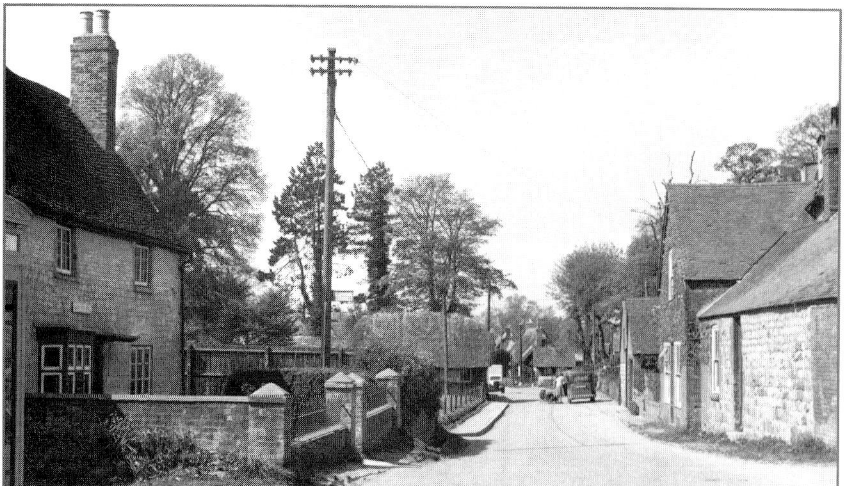

◄ **Avebury, High Street c1950** A80008
In the 18th century, many of the standing stones were broken up and used as boundary markers; they were also integrated into many cottage walls. Evidence of this can still be seen by the observant. The name comes from the Saxon 'Affa's burg' (fort).

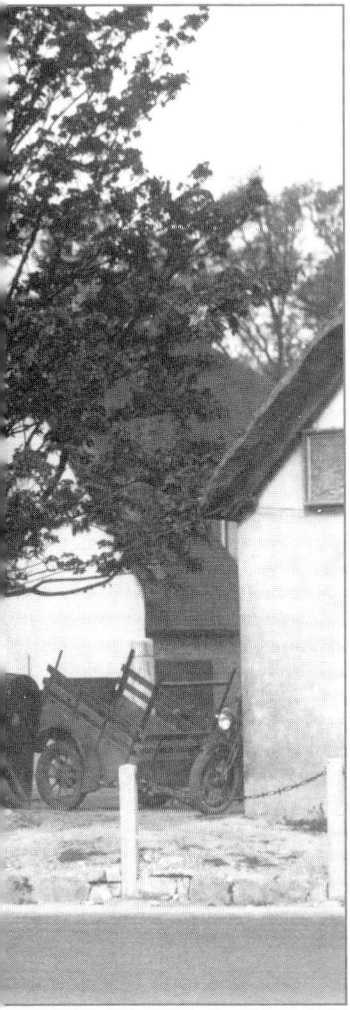

Avebury
The Red Lion Hotel c1950
A80005

This tiny village has a huge reputation as the home of the Avebury complex: a large circular bank and ditch surround the famous stone circle, which is thought to have been erected 4,000 years ago as a ceremonial centre. Here we can see the delightful Red Lion public house standing in the centre of the circle; at this time Leslie Lees was proprietor. The pub boasts an 80-foot well in one of its dining rooms.

Badbury
The Village c1960
B818007

The name comes from the Saxon 'Badda's burg' (fort); the village is thought by some to be Mount Badon, site of a battle between the British under Arthur and the Saxons.

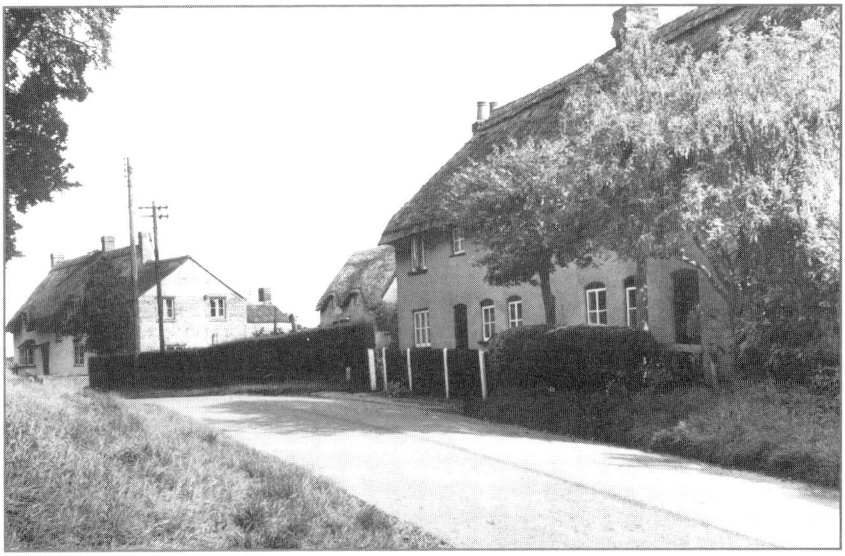

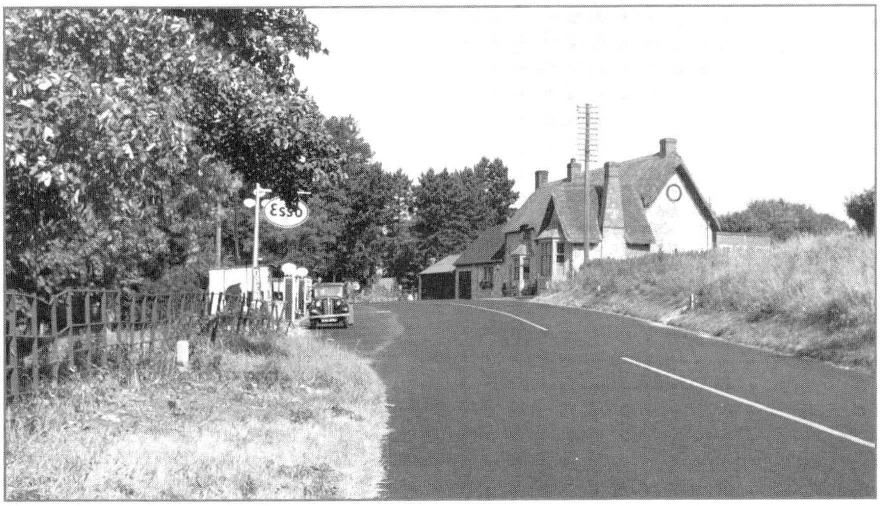

Beckhampton
The Village c1950
B292013

Recent excavations at Avebury have revealed the remains of an avenue of megaliths that lead from there towards Beckhampton. The two sites are connected, and Beckhampton has two massive standing stones of its own (one is 62 tons in weight), known as the Devil's Quoits.

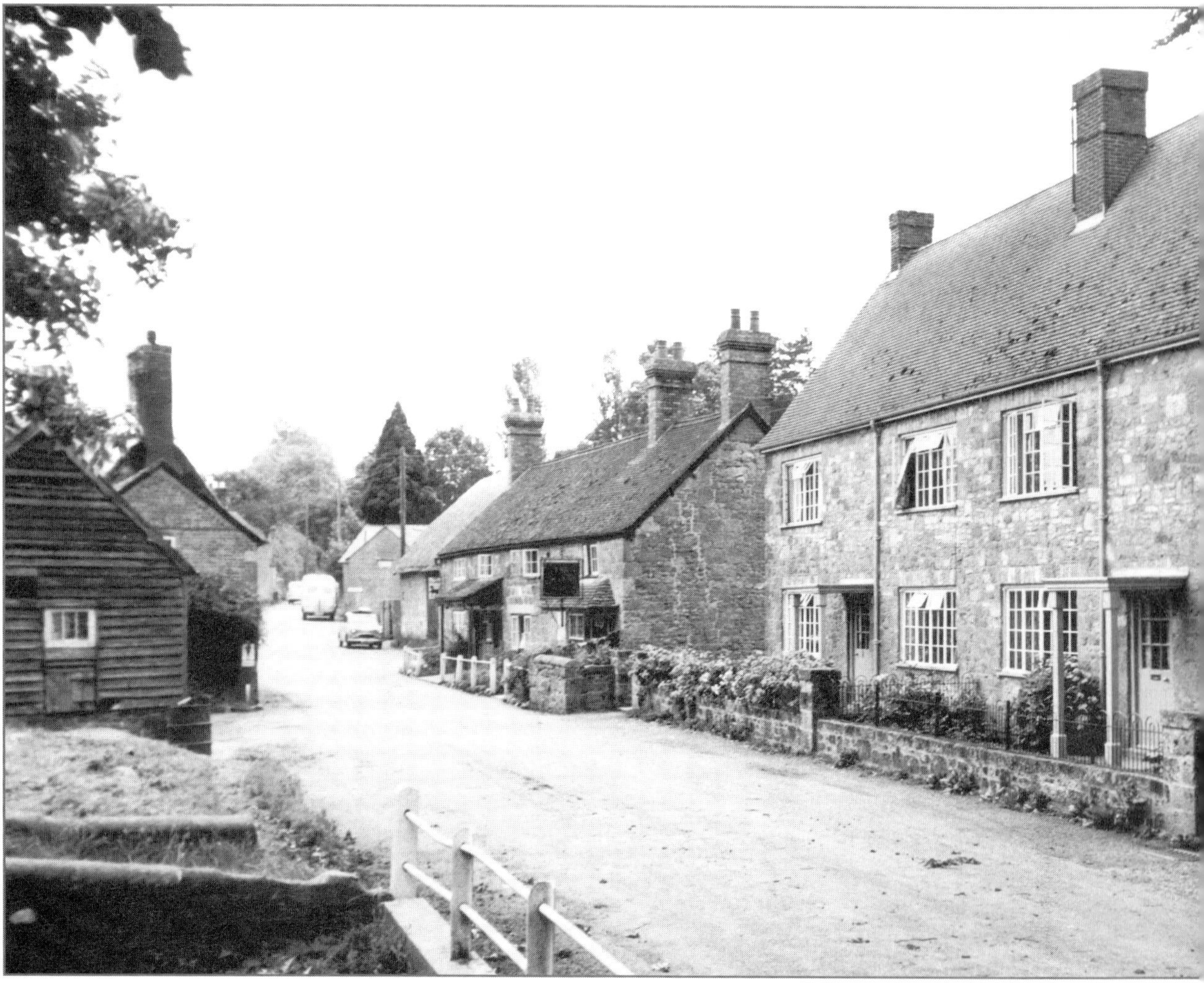

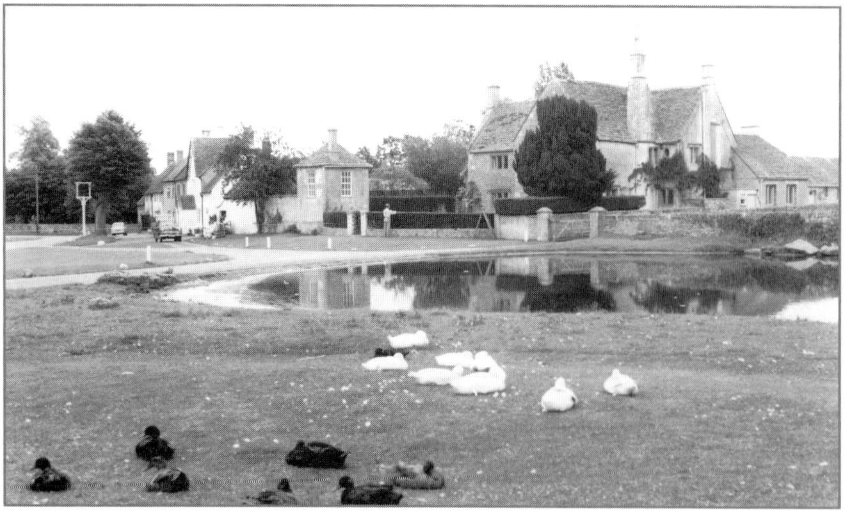

Biddestone
The Village c1955
B371002
Biddestone is very much the archetypal English village: handsome, stone-built houses are clustered around the green and the duck-pond. The 17th-century local grey stone Pool Farmhouse, with the gazebo built into the wall, is centre right. The village name comes from the Saxon 'Biedin's tun' (settlement).

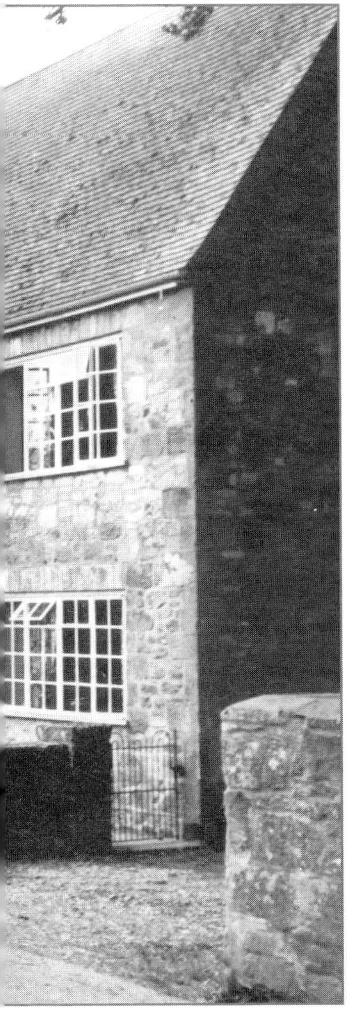

◄ **Berwick St John The Village c1950** B370002

This village is at the head of the Ebble valley. Some two hundred years ago, John Gane, a vicar of Berwick, made provision in his will for the church bell to be rung every fifteen minutes at 8pm through the winter months to guide any travellers lost on the downs. The practice is now discontinued. The name of the village derives from the Saxon 'berewic' (barley farm). Note the pub sign on the right for the Talbot Inn.

▼ **Bowerchalke, The Bell Inn c1960** B373001

Almost completely surrounded by hills, this village was first known as Cealcun in 826. Bower comes from the Saxon for borough. Local legend also has it that somewhere on Bowerchalke Down there is a buried golden coffin with a curse - on the men who dug it up in the first place - firmly attached.

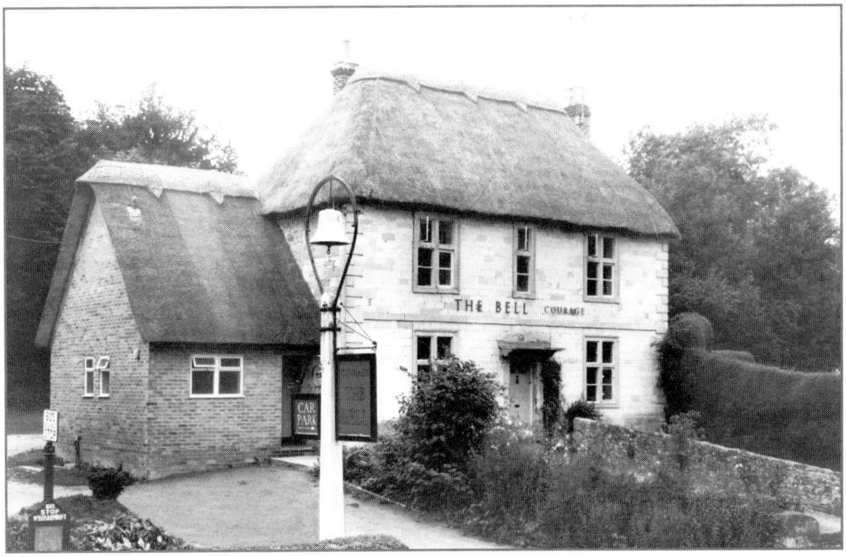

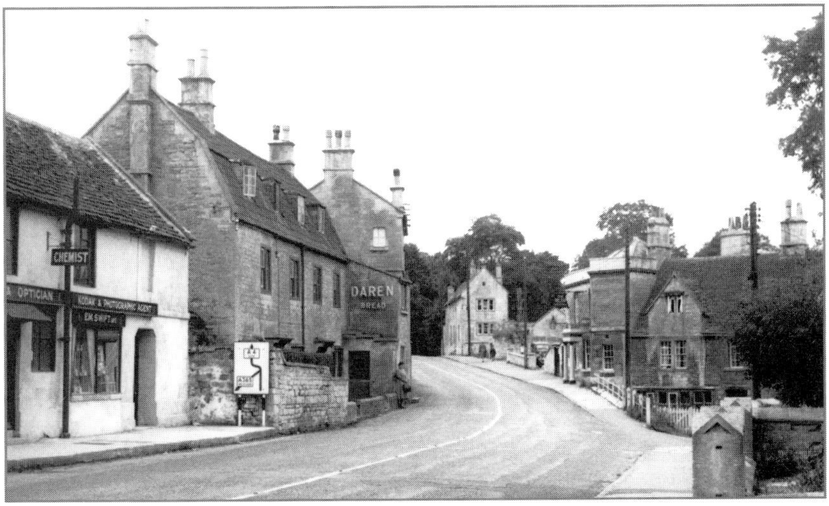

◄ **Box, The Village c1950**

B374004

According to legend, the 8th-century St Aldhelm threw down his glove here and said that if men were to dig where it fell, they would find treasure. Perhaps the diggers did not expect St Aldhelm's 'treasure' to be stone, but it has certainly been a source of prosperity for the village for many years; the industry employed nearly 700 men in 1900. The Bear public house can be seen to the right.

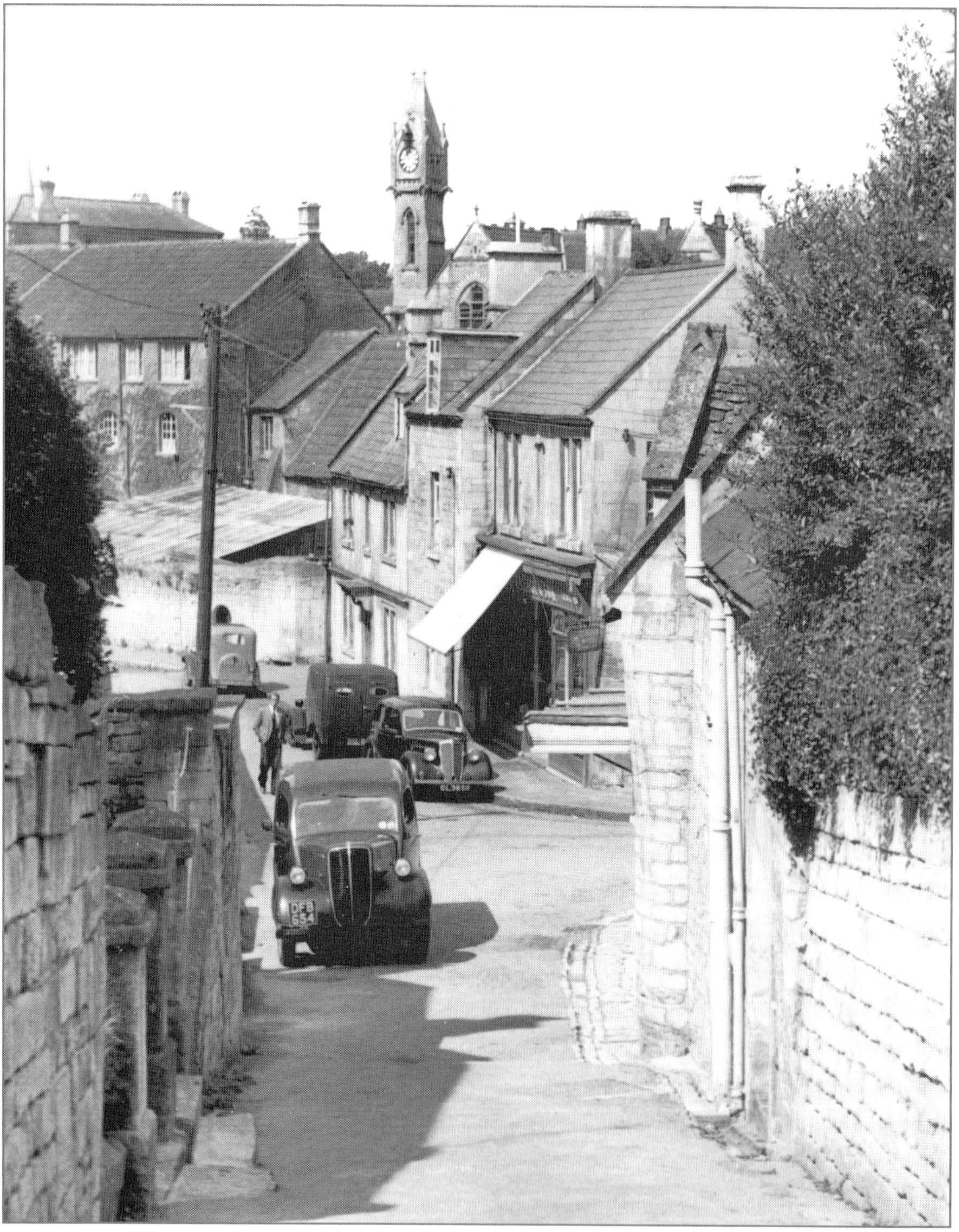

Box, Glovers Lane c1950 B374022

The village is set into a steep valley carved out by the By Brook. A Roman villa was excavated nearby. The village is famous for being a source of fine stone, but it also once had thriving brewing and tallow industries. The Reverend W Awdry, famous for his 'Thomas the Tank Engine' books, once lived in the village.

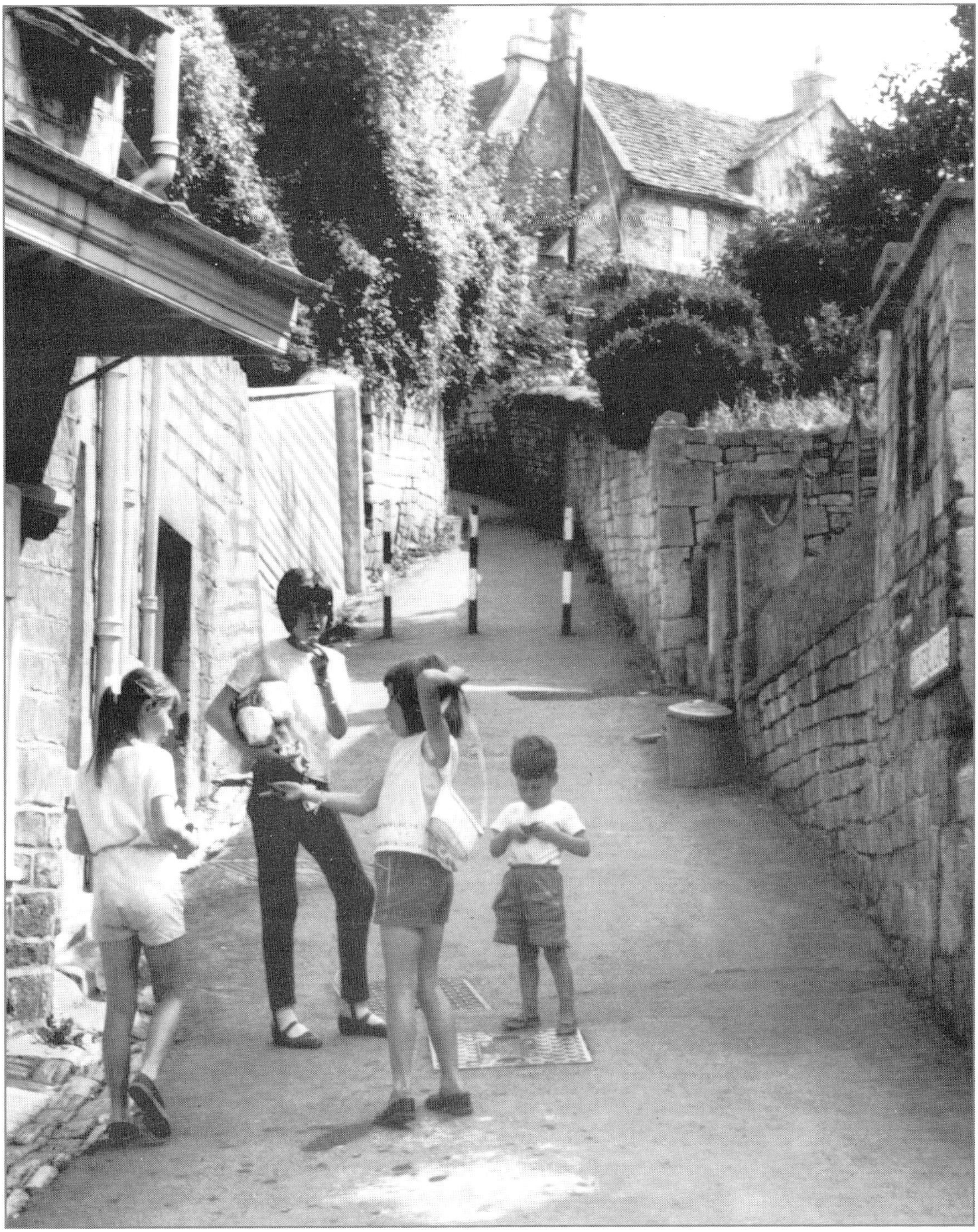

Box, Glovers Lane c1965 B374033
The village is also famous for Brunel's Box Tunnel, through which the train service to London travels. Brunel employed 1,200 men at the beginning of the project, and this rose to 4,000 by the time the two ends of the tunnel were joined. 100 men died during its construction. The village name simply derives from the Saxon for box-tree. It was listed as Bocza in 1144.

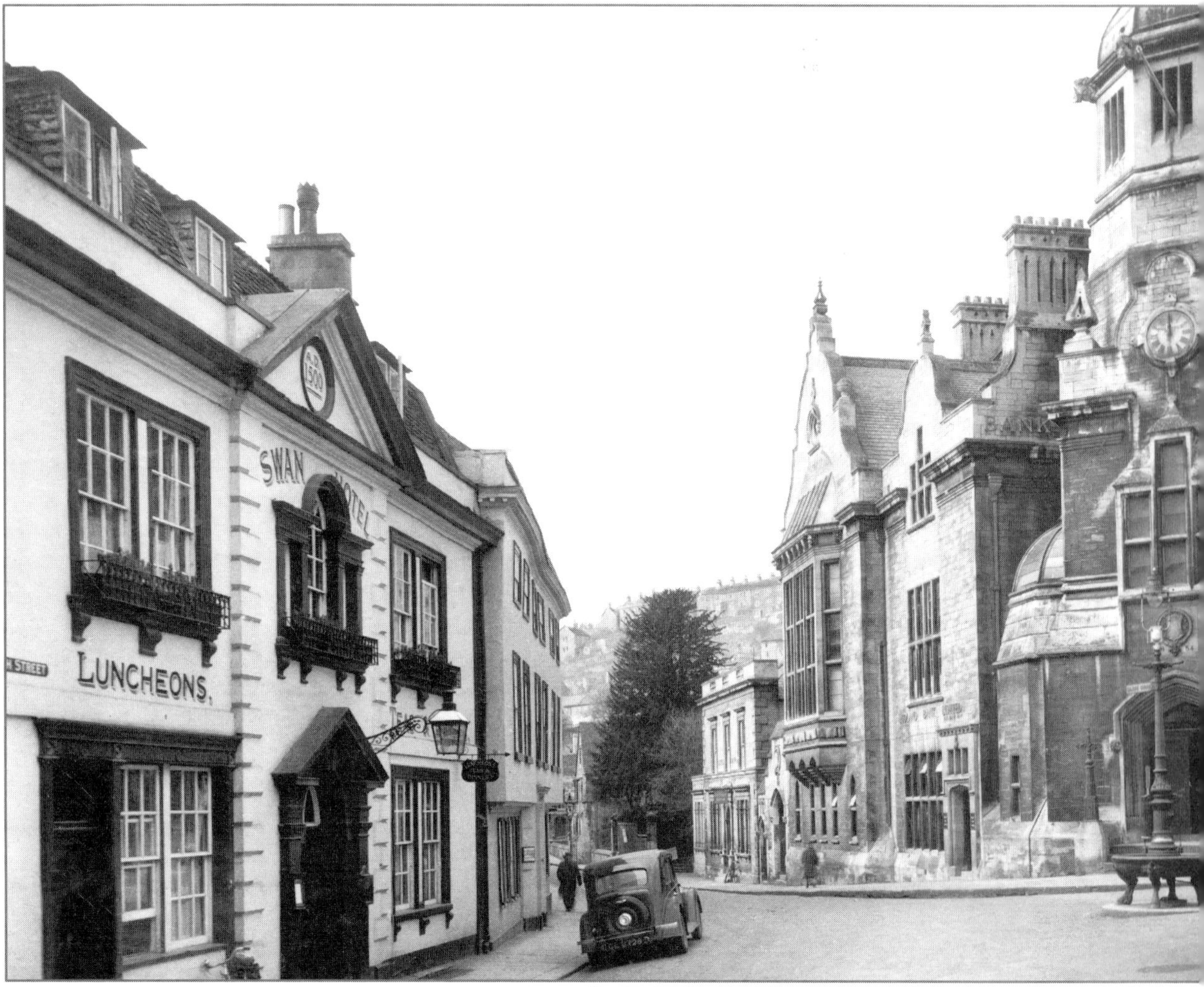

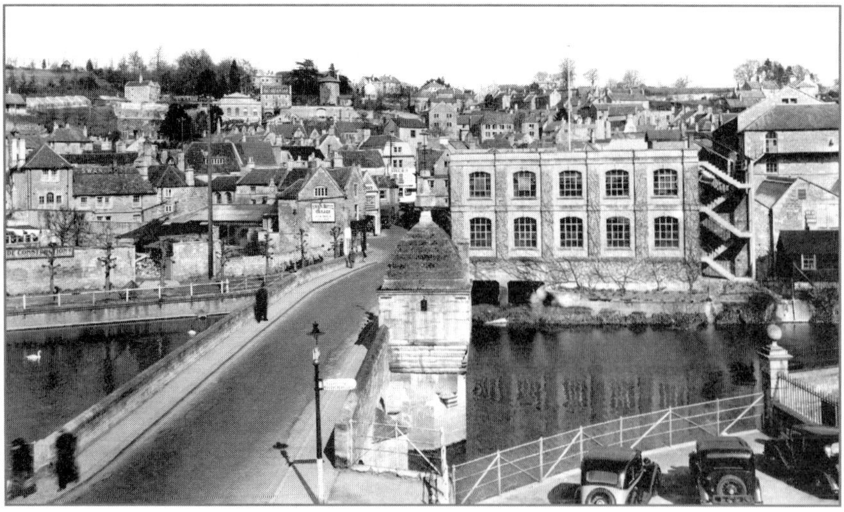

Bradford-on-Avon
The Bridge c1945 B174016
This lovely wool town on either side of the river Avon derives is name from the Saxon for broad ford on the river Avon, and was famous for its broadcloth weaving industry. The bridge was first erected in the 14th century and then rebuilt in the 17th. The structure on the left of the bridge was the town lock-up; it was originally a chapel. The mill buildings on the river date from the 19th century, and were first used for cloth manufacturing.

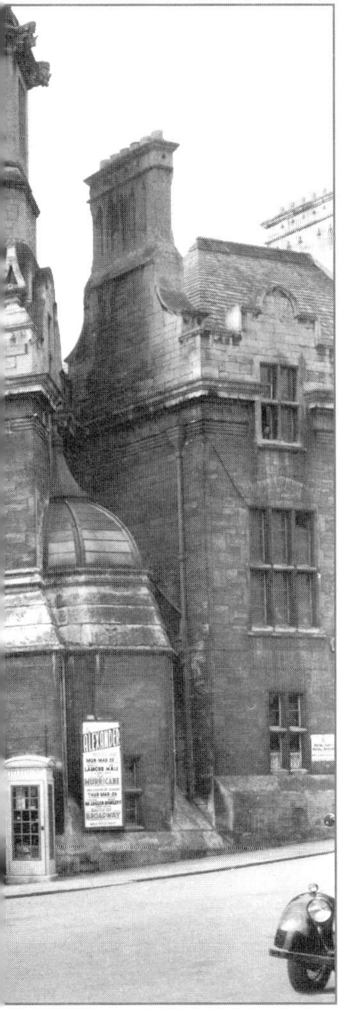

Bradford-on-Avon Church Street c1945

B174012

The Swan Hotel to the left is dated 1500. A branch of the Midland Bank can be seen immediately to the left of the ornate building on the corner. To the right of it is The Alexander, advertising Dorothy Lamour and John Hall in 'The Hurricane'.

Bradford-on-Avon, The Canal c1955

B174039

John Rennie's extraordinary feat of engineering was built not for the present-day leisure industry, but for trade. The 'navigators', or 'navvies', who did all the hard work, led grim lives. 'The life of a canal labourer was very hard, though compassion was shown to one such person who had his leg broken by a fall of earth. The committee directed that he should receive proper care and attention at their expense and that he be given the sum of five guineas 'as an act of charity', but this was not to be regarded as a precedent'. (Kenneth Clew, 'The Kennet and Avon Canal'). The canal opened in 1810.

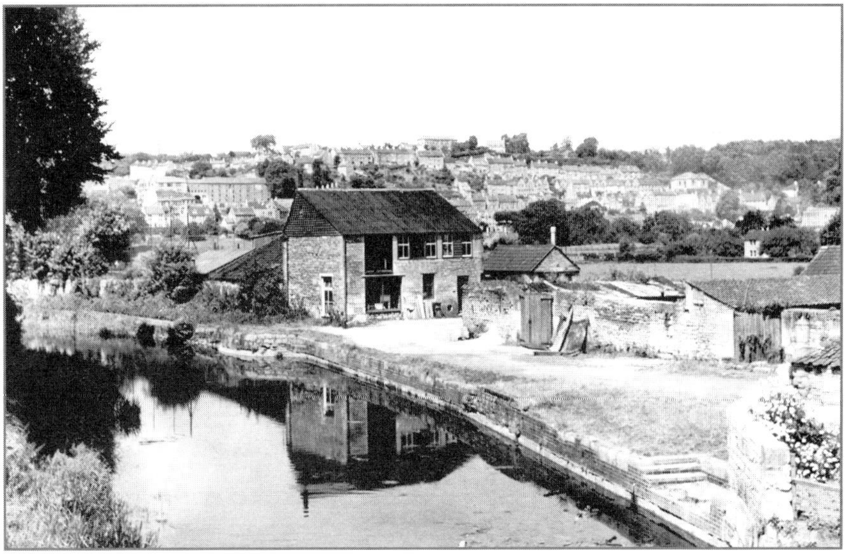

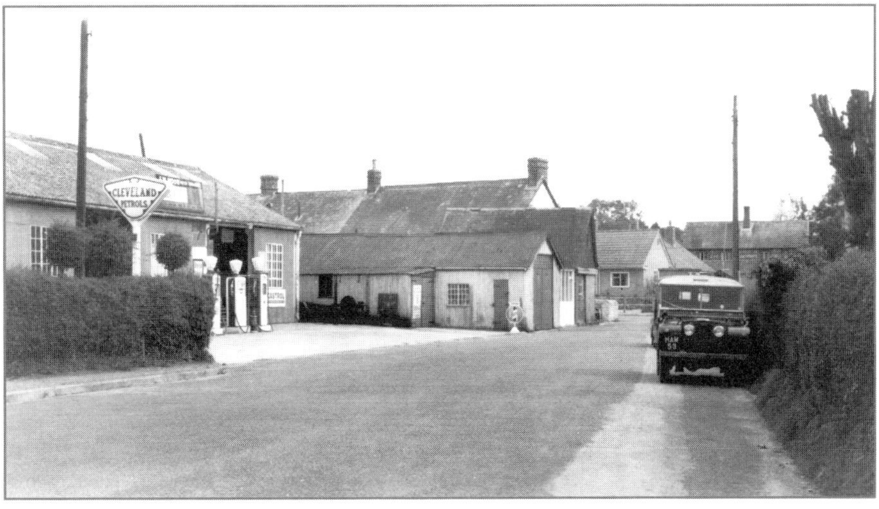

Broadchalke The Village c1955

B376007

The village is the largest in the valley; it was once predominantly abbey land until the Reformation, when it was passed to the earls of Pembroke. Moon Motor Engineers can be seen to the left behind the petrol pumps; it is still operating as a garage.

▼ **Broadchalke, The Post Office c1955** B376016

Note the 'Echo' headline on the advertising board, and the proprietors' name (H B & G M Mitchell) above the door. John Aubrey once had a farm here. He wrote: 'There are not better trouts (two feet long) in the kingdom of England than here. The water of this streame washes well, and is good for brewing. I did putt in craw-fish, but they would not live here; the water is too cold for them'.

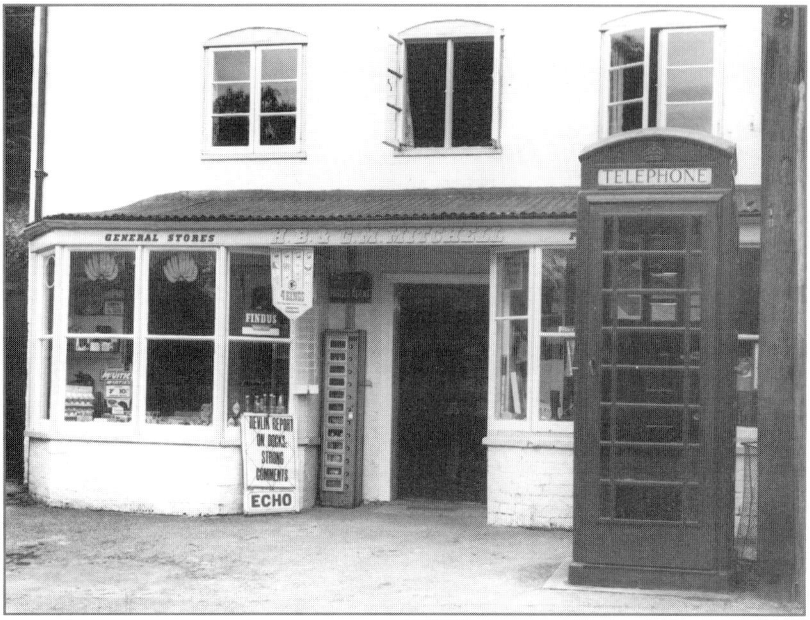

▼ **Broad Hinton, The Post Office and The Street c1945** B377008

As with many Wiltshire villages, folklore abounds here - a man apparently witnessed his own funeral taking place at the church. The village name derives from the Saxon 'heahtun' (settlement).

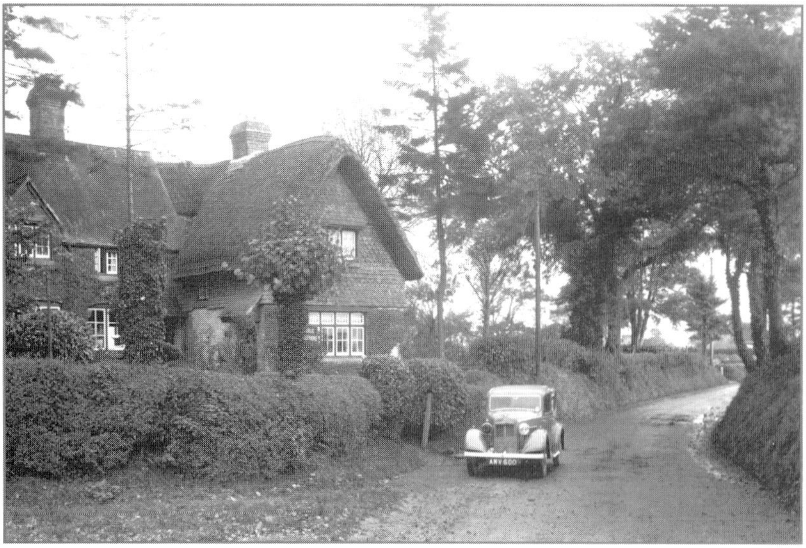

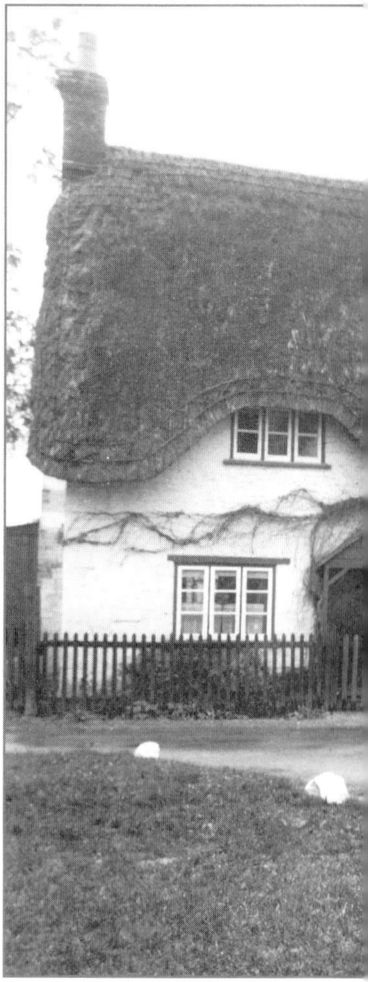

▲ **Broad Hinton, Cottages and the Village Well c1945**

B377002

The village is home to one of Wiltshire's famous white horses: it measures 90 ft by 90 ft, and was cut by a parish clerk in the Victorian era. In the church there is a monument to Sir Thomas and Lady Anne Wroughton and their three children. The curious thing is that only she has hands - not an omission, but a reference to the local tale that he, on returning home, was so incensed to find his wife reading her Bible instead of preparing his meal, that he ripped the book from her hands and flung it into the fire, whereupon his and his children's hands promptly withered away.

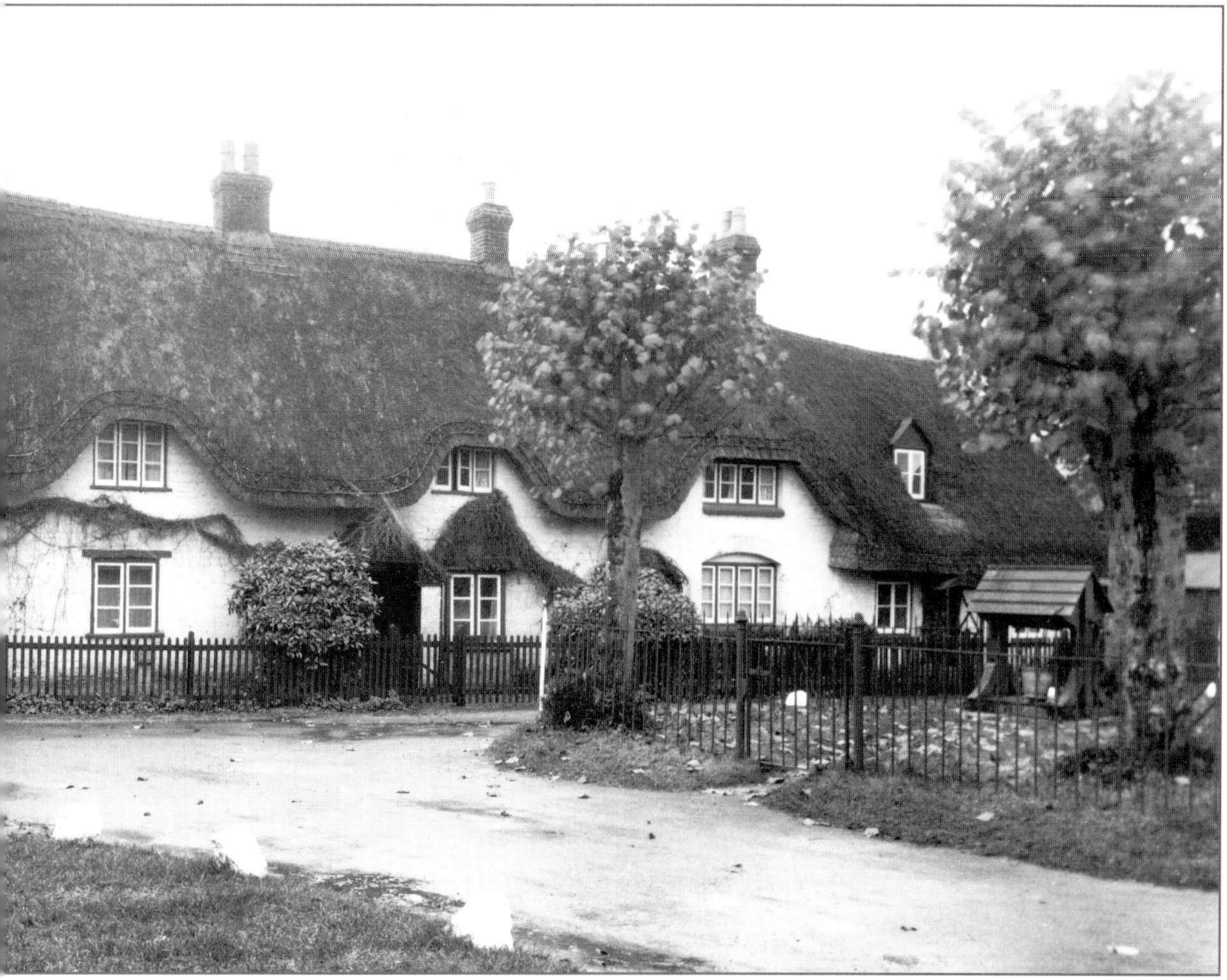

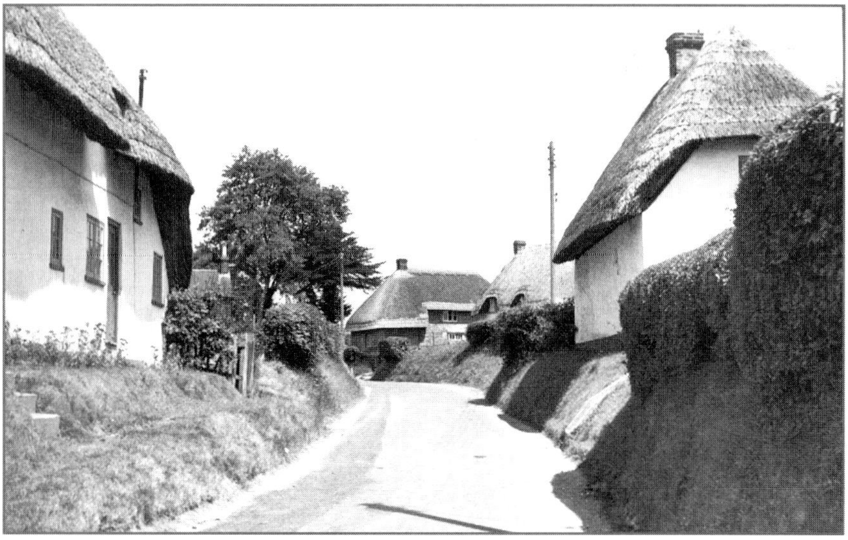

◄ **Brunton**
The Village c1955 B815006
This picturesque village, complete with sunken lane, epitomises the classic thatched English village found so often in rural Wiltshire.

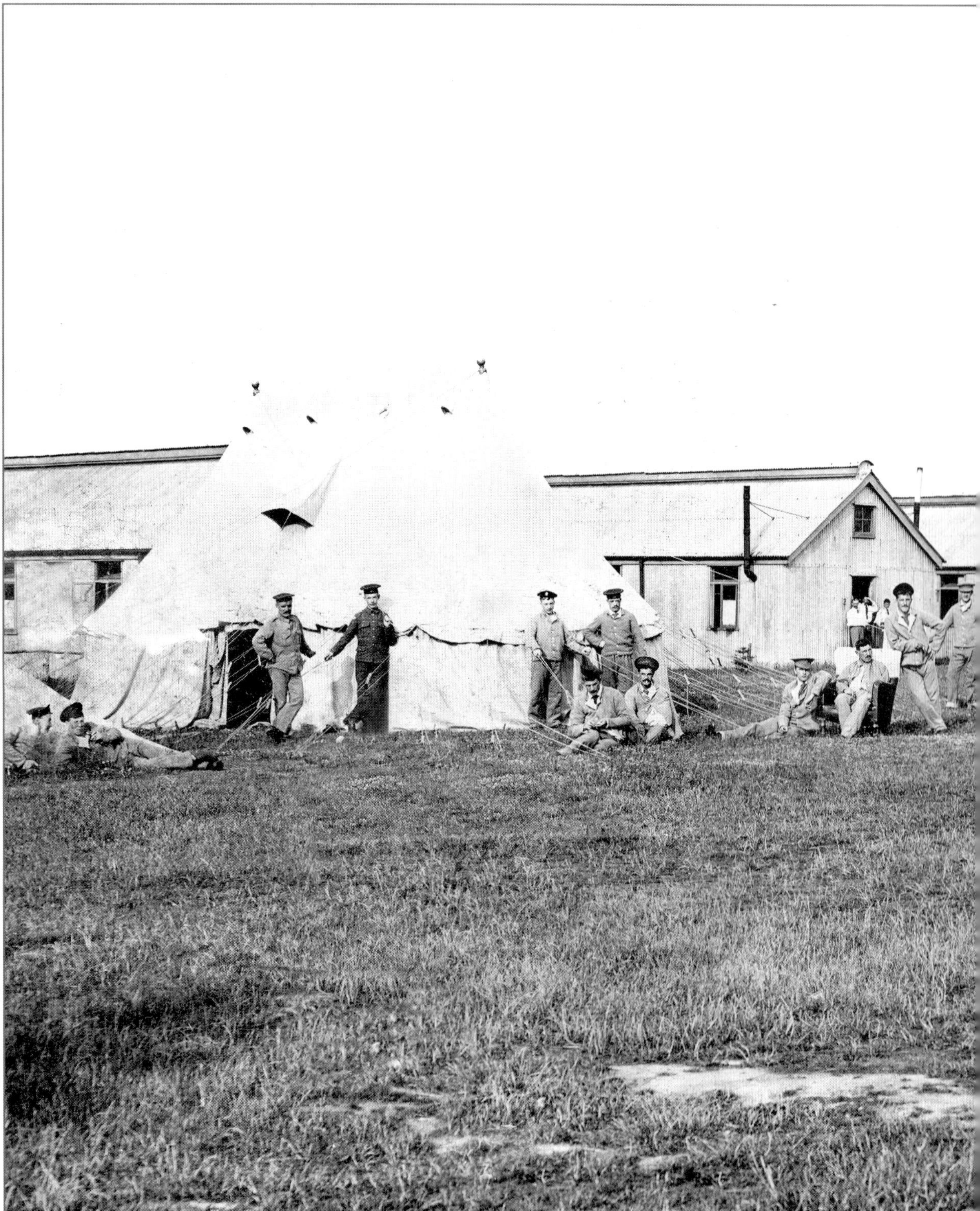

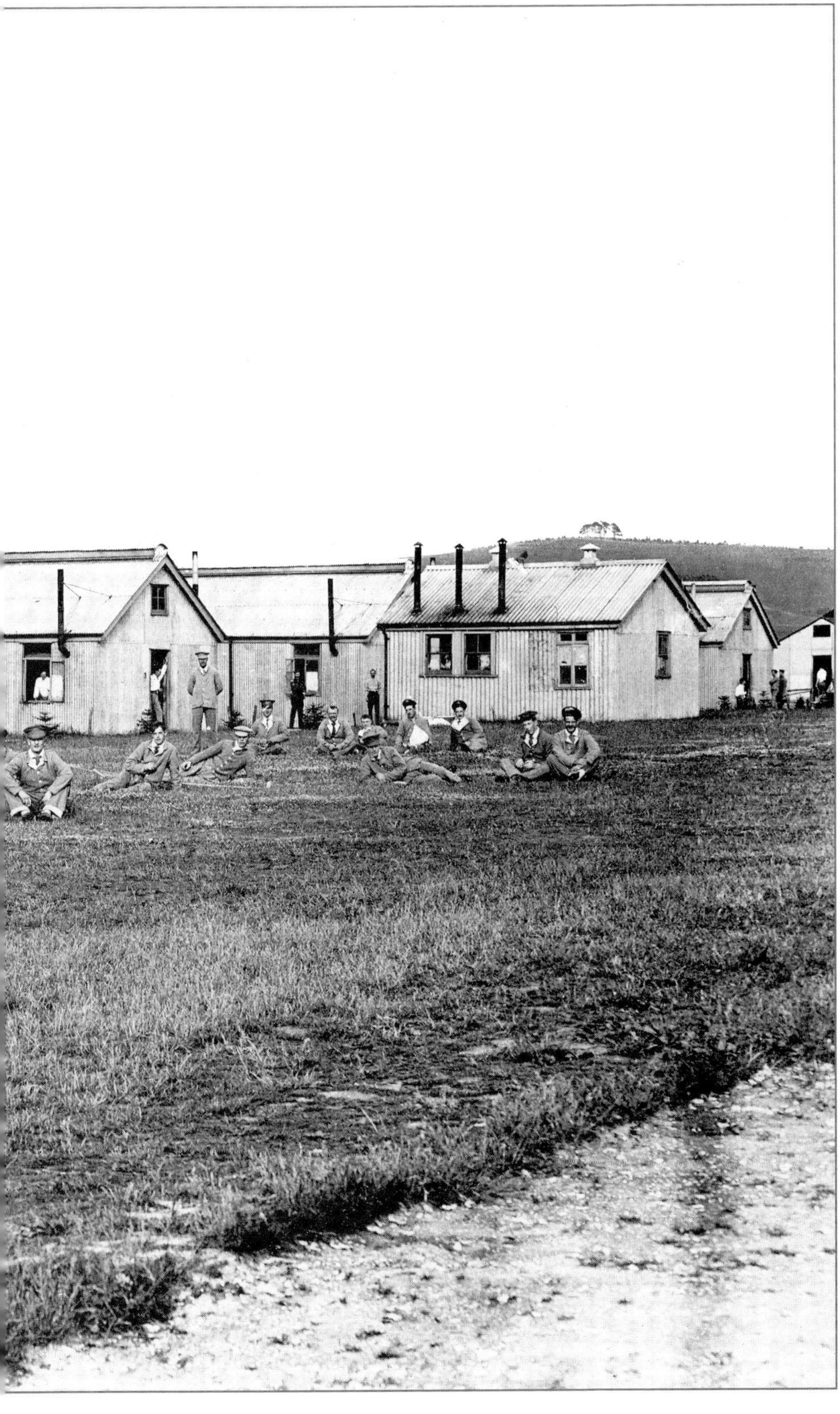

Bulford, The Military Hospital, Bulford Camp c1945 B378012
Bulford has been host to the army since the early 20th century; the large Bulford Camp can be found below Beacon Hill. Tank crossing points along the roads are a frequent reminder of this - a sight familiar to the author's father, who was once stationed here.

▼ **Bulford, Bulford Camp**
The Post Office and the Church c1945 B378001
Set in a sheltered hollow between Salisbury and Pewsey, the village name derives from the Saxon: the ford where the 'bulut' (cuckoo flower or ragged robin) grows. The army presence is a significant feature of the area, and Bulford Camp is part of the 43,500 acres which the Ministry of Defence owns.

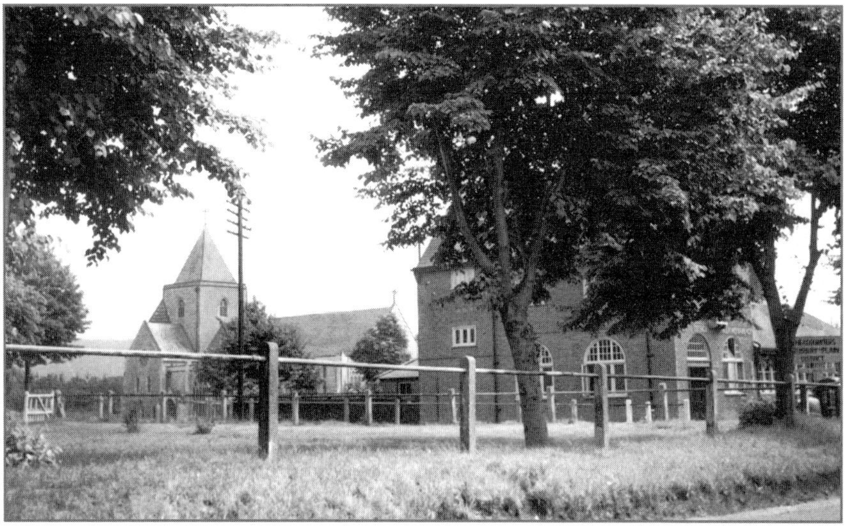

▼ **Calne, High Street c1950** C228007
Calne is a stone-built town centred on its market place. The town's name derives from the Welsh word 'ceilog', and means loud river. Note Buckeridge Grocer's shop on the right, and Phillips Outfitters on the left with the bicyle parked outside.

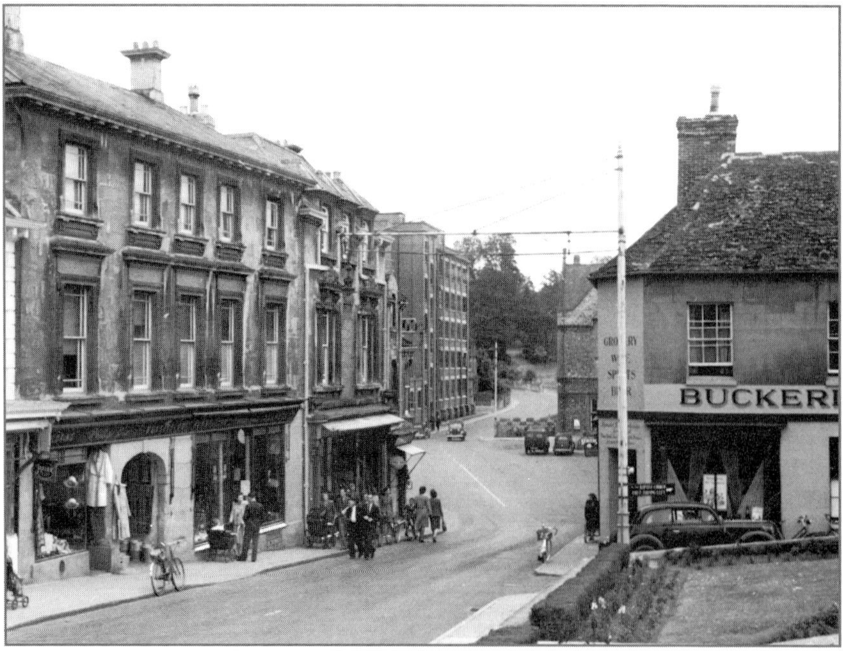

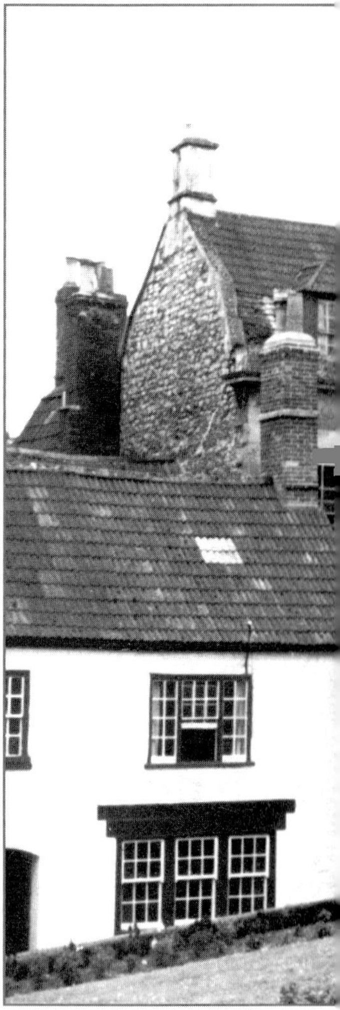

▲ **Calne, The Town c1950**
C228008
Calne has its fair share of famous sons. Doctor Joseph Priestly discovered oxygen while living in the town from 1772 to 1779, and Walter Goodall George, the world record-holder for the mile from 1886 to 1915, was born here.

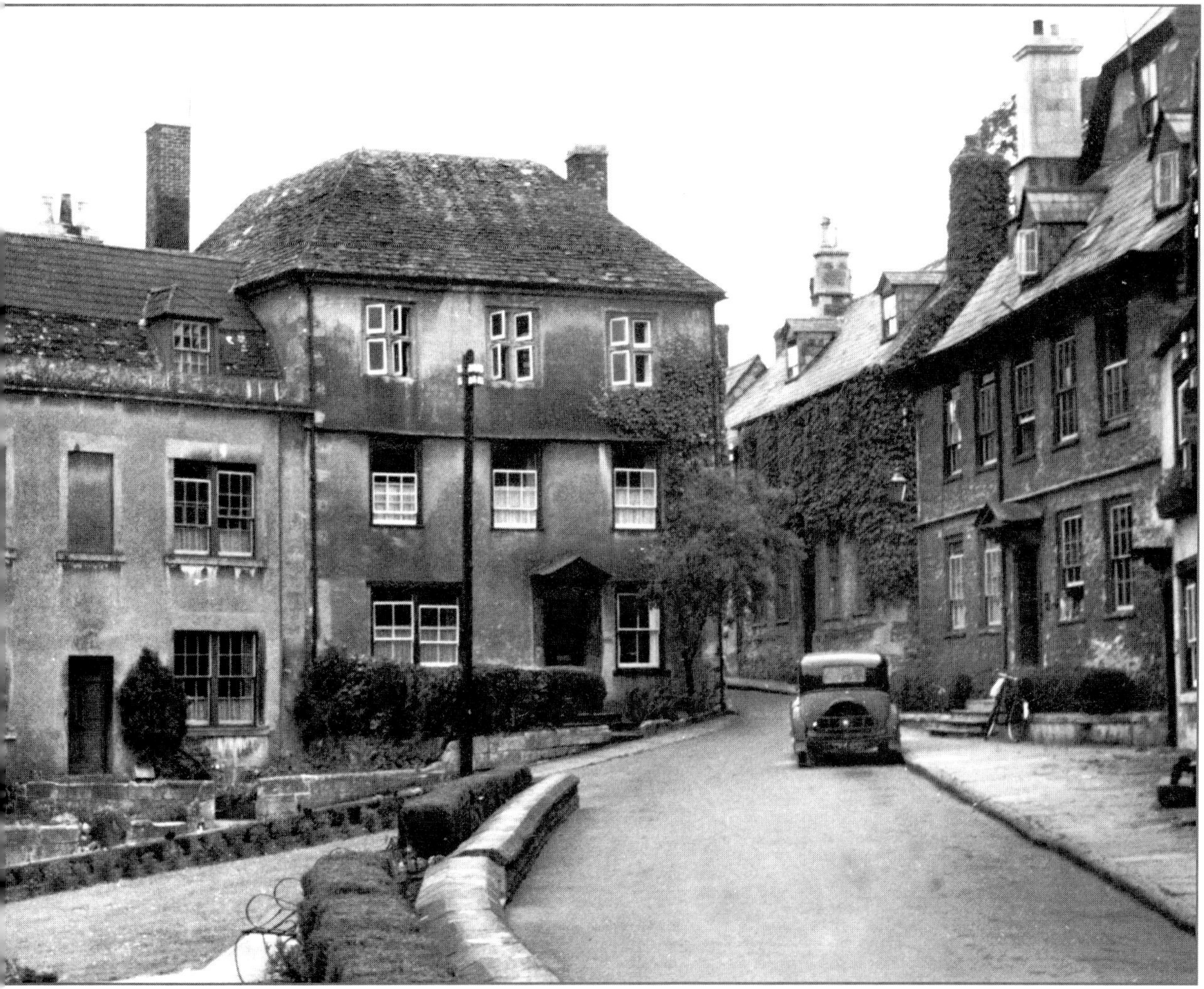

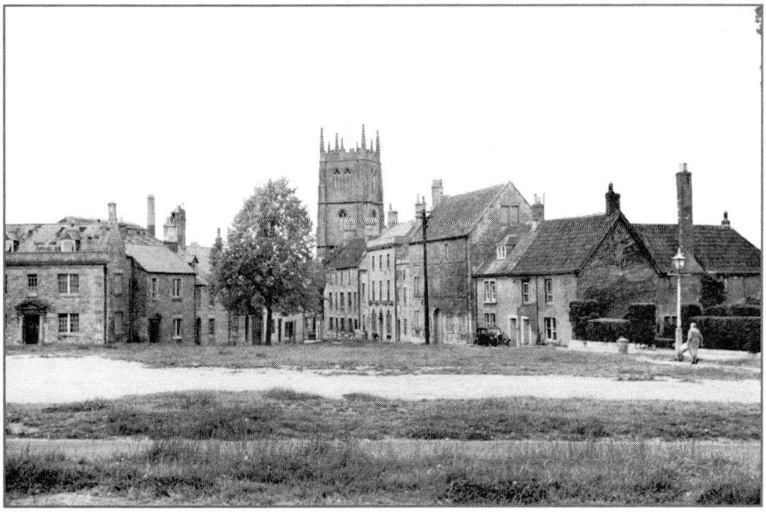

◄ **Calne, The Green c1950** C228020
The tall pinnacles of the Church of St Mary in the centre surmount a 17th-century tower, thought to be the work of Inigo Jones, and a replacement for the one that collapsed in 1638 (one bystander apparently died of fright). Around the Green can be found a row of 17th-century almshouses. The Witanagemot (the council of England in Anglo-Saxon times) met in Calne in 978 to debate the celibacy of the clergy. Archbishop Dunstan, who was advocating celibacy, was left safe on a beam when the floor collapsed. It was deduced from this that God favoured his view.

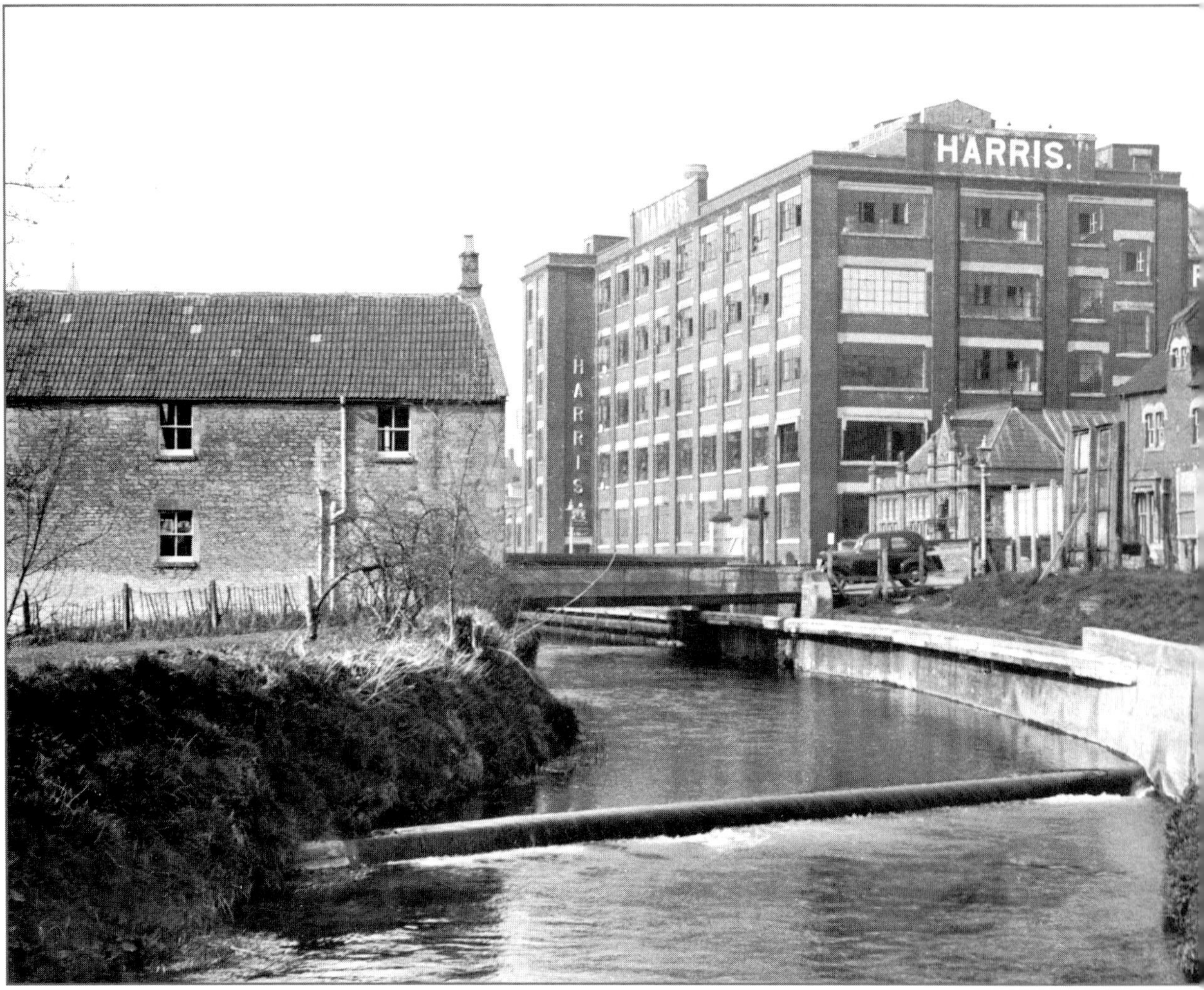

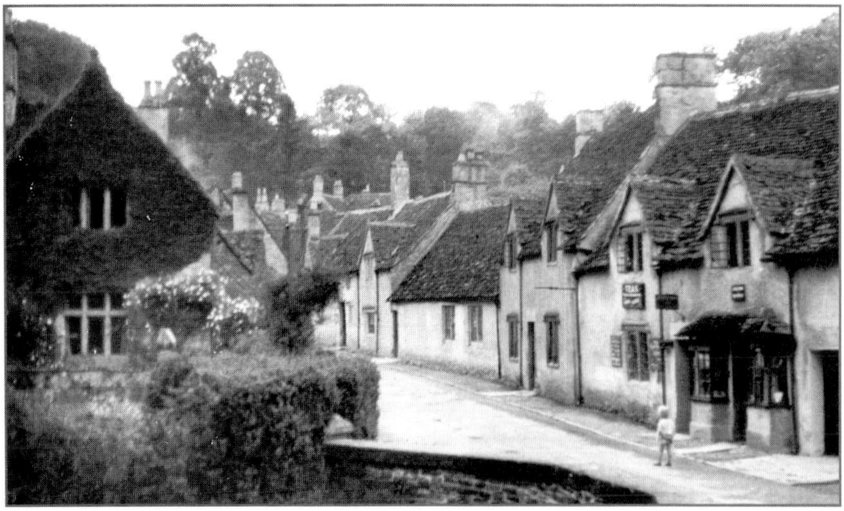

◄ **Castle Combe Main Street c1950** C43002

Castle Combe is stunningly beautiful - and there seems little more that can be said. It has survived the Hollywood invasion which, it seemed, threatened to turn it into a permanent film set ('The Story of Dr Doolittle', etc) and is today as beautiful as when it was voted England's most beautiful village in 1962. Originally owned by the Scrope family in the reign of Richard II, the village was also famed for 'Castlecombe', a red and white cloth.

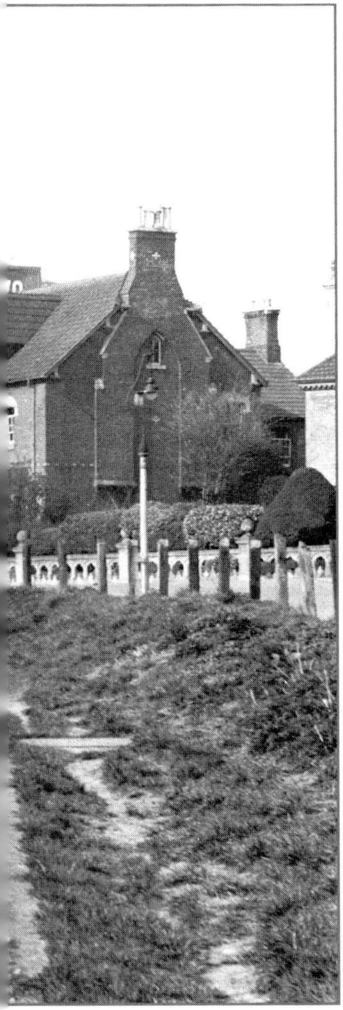

Calne, The River and the Harris Bacon Factory c1955

C228029

Now demolished, the C & T Ltd Bacon Factory shown here once overshadowed the town. Harris's has been in the town since 1770, and was once a significant employer. Its removal has made way for redevelopment in the town centre. The town was also known for broadcloth and other fabrics - there were once twenty spinning and fulling mills in the town.

Castle Combe The Old Cross c1950

C43001

Note the stone-tiled, pyramidal roof of the Market Cross. Its origins are unknown, but records refer to it by 1590. Note the steam bakery sign further up the street. The village name derives from the Saxon 'cumb', meaning short, broad valley.

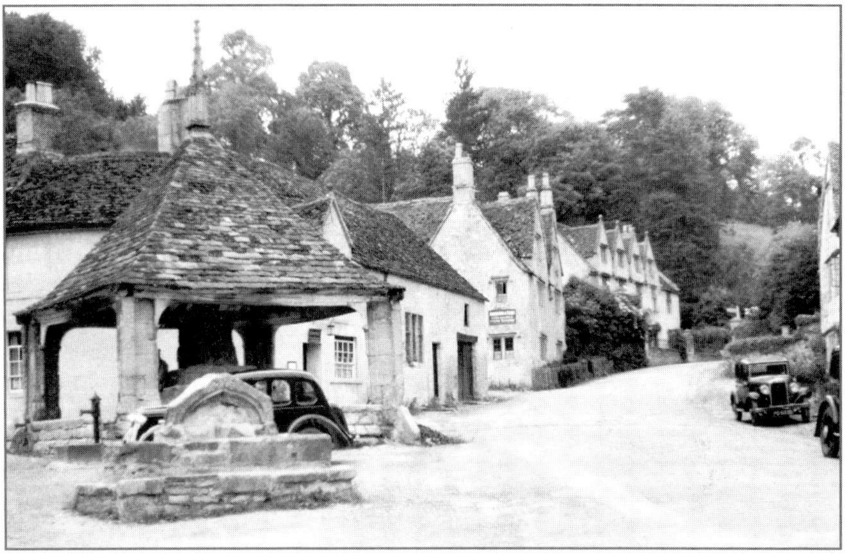

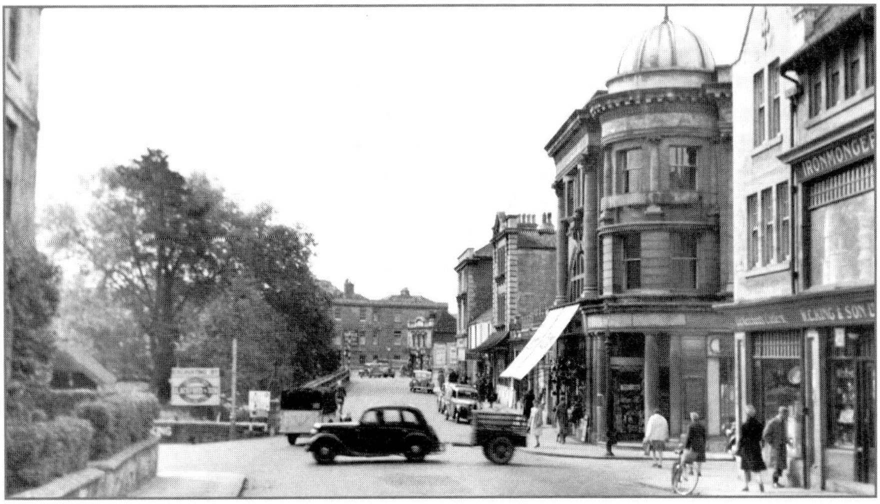

Chippenham The Town Centre c1950 C294003

This town on the banks of the river Avon, straddling the London to Bath road, started life as a market town - the name perhaps derives from 'cheaping', a market. The domed building, centre right, is now an Oxfam shop. Note King & Son Ironmongers on the right.

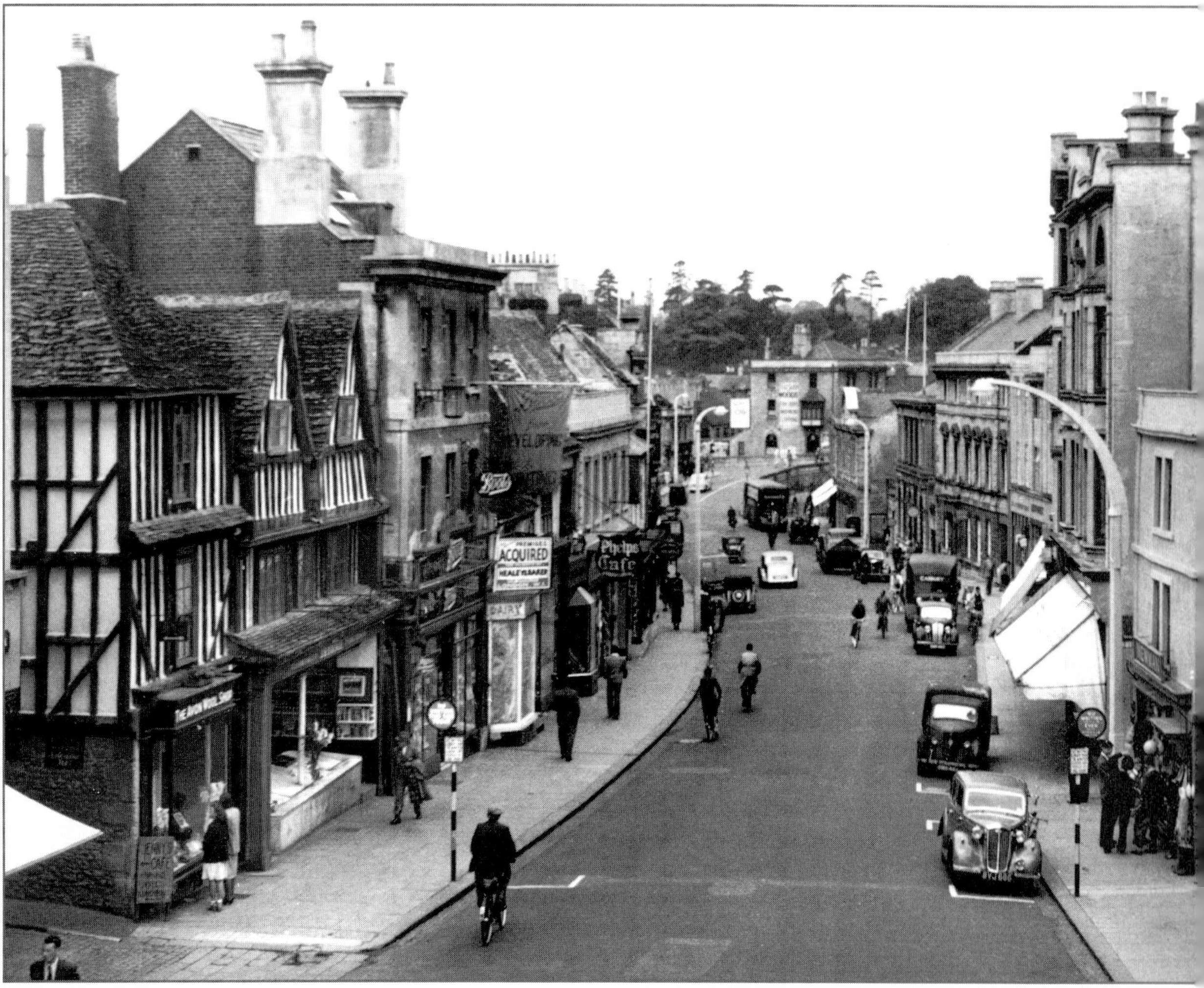

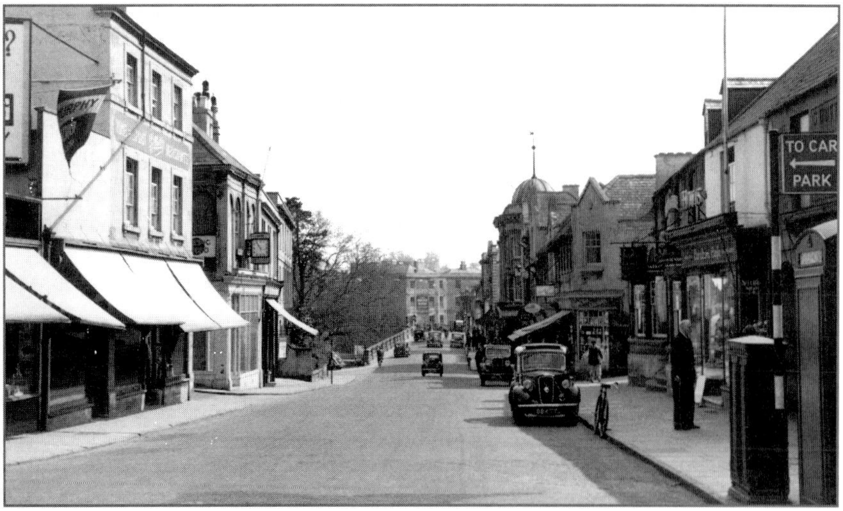

◄ **Chippenham**
New Road c1950 C294042
The bridge that can be seen in the centre of the picture has since been replaced by another in 1966. There has been a bridge on this site for over three centuries. The town has many famous sons, one of whom, Ludovic Muggleton, founded a 17th-century religious sect which rejoiced in the name of 'the Muggletonians'. Note the Carlton Cafe on the right, and Bridge House beyond the bridge.

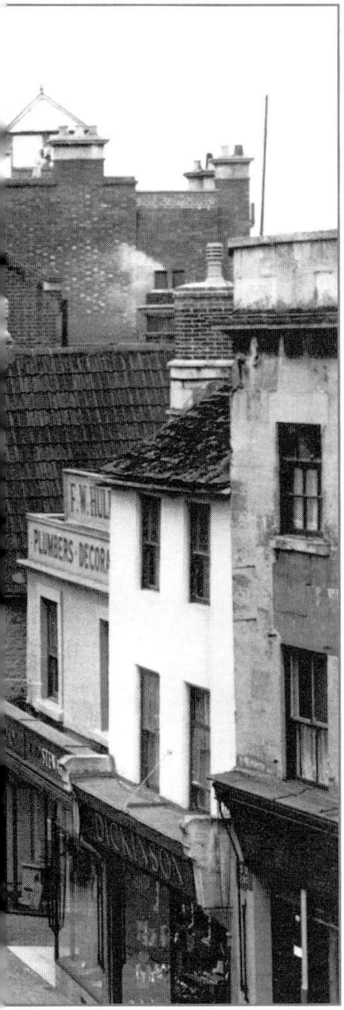

Chippenham
High Street c1950 C294006
King Alfred the Great is reputed to have given Chippenham to his daughter Elfrida, and he enters Chippenham's history again in an account from the Anglo-Saxon Chronicle in 877, this time less happily: he narrowly escaped capture by invading Danes while he was in the town feasting at Christmas. The Boots shop on the left is still trading, and the building seen over the bridge is an Oxfam shop.

Chippenham
The Post Office c1960
C294063
This building still carries out the same function today, and the church spire behind is of the parish church of St Andrew - 'The Church in the Market Place'.

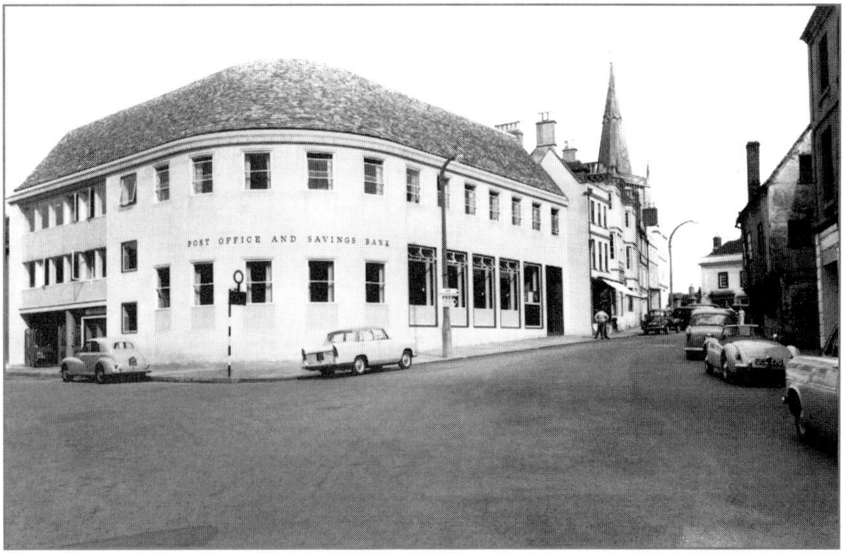

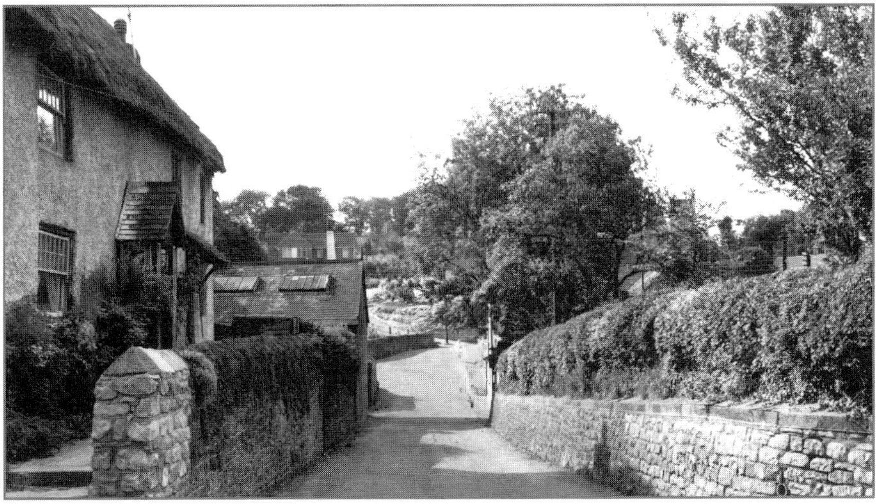

Chiseldon
High Street c1960
C220008
Just south of Swindon and set in a sheltered hollow with chalk- and sarsen stone-built cottages, the parish of Chiseldon was the birthplace of the essayist, novelist and nature writer Richard Jefferies. The copse of trees in the village comprises the survivors of the group of trees he called 'one of my thinking places'.

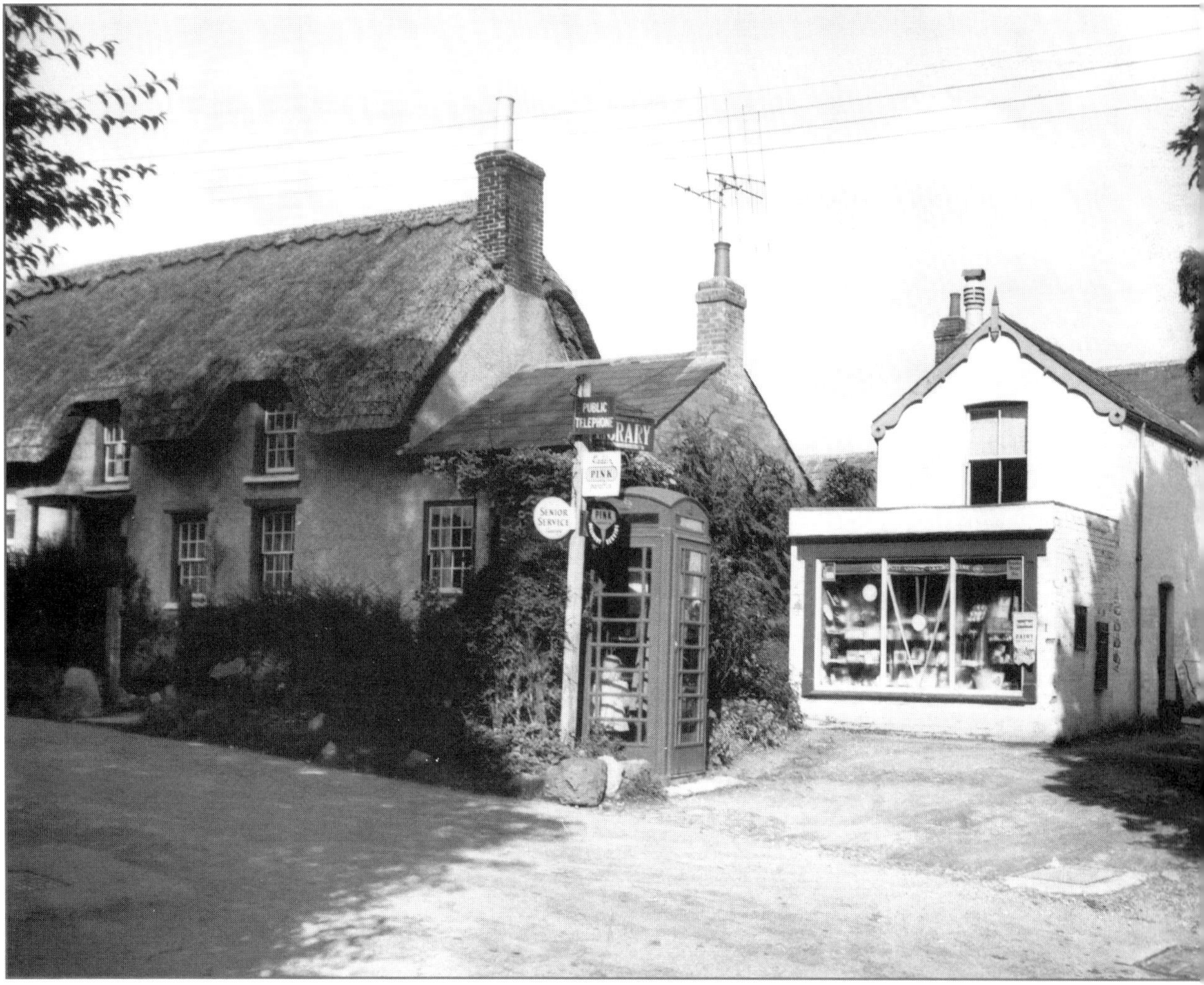

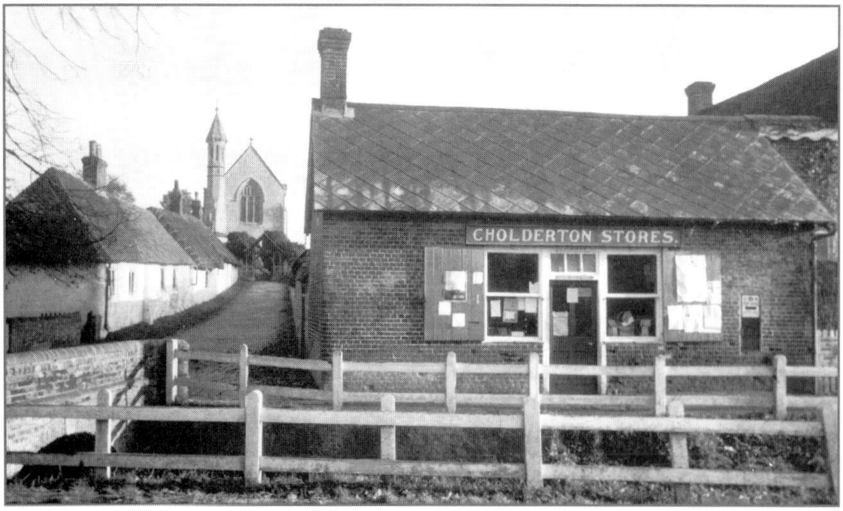

◄ **Cholderton, The Church and the Post Office c1955**

C296001

On the edge of Salisbury Plain, the village derives its name from the Saxon, meaning the settlement of Ceol. Note the one-storey cob cottages on the left, and the church of St Nicholas beyond. The Rev Thomas Mozley set about restoring the church in 1840, and located a replacement roof in Ipswich - he brought it back to Cholderton at vast expense, most of it paid personally, and built his new church under it.

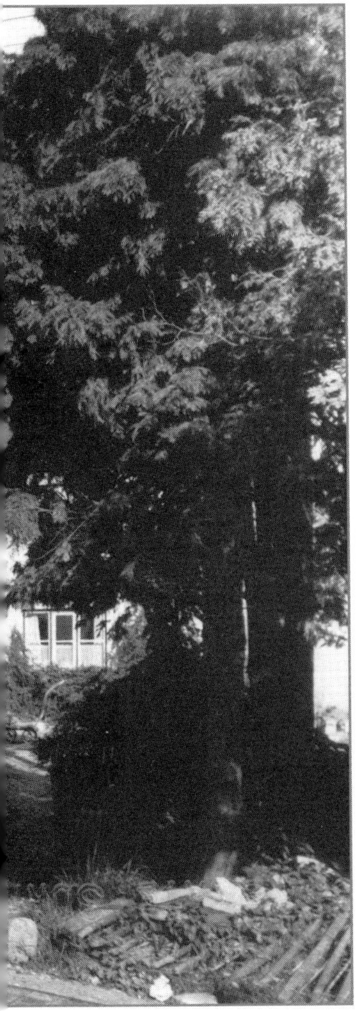

◄ **Chiseldon**
The Post office c1960
C220015
Note the advertising placards on the post by the telephone box - a method not seen today. The village name comes from the Saxon 'ciseldenu', meaning gravel valley.

▼ **Colerne**
High Street c1955 C297001
The church, in the centre of the picture, is St John the Baptist; it dates from the 1190s, although the present tower was built in 1450. Although the village was once famous for brewing, it has another claim to fame - it is the home of 'stowball' or 'stobball', a game similar to golf played on nearby Colerne Down. The jet fighter base of RAF Colerne, established in 1945, was closed in 1976. The village name derives from the Saxon 'col' (charcoal or coal) and 'aern' (house).

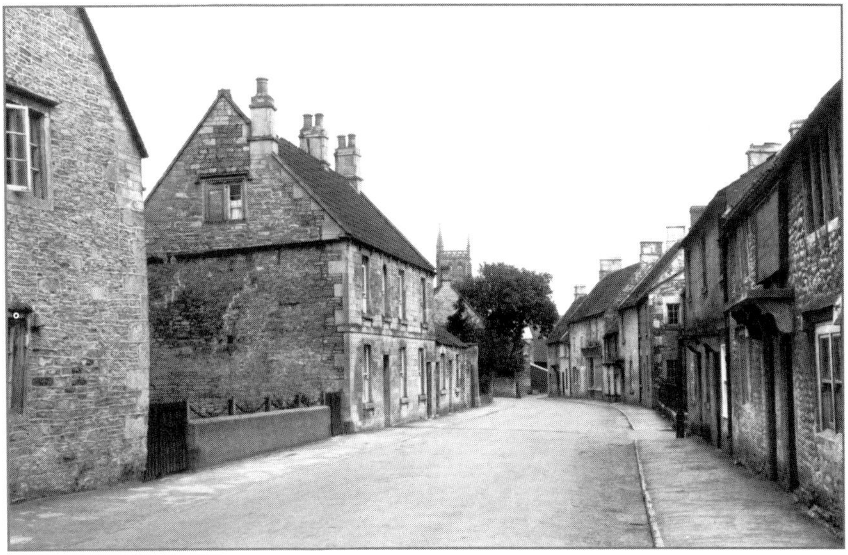

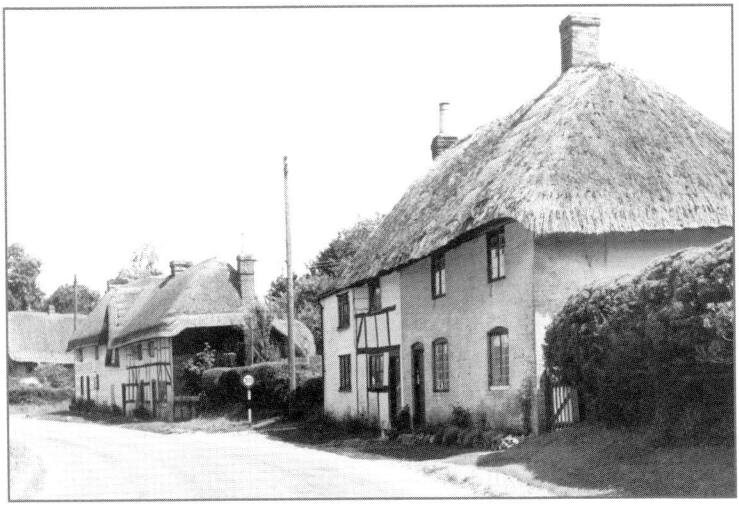

◄ **Collingbourne Ducis**
The Village c1955 C223004
Both this village and Collingbourne Kingston were once medieval forest villages. The village name derives from the river Coll and the Saxon 'burna' (stream). Ducis derives from the owners, the Dukes of Lancaster. One of the village's sons, William Collingbourne, wrote satirical verse, for example 'The Cat, the Rat and Lovel the Dogge, Rule all England under a Hogge'. King Richard III's ministers Catesby, Ratcliff and Lovell were insulted, the king (whose crest was a boar), was insulted, Collingbourne was found guilty of sedition and hanged. The price of creativity!

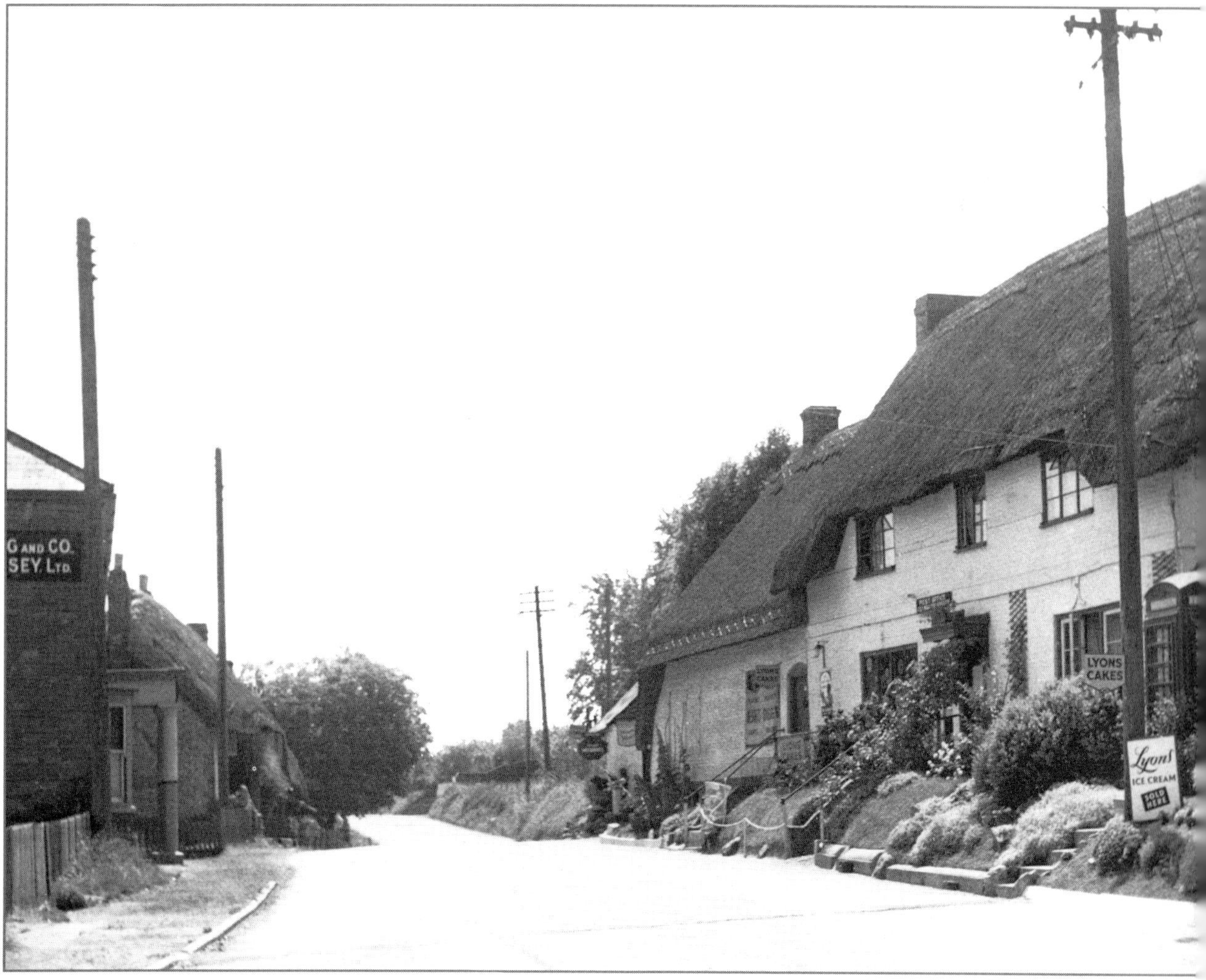

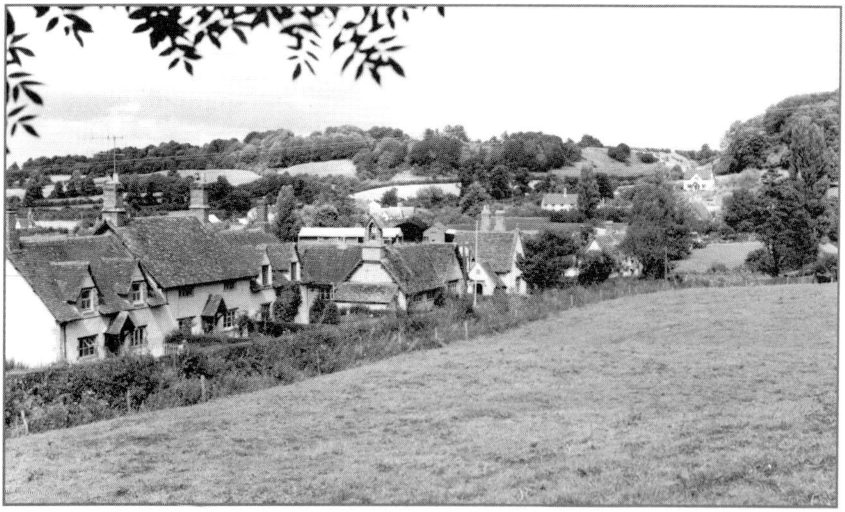

Compton Bassett
General View c1960
C696002
This beautifully-kept village was the home of the Heneage family for many generations. The village name comes from the Saxon 'cumb' and Bissett (a 12th-century landowner).

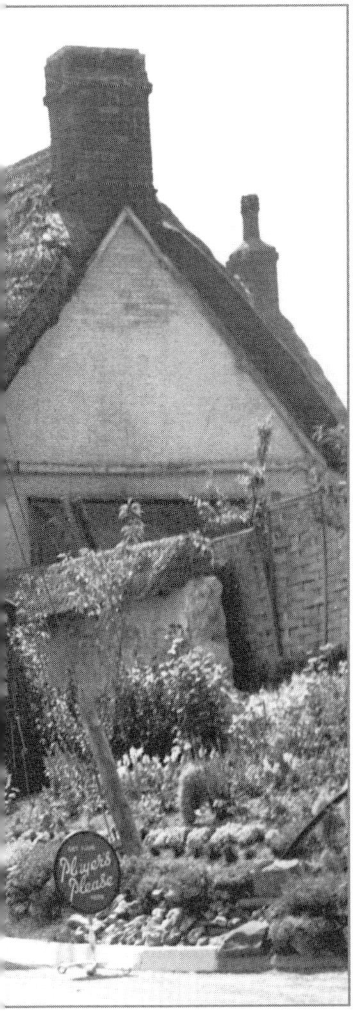

◀ **Collingbourne Kingston The Village c1955** C298004
This is a much smaller village than Collingbourne Ducis, but it has a big reputation for hospitality: in 1604 the rector and eighteen parishioners petitioned for a victualling licence for the comfort of travellers who had sought refuge in the village after being lost on the Downs. The Kingston part of the name indicates that this village was part of a royal manor.

▼ **Corsham, High Street 1948** C162011
Stone quarries existed in the village from early times; in 1801 it was voted eighth most popular village in the county. The village exhibits a broad mix of architecture from Georgian houses through to 15th-century former weavers' cottages.

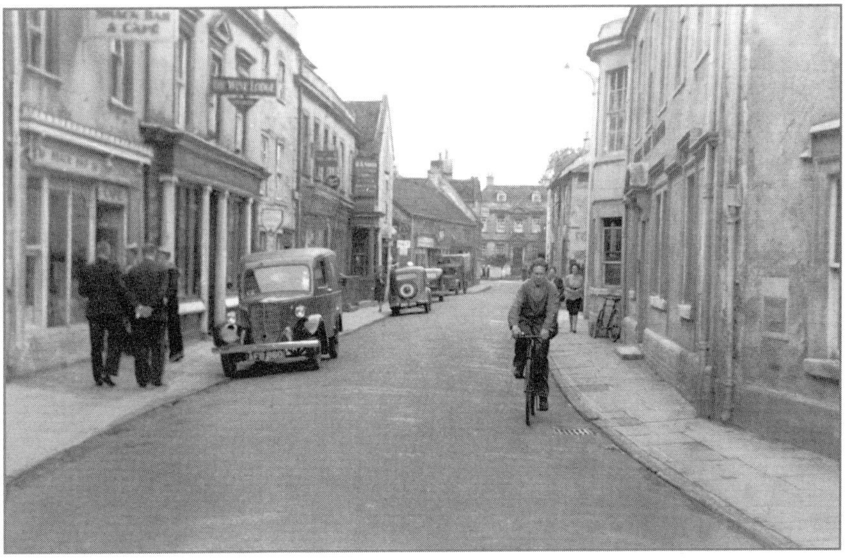

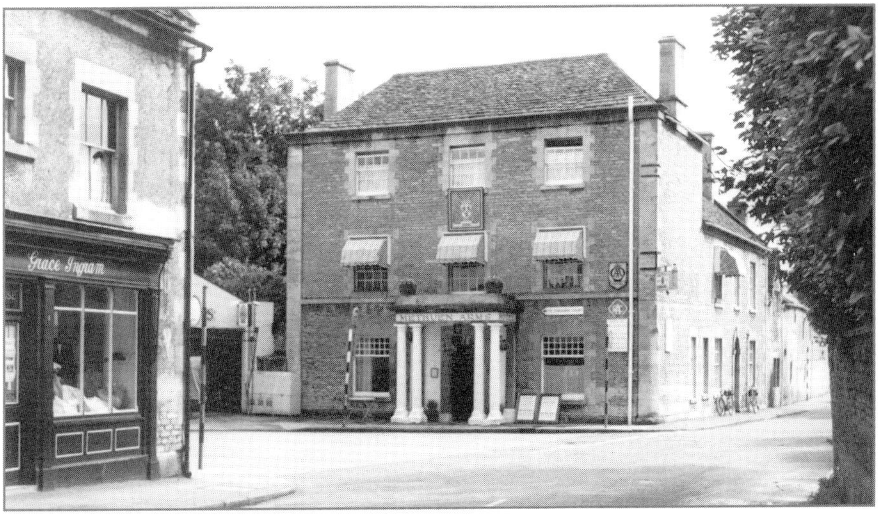

◀ **Corsham The Methuen Arms c1955** C162012
The public house and hotel bears the crest and name of the Methuen family of Corsham Court; the inn was built in 1582, but was known as the Red Lion Inn in 1809. Before that, it was the site of a house, Winters Court, dating from the 15th century. The village grew because of the weaving industry; it derives its name from the Saxon 'Cosa's ham' (village).

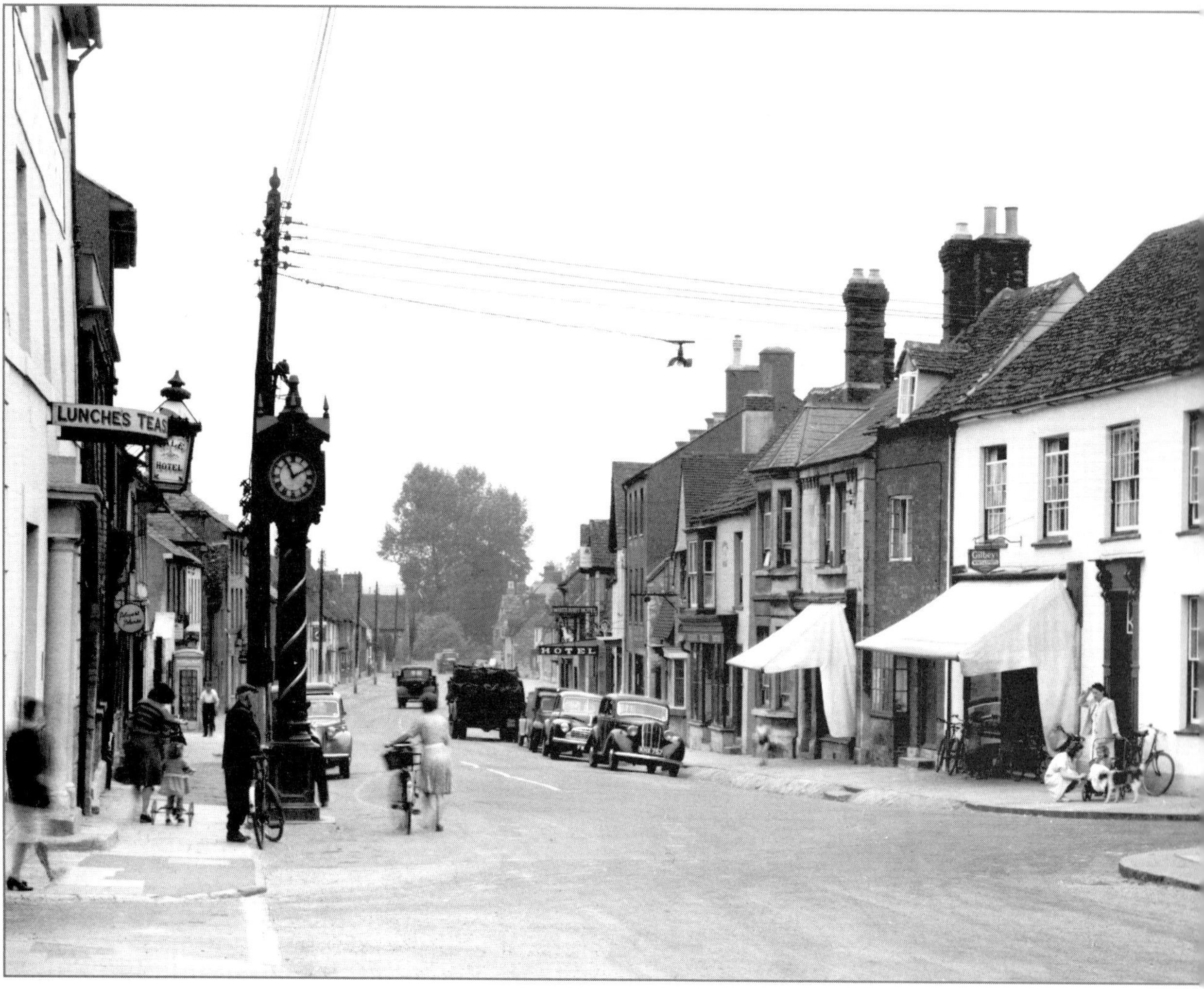

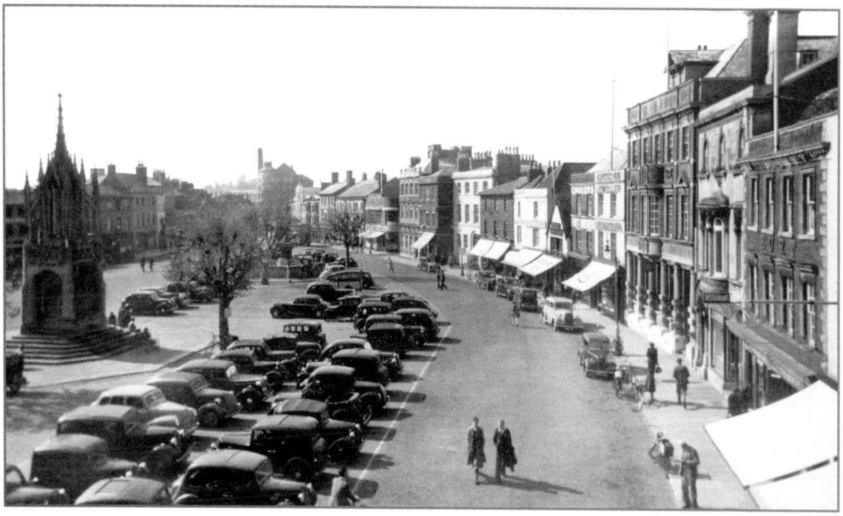

Devizes, The Market Place c1950 D28052
The town is very near the centre of the county. It did not come into being until after the Norman conquest. The Cross seen on the left was built in 1814 by Benjamin Wyatt; it tells the 1753 tale of Ruth Pierce of Potterne, who swore that she had paid for her third share of wheat and wished to drop dead if she was lying. She did just that, with the money still clutched in her hand. Note Lloyds Bank on the right, the Cheesecake Cafe and Cole & Son, Gunmakers.

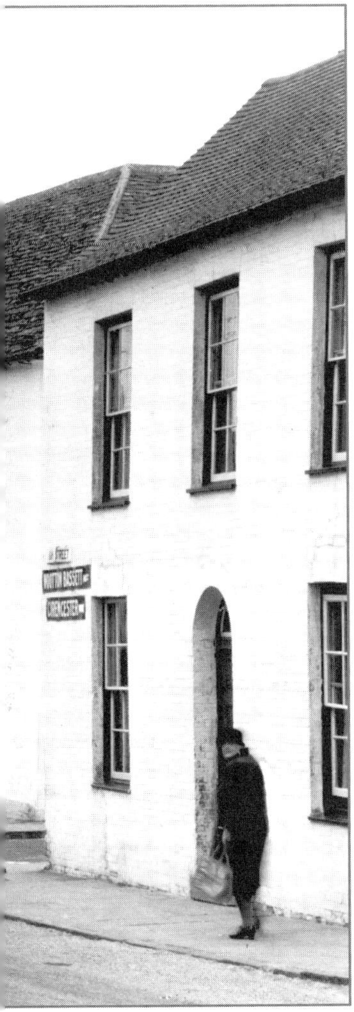

Cricklade, High Street c1950 C300003
This is the most northern Wiltshire town. There is much evidence of Roman occupation all around this area. The name literally means crossing place by the hill, from 'cruc' (hill) and 'gelad' (crossing). Note the White Hart Hotel on the right, and the Vale Hotel on the left by the magnificent clock.

Devizes, The Brittox c1960 D28073
The Brittox dates from 1300; the name simply means fortified place, probably inspired by the proximity of the castle walls. The town derives its name from its location, between Salisbury Plain and the Marlborough Downs where three boundaries met - 'ad divisas' (at the boundaries); it was Divisas in 1139.

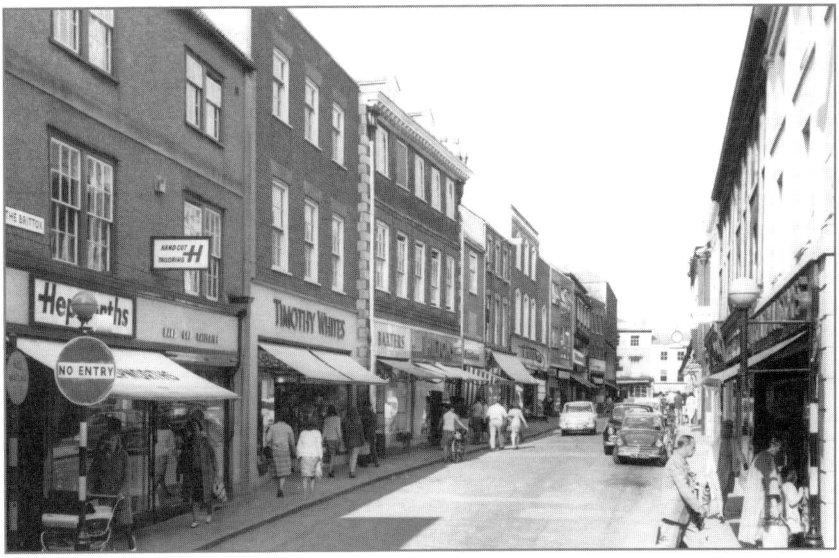

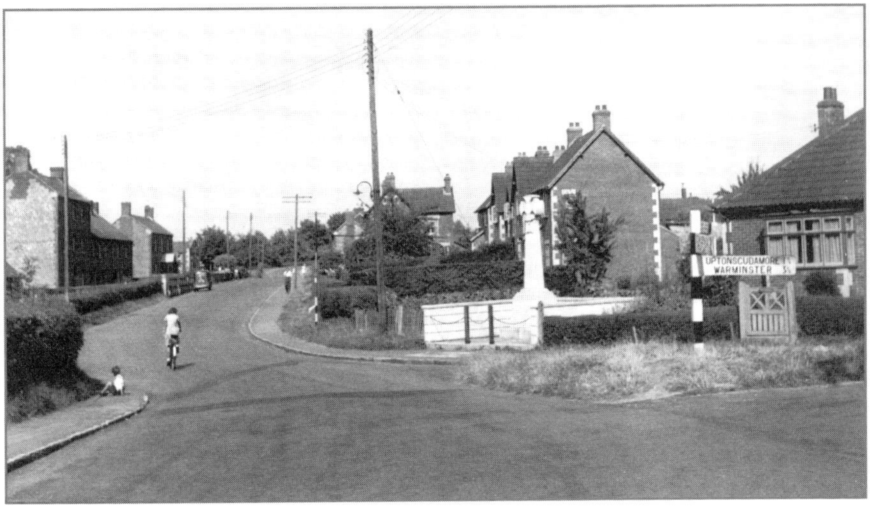

Dilton Marsh The War Memorial and High Street c1955 D111002
The name comes from the Saxon 'Dylla's tun' (settlement). The later addition of Marsh is self-explanatory. The village was a prosperous centre of weaving until the mechanisation of the process put an end to cottage-based manufacturing. The war memorial is to the village's dead of the Great War.

▼ **Downton, High Street c1955** D112007

An ancient borough on the Wiltshire/Hampshire border, the village thrived on its cottage industries, which included lace-making, flour-milling and paper-making. Tannery House was indeed once a tannery, having been taken over by the Downton Tanning Co in 1930. The name of the village derives from the Saxon 'dun' (hill) and 'tun' (settlement).

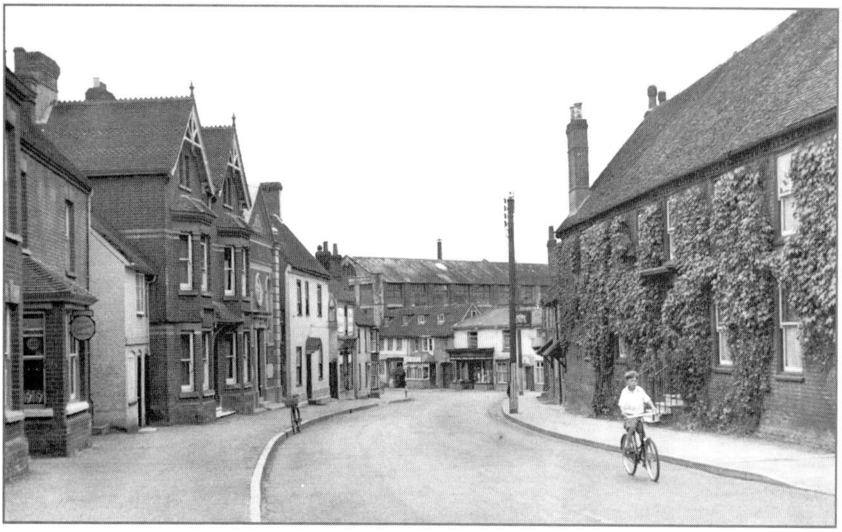

▼ **Durley, The Post Office c1955** D113002

The little and little-known former forest village of Durley is neatly concealed within Savernake Forest.

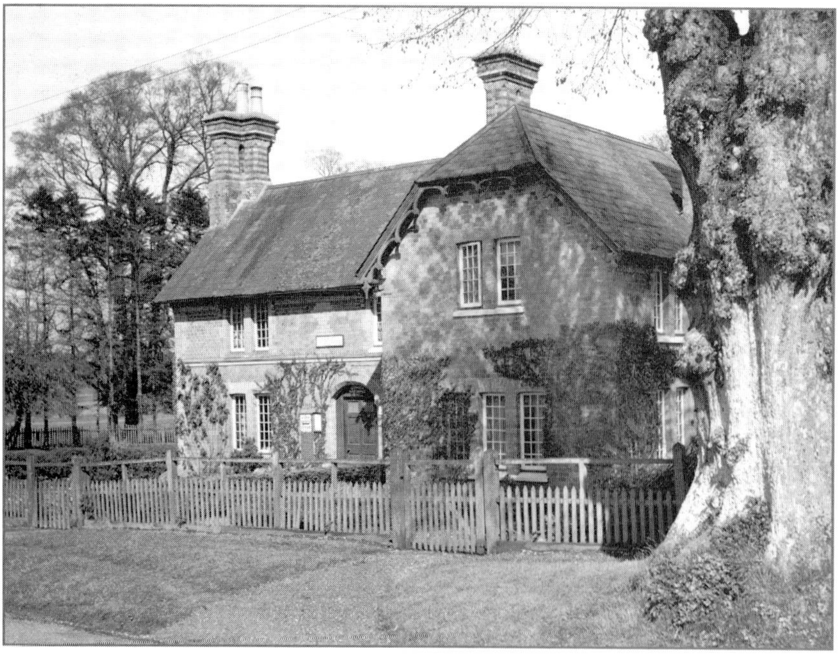

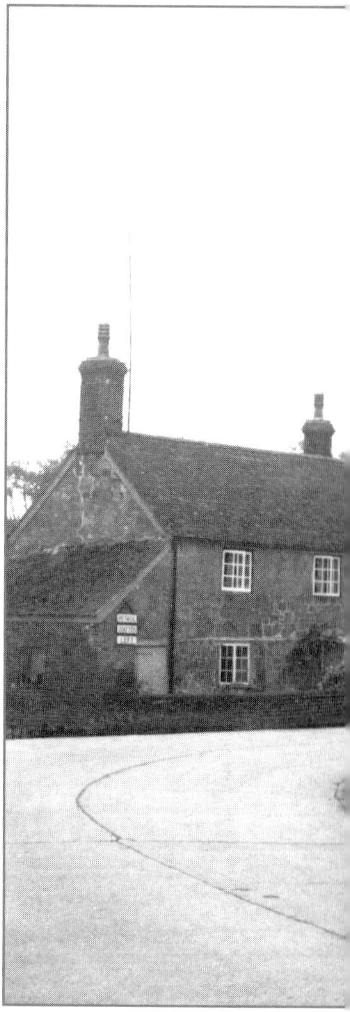

▲ **East Knoyle, The Post Office c1955** E163004

Once run by a Mrs Stamp, it was called Wren's Shop to commemorate the fact that Sir Christopher Wren was born here in 1631 or 1632. His father, Dr Wren, as well as being the vicar, was a Royalist during the English Civil War and was tried for designing ecclesiastical plasterwork that offended the Puritan victors. He was fined forty pounds and his living was sequestrated.

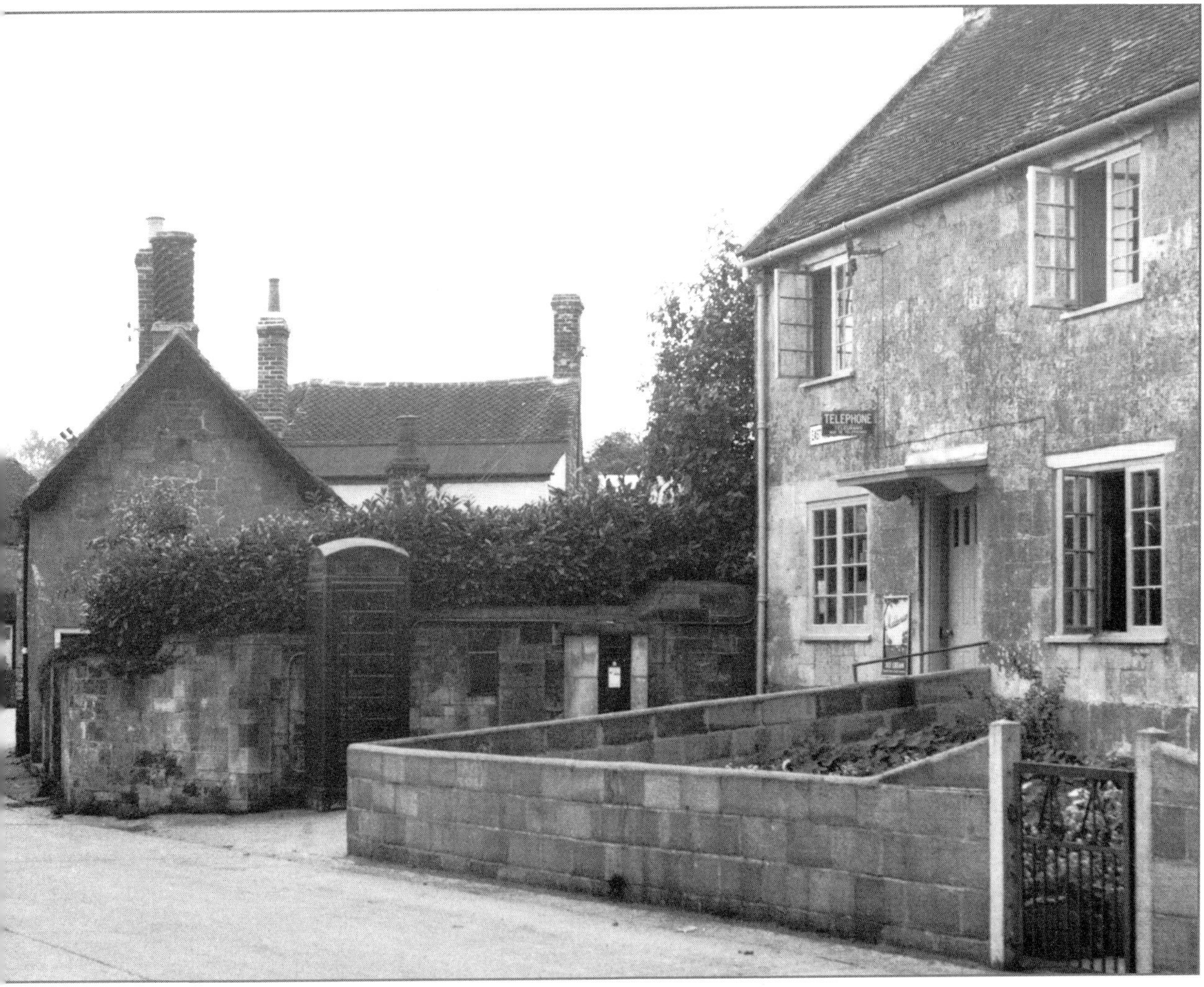

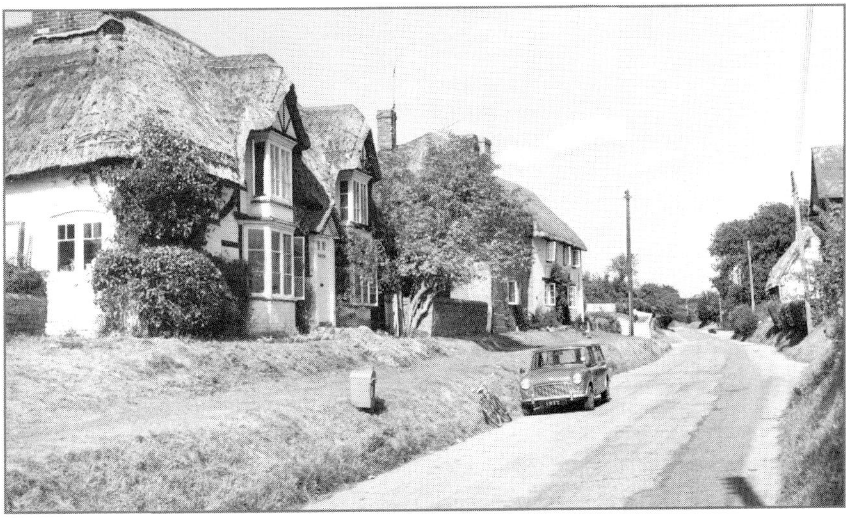

◄ **Easton Royal**
The Village c1960 E94016
The name was Estone in the Domesday Book, and the Royal comes from part of the parish being in the royal forest of Savernake.

▼ **Erlestoke, The Village c1950** E42003

Originally Stoke or Stokes, the prefix Erl may come from Earl Harold, who held the manor prior to the Conquest of 1066. Some of the houses on the main street were built to replace the original cottages, which were pulled down to make way for the rebuilding and landscaping of Erlestoke Manor prior to 1791. Many of the panels or statues over the doors were recovered from the demolition of the original Manor.

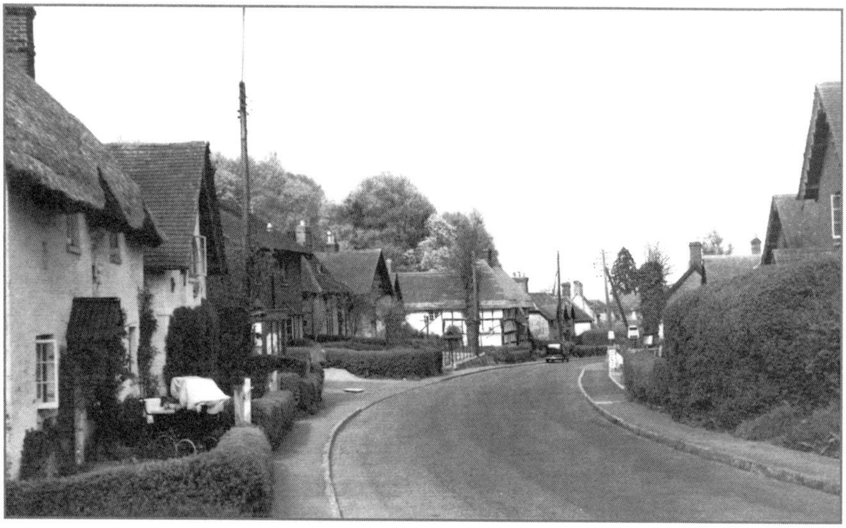

▼ **Figheldean, The Post Office c1950** F95007

Now a private residence, the Post Office shown here has moved.

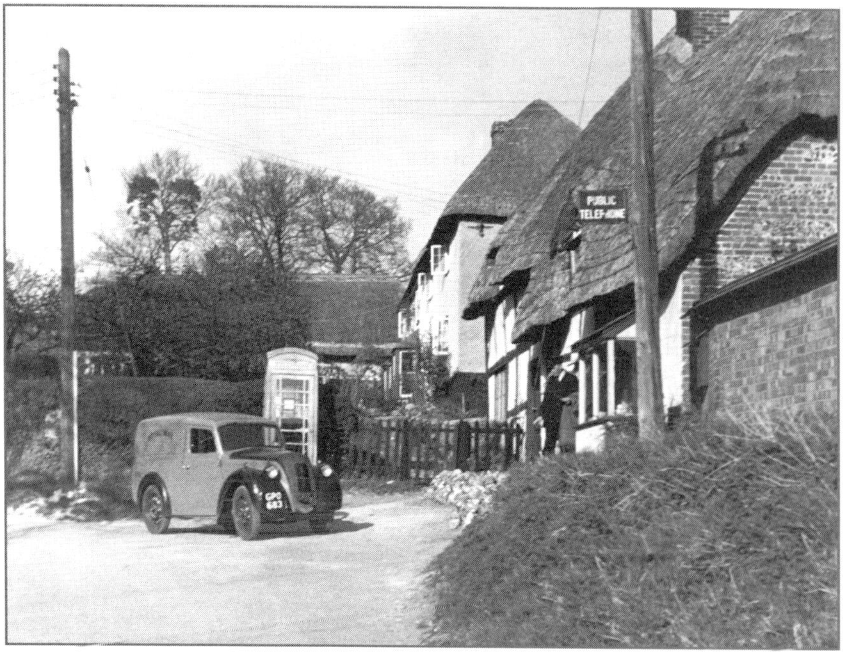

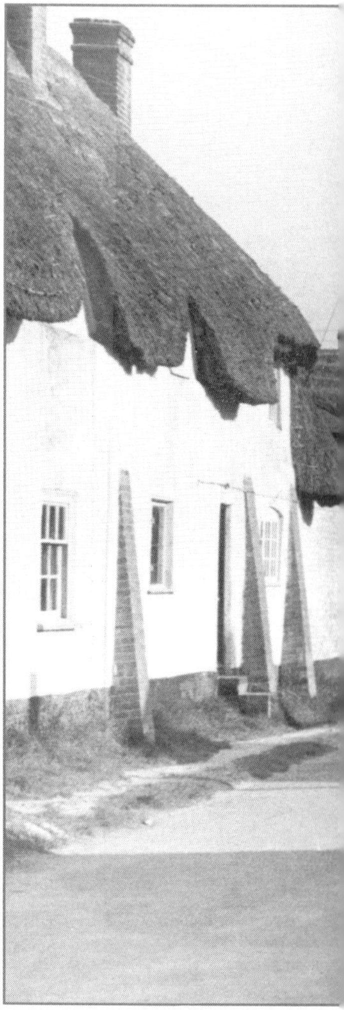

▲ **Figheldean The Village c1950**

F95014

The name derives from the Saxon 'Fygla's denu' (large valley).

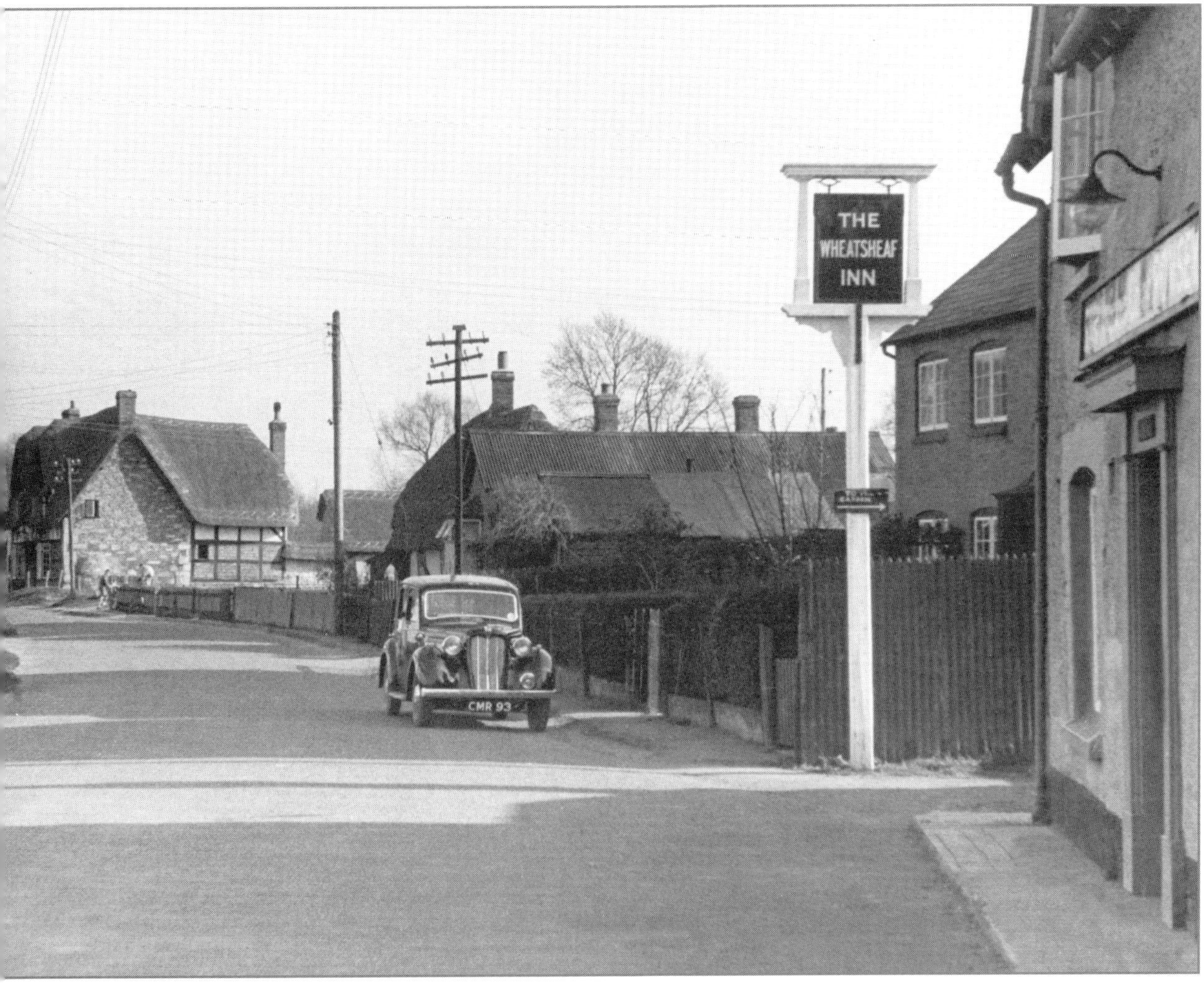

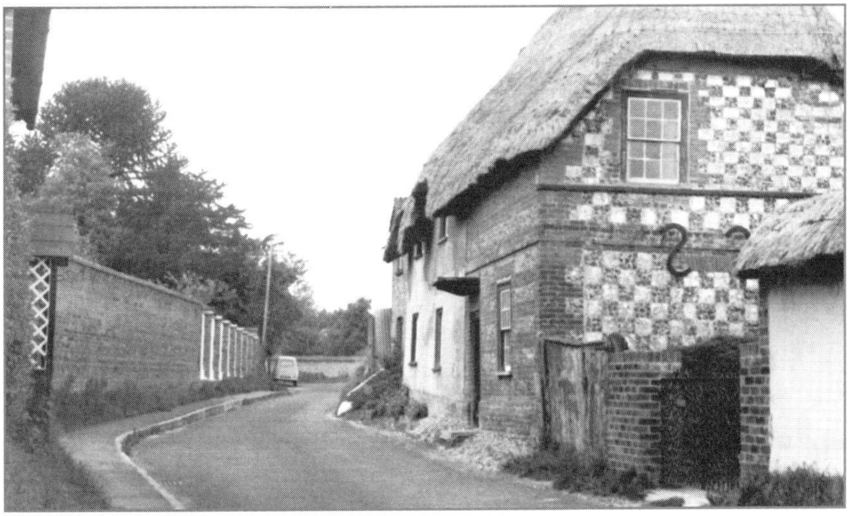

◄ **Fittleton, The Village c1955** F217023
The building on the right still looks the same today, but the single-storey building to the right of it is no longer there; it has been replaced by a new-built house. The name derives from the Saxon 'Fitela's tun' (settlement).

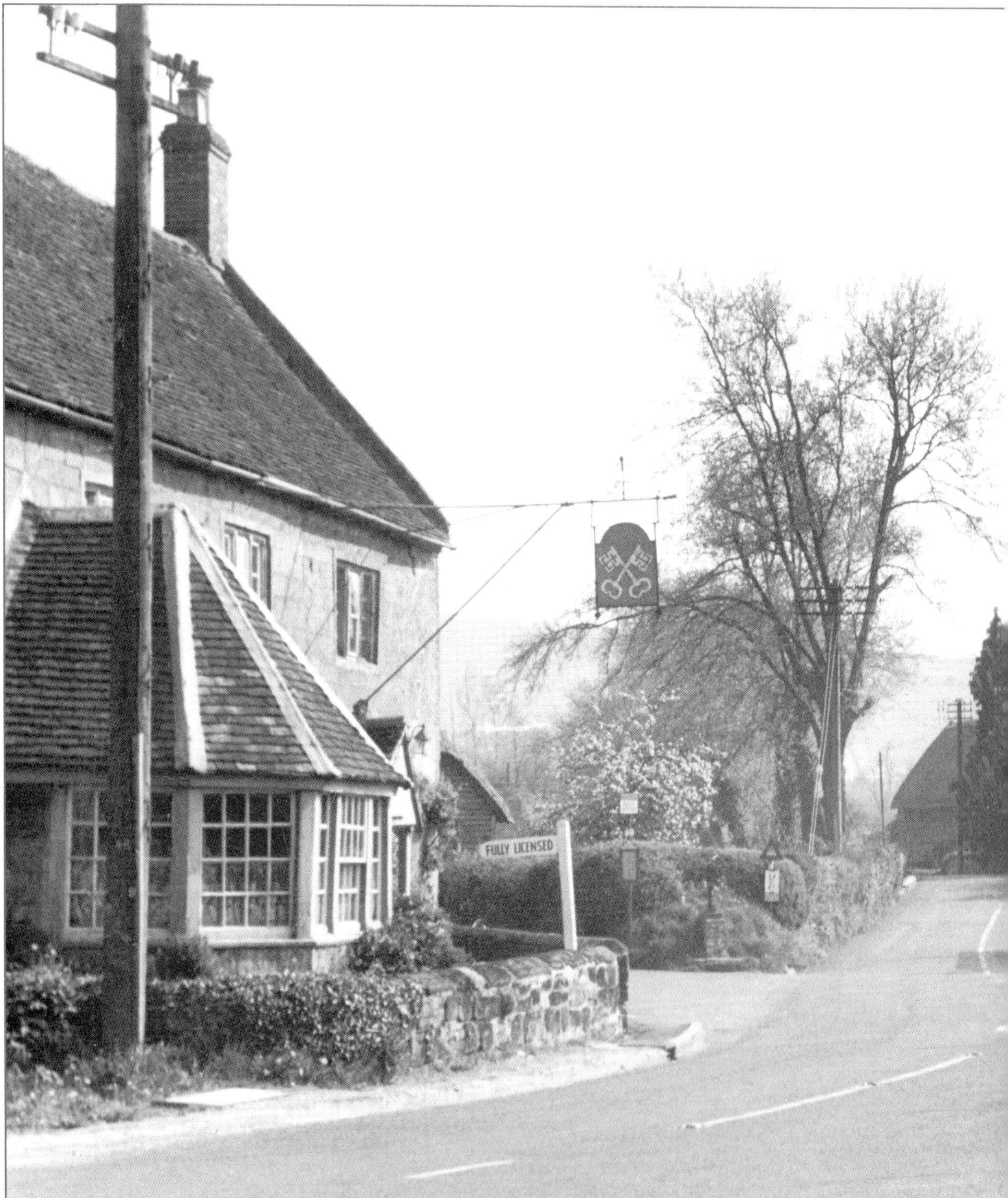
FULLY LICENSED

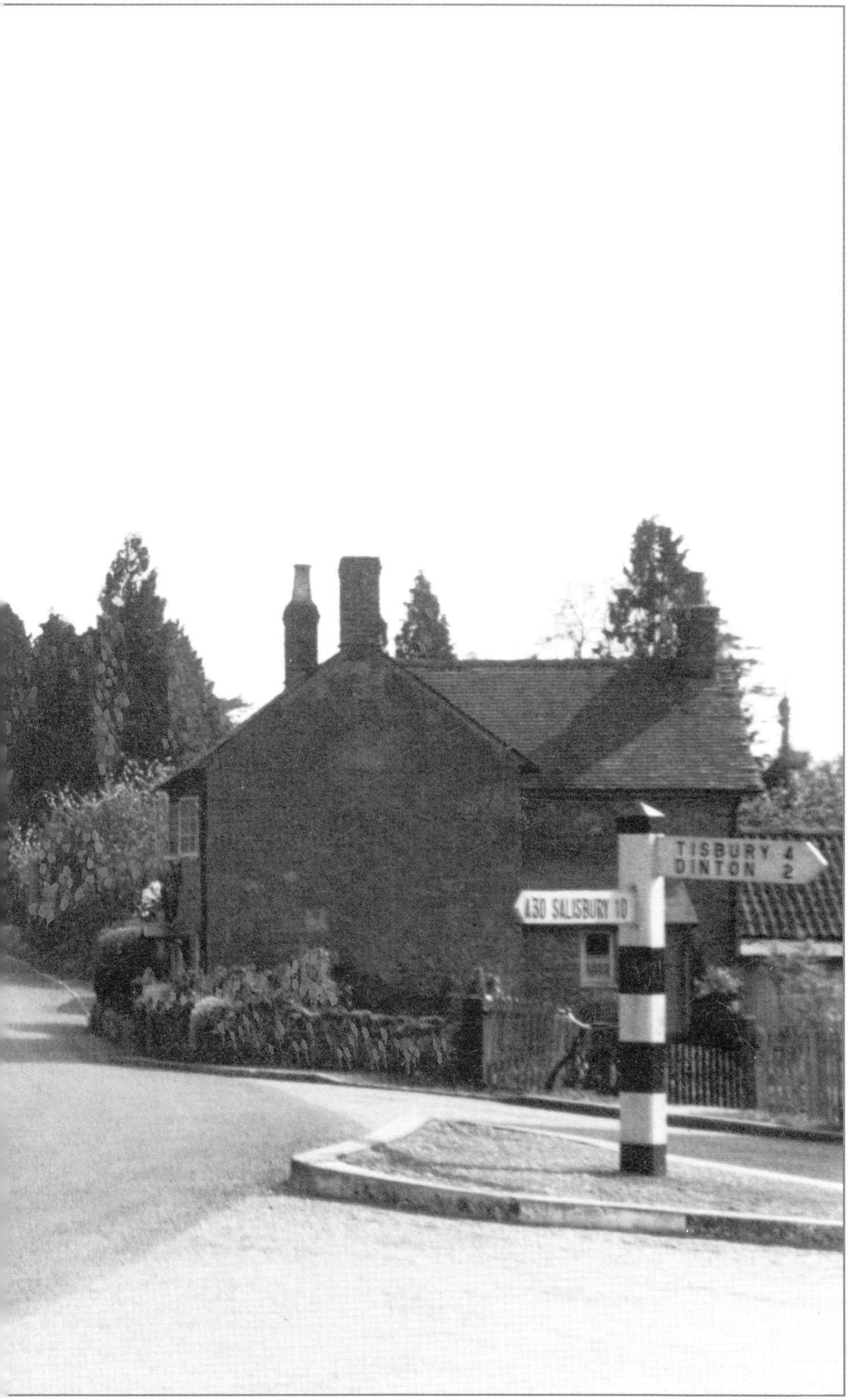

Fovant
The Cross Keys c1955
F96013

The village has kept its ancient Celtic name. It became the refuge of the Abbess of Wilton and her thirty nuns after she was pensioned off with £100 after the Dissolution of the Monasteries.

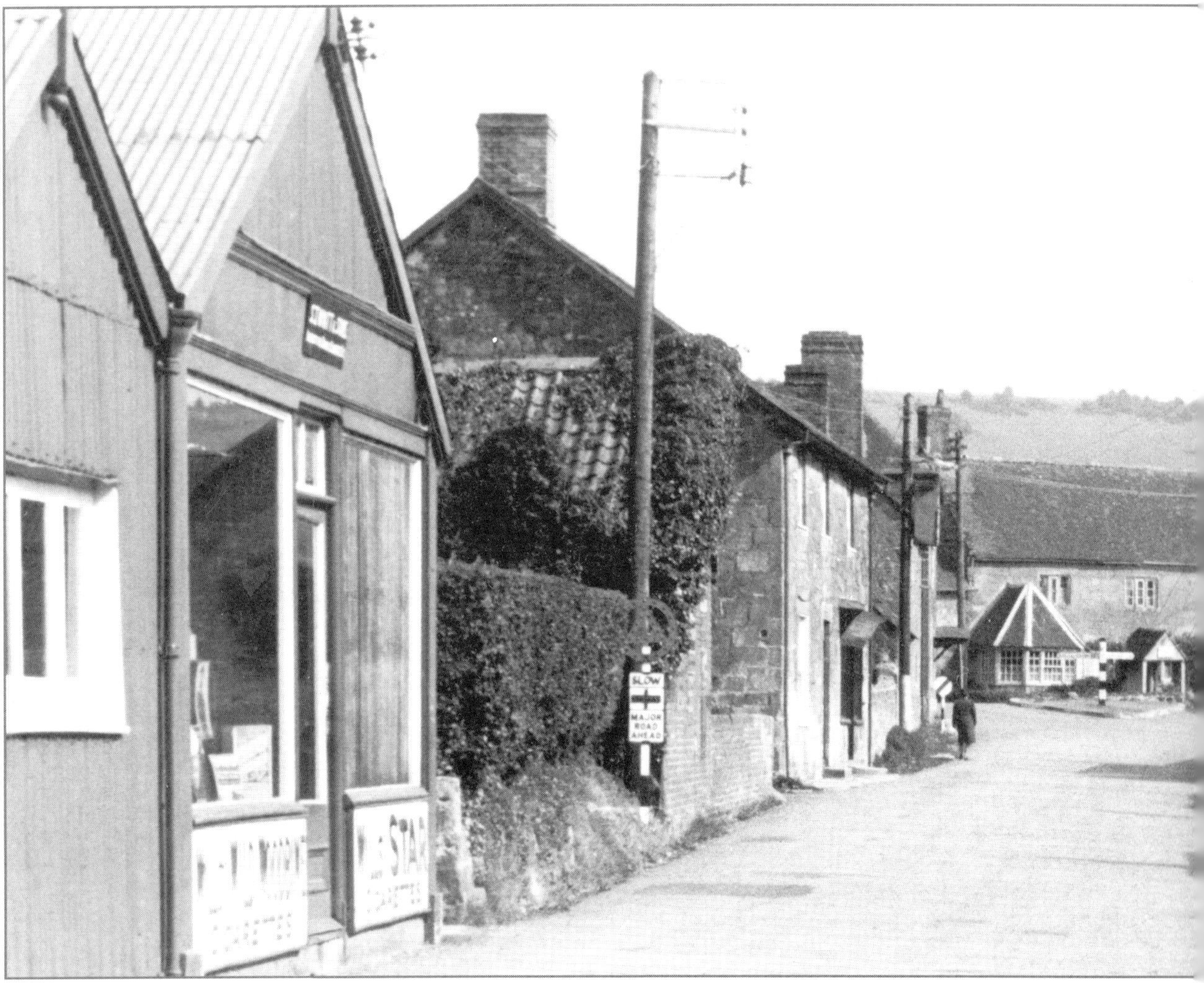

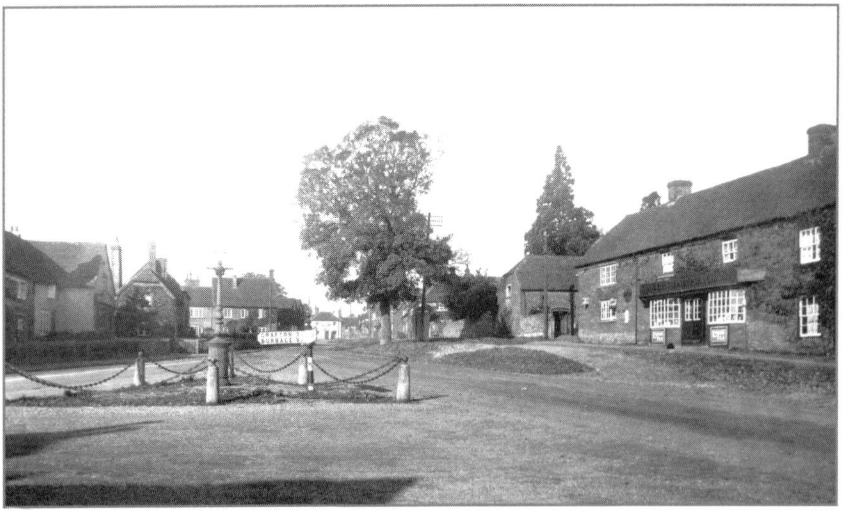

◄ **Great Bedwyn High Street c1955**

G132004

Very little romance surrounds the name of this village - it simply means the place where bindweed grows! The village was, however, a significant market town; it even struck its own coinage in Saxon times. Until the Reform Act of 1832 it was a rotten borough, and sent two members to Parliament.

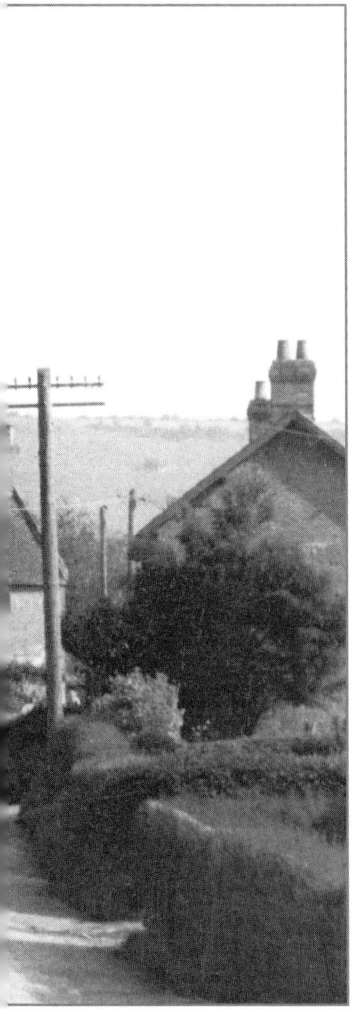

◄ **Fovant, The Village c1955**

F96014

A significant military presence during WWII has left its mark - the Wiltshire Regiment proudly cut its regimental badge into the chalk above the village. This was not the first - the London Rifle Brigade cut theirs in 1916, and from 1915 to 1917 over thirty regiments passed through Fovant, many adding their emblems in the chalk. Note the cigarette advertisements on the left for Wills Wild Woodbines and Wills Star.

▼ **Great Bedwyn, Station Approach c1955**

G132010

Though seemingly sleepy today, it was apparently not always thus. In 1648 a petition was sent expressing concern over the number of alehouses and the effect this was having on the village's servants - 'they go and abide in the alehouses and continue there two or three days'.

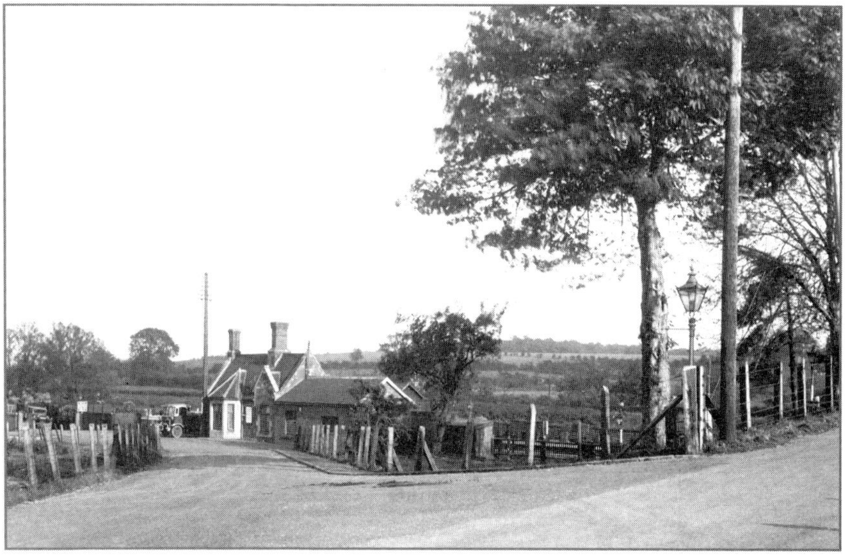

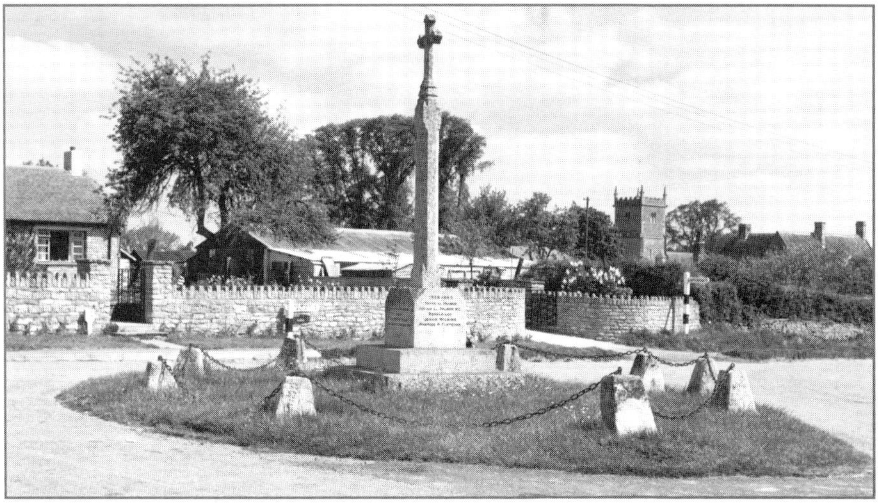

◄ **Great Somerford The Memorial c1955**

G133003

The name is significant. The ford, passable principally in the summer, was responsible for the death in 1605 of the village's rector, Richard Atwood, when he tried to reach the village in the winter floods. The church tower is that of St Peter and St Paul.

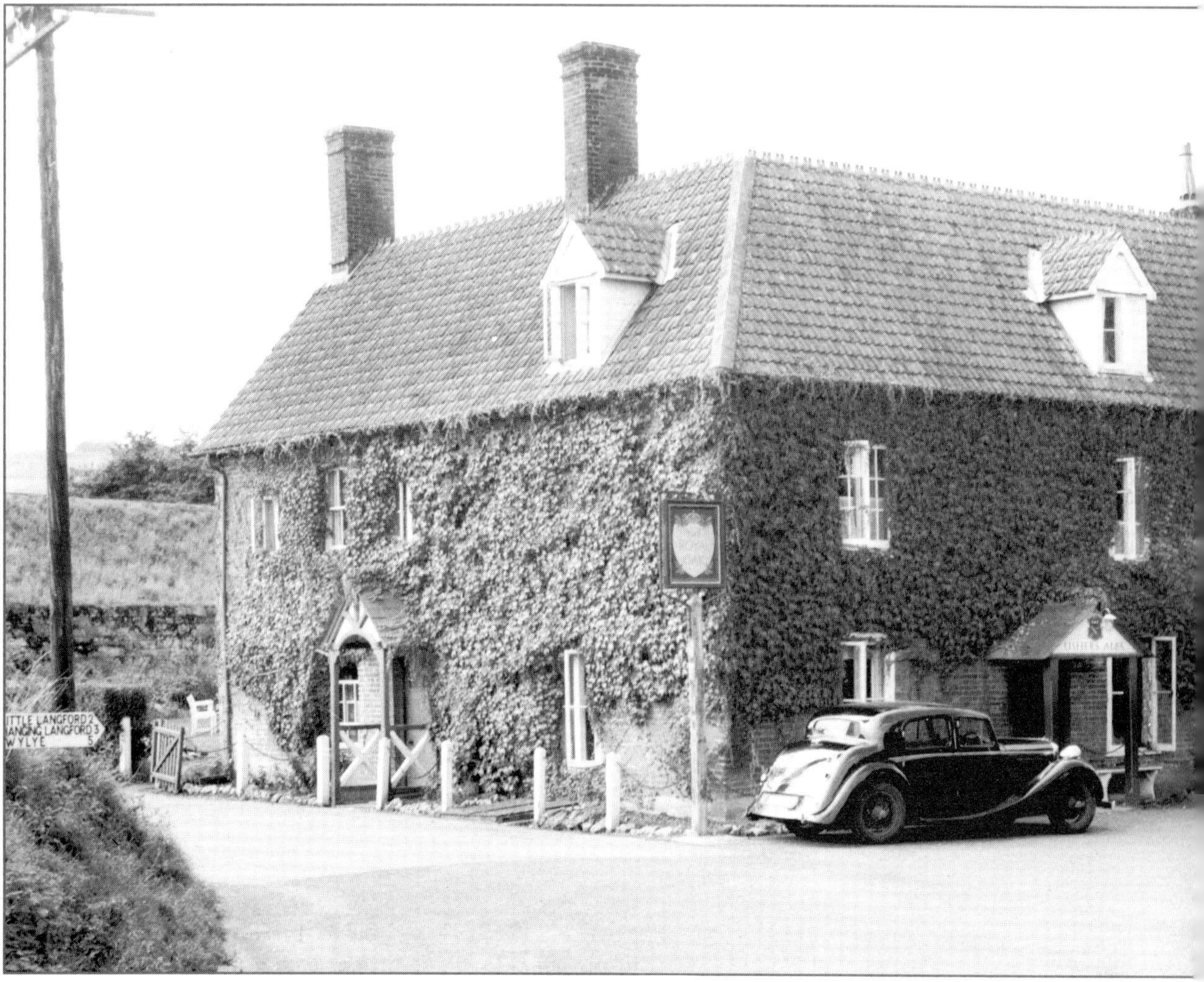

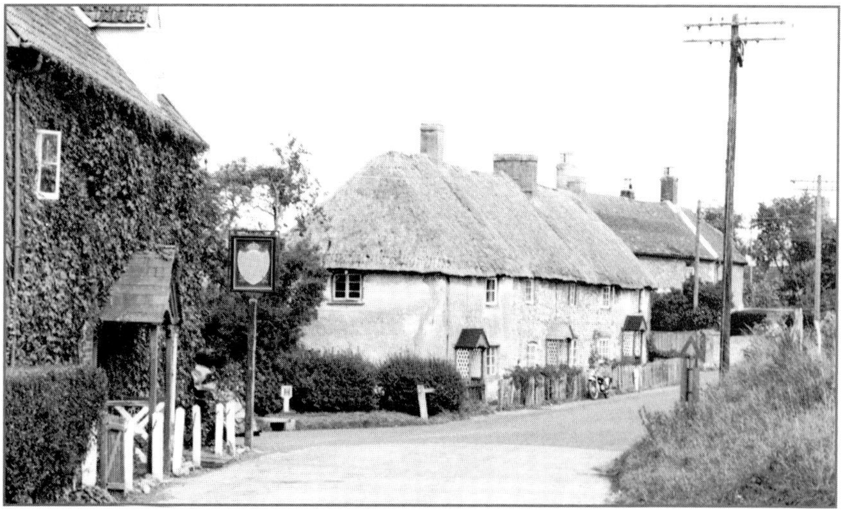

Great Wishford Lotmore Cottages and the Royal Oak c1950

G340003

Here we have another view of the Royal Oak, on the left, and the cottages beyond. The name derives from the Saxon for ford by the wych-elm.

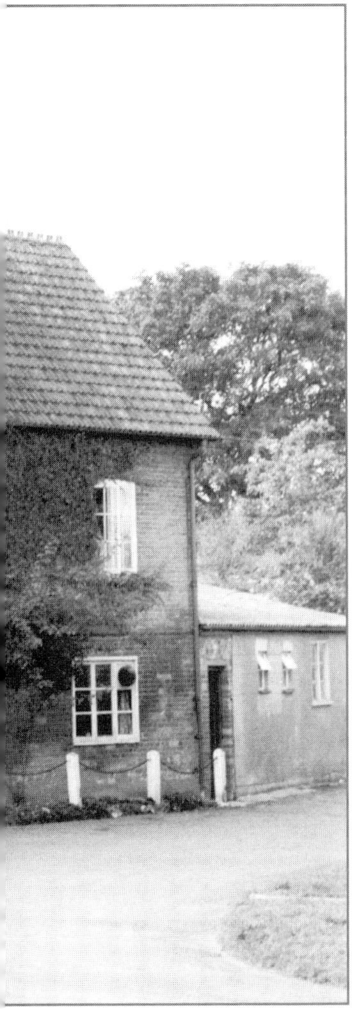

Great Wishford, Royal Oak c1950
G340001
On 29 May the residents of Great Wishford celebrate Oak Apple Day by processing into the nearby Groveley Woods to collect firewood. This assertion of ancient rights is accompanied by the cry of 'Groveley! Groveley! Groveley! and all Groveley!': this is said to refer to the victory of the villagers over the local landowner, the Earl of Pembroke, who tried to curtail their right to gather wood in Groveley Wood. However, documentary evidence suggests that this practice has gone on for many years before then, and may be connected with the prehistoric festival of the green woods.

Haxton, The Pound c1955 H486020
I am informed by a 81-year-old resident that there are moves afoot to re-name this 'The Green'. She says it has always been 'The Pound', so 'The Pound' it shall be. The village survives today very much as seen in this photograph.

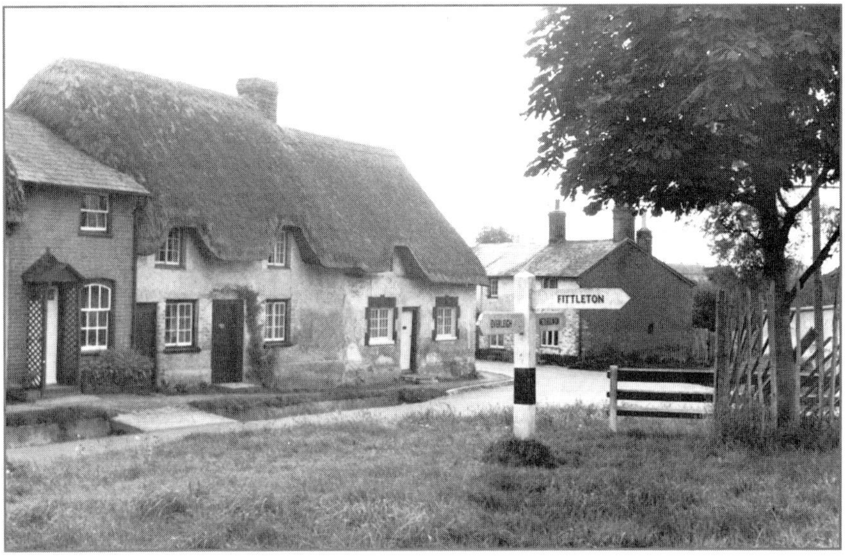

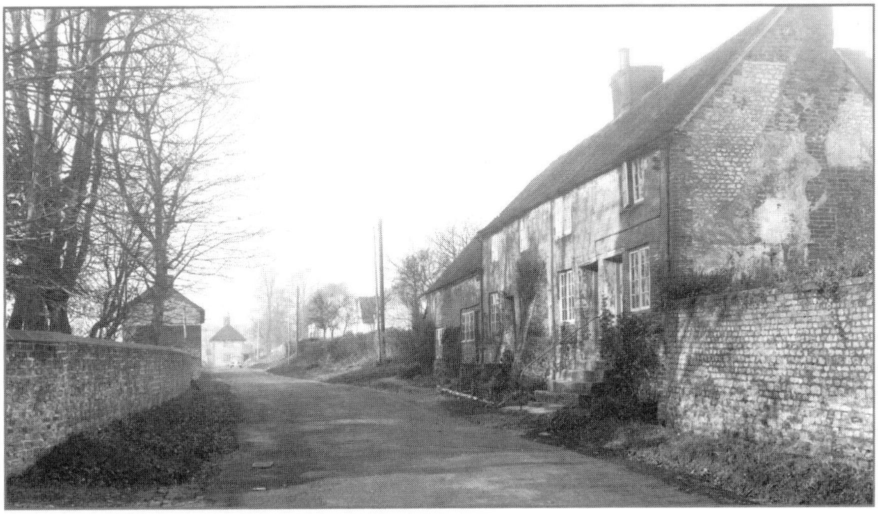

Heytesbury, Little London, Old Houses c1955 H235007
The house on the right used to house a laundry; it is now much converted but still recognisable, and its surroundings have changed very little. The name of the village derives from 'Heahthryth's burg' (fort). Little London is thought to come from the fact that the Burgesses who elected the Members of Parliament lived in houses concentrated in that area.

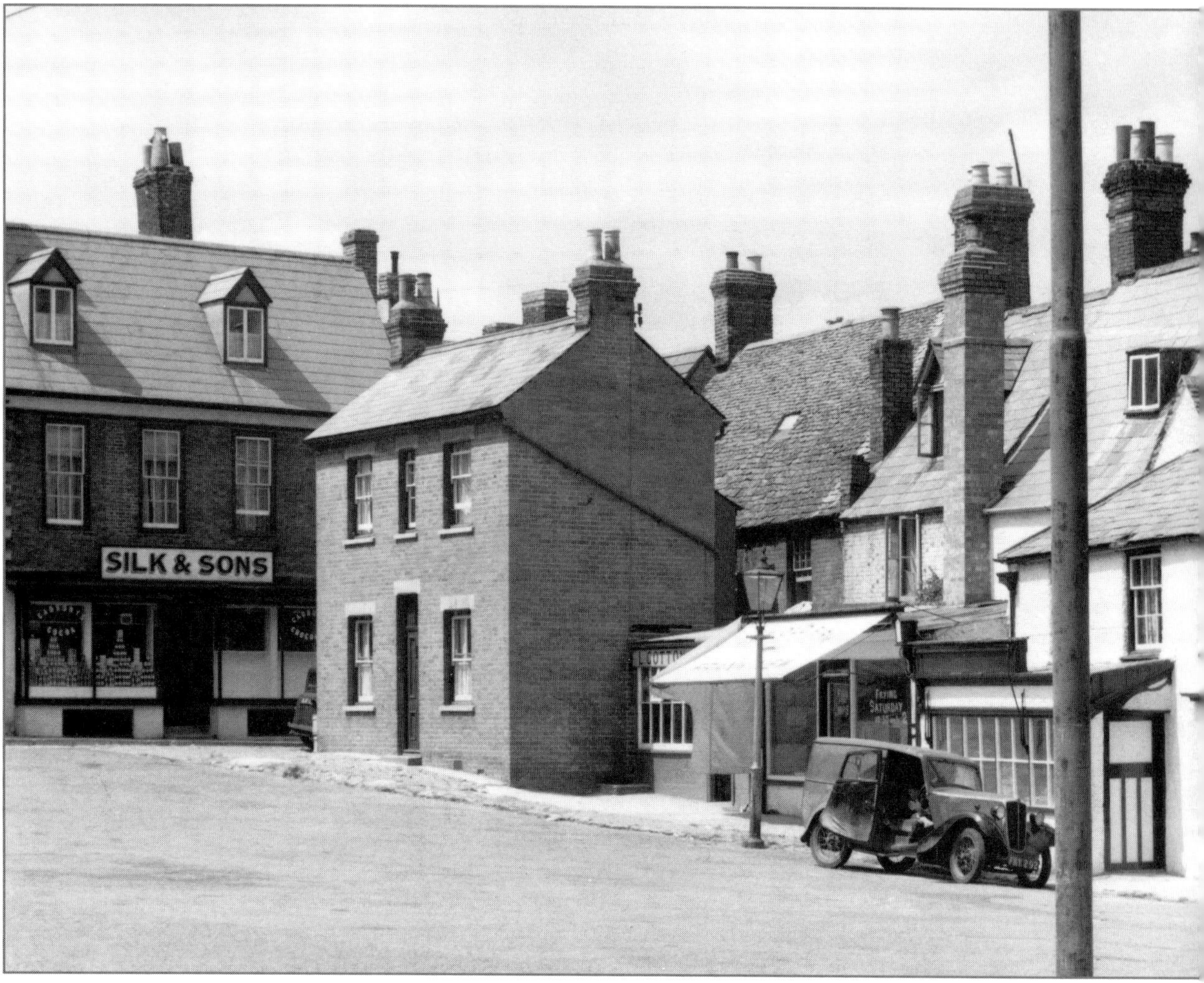

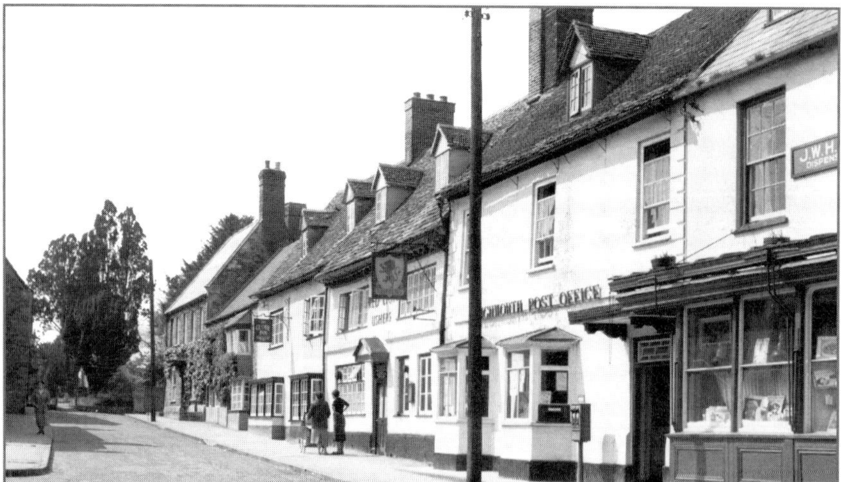

◄ **Highworth Sheep Street c1955**

H157018

Moving up the street, on the right we can see J W H Bran's Chemist shop, the Red Lion and the Globe Inn. Highworth was once of greater significance than neighbouring Swindon, which now overshadows it. It is amusing to note that Swindon's first postal address was 'Swindon, near Highworth'.

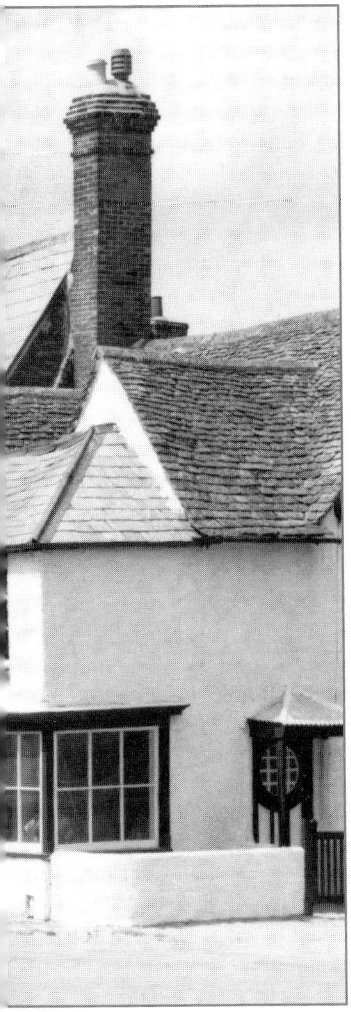

◄ **Highworth, The Market Place c1945** H157004

Note the Silk & Sons shop advertising Cadbury's Cocoa in the window. The original name for the village was simply Worth, the Saxon for homestead. A local legend has it that Oliver Cromwell once fired canon at the Highworth Church from Castle Hill. The scars on the church can be seen, although the three-mile range with 17th-century ordnance makes Castle Hill as a source of the artillery fire somewhat unlikely. What is certain is that Highworth was loyal to Charles I in the Civil War.

▼ **Horningsham Old Cottages c1955**

H487007

The village was created out of the forest of Selwood. These former almshouses on Church Street in the village can be seen today exactly as in this picture.

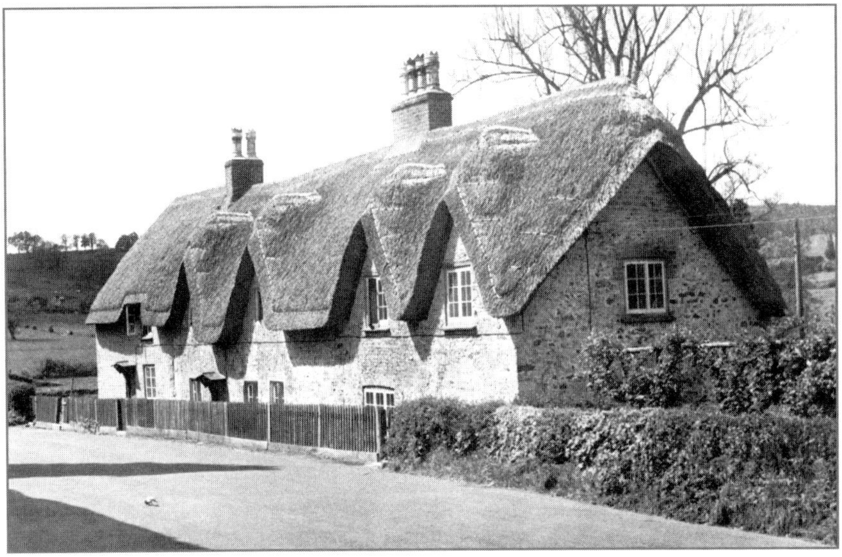

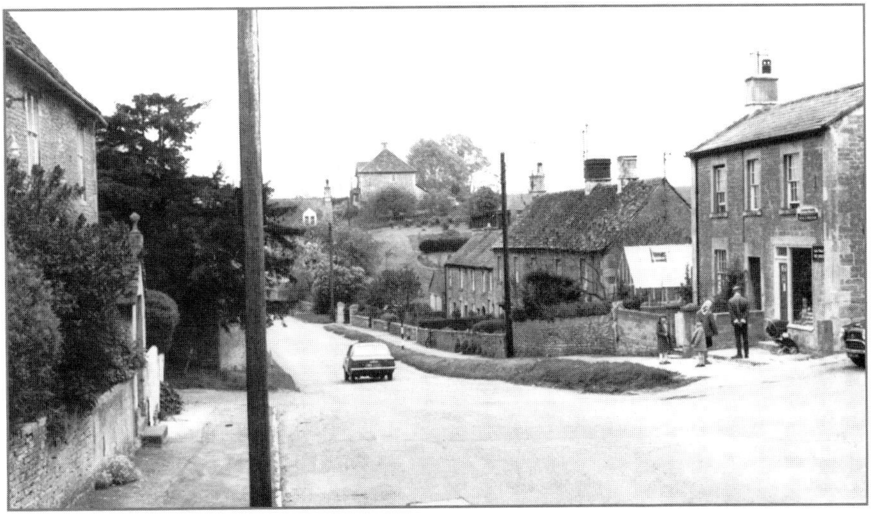

◄ **Kington St Michael The Village and the Post Office c1960**

K168018

The village has two very famous sons: John Aubrey, born in the parish in 1626, and John Britton, born in 1771. Both are commemorated in a stained glass window in the church. The name of the village probably simply comes from the Saxon 'cyning' (king's) and 'tun' (settlement). The Post Office shown here still exists.

▼ **Kington St Michael, The Village c1960** K168007
The village is on the Wiltshire/Gloucester border, very near the Roman Way. Note the poster on the gate on the right advertising a 'Grand Spring Bazaar'.

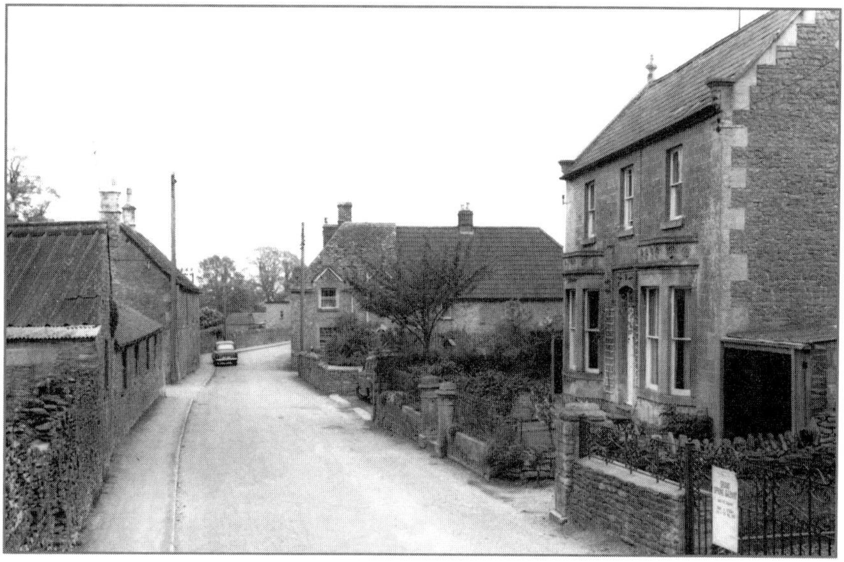

▼ **Limpley Stoke, The Lower Village c1955** L47019
This view shows the Post Office and General Stores. The village is divided into Upper, Middle and Lower. The village name of Stoke comes from the Saxon 'hangian' (outlying) and 'stoc' (farm). Limp may be a personal name, and ly is from the Saxon 'leah' (clearing).

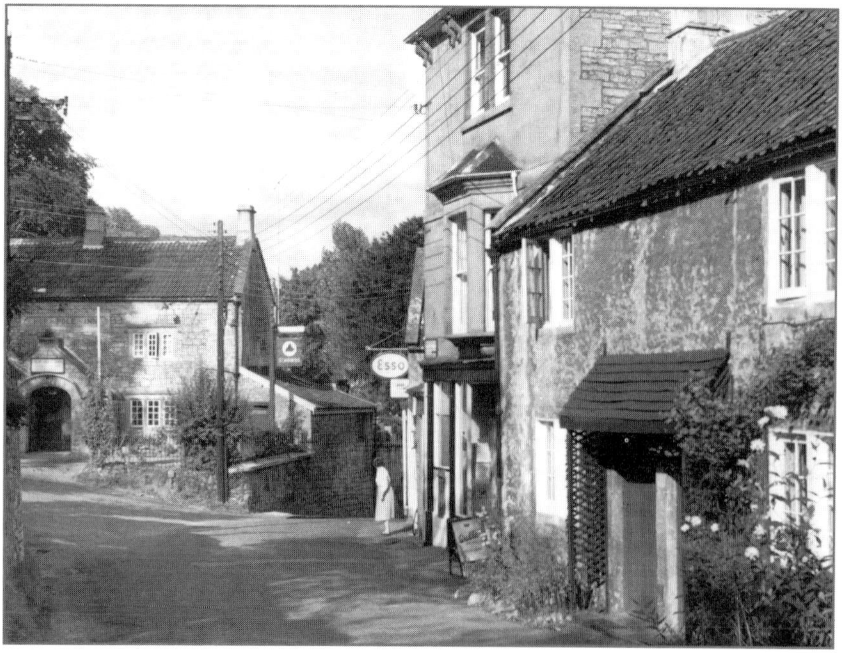

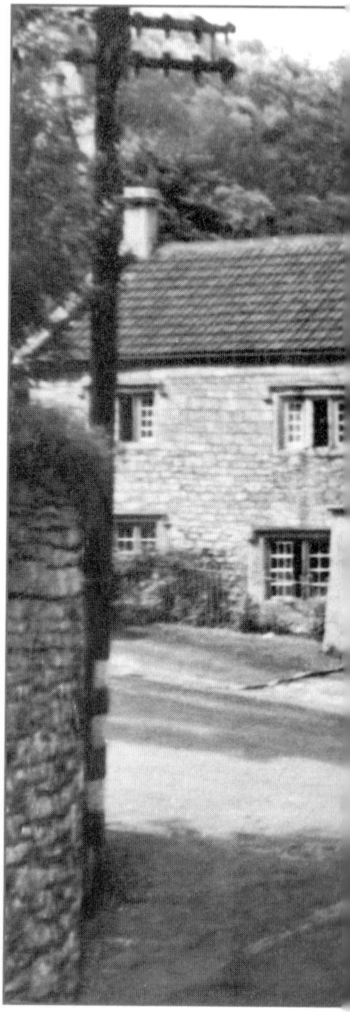

▲ **Limpley Stoke The Hop Pole Inn c1950** L47004
Note the pub sign declaring Simonds Ales. The village was originally called Hanging Stoke, and if you visit the village you can easily see why.

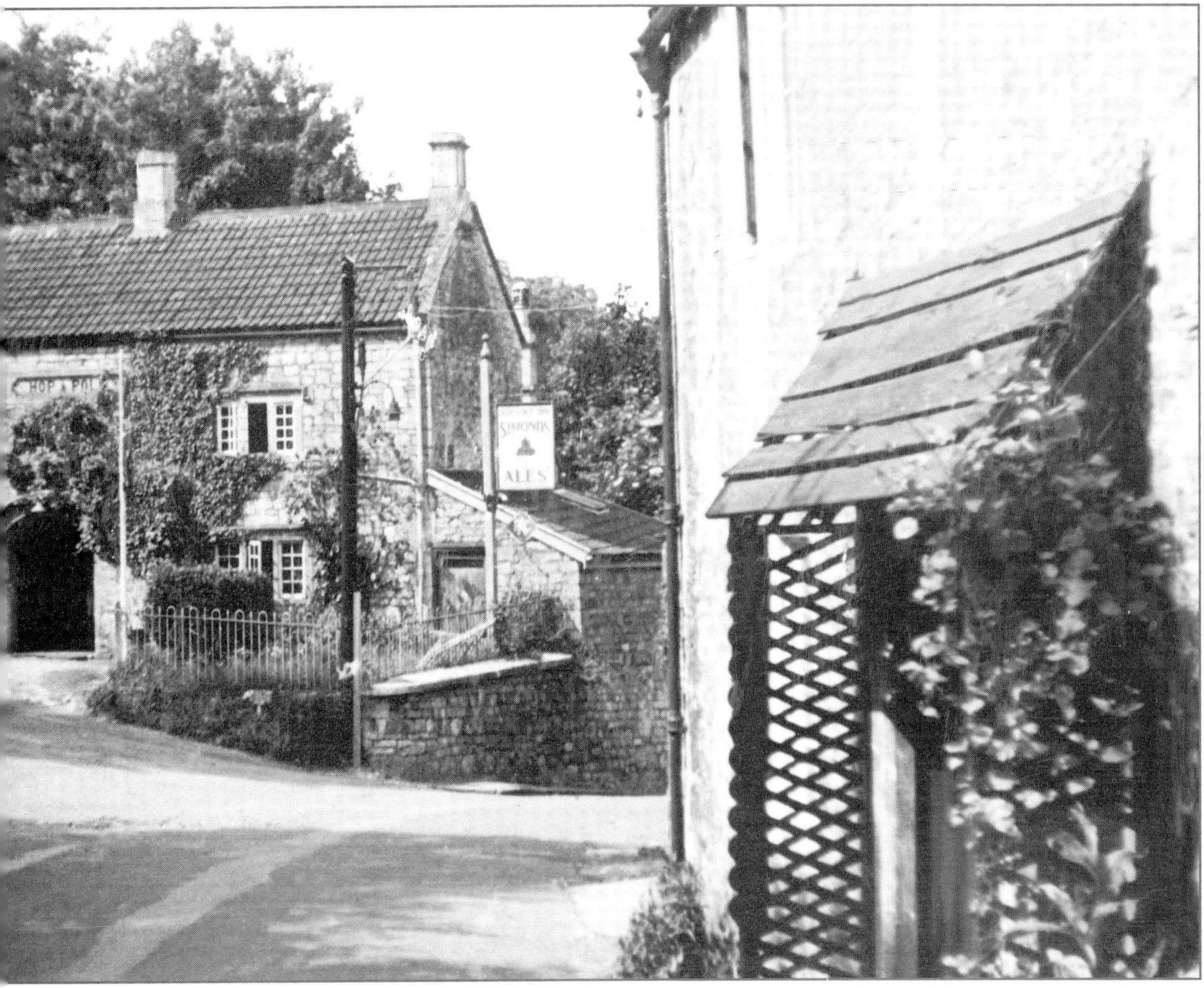

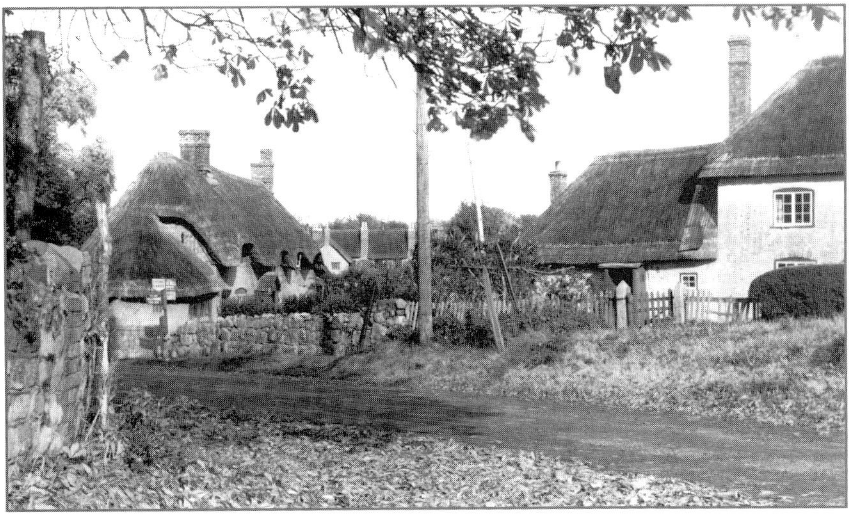

Lockeridge, The Village c1955 L189006

This is not really a village at all, as it has no church. The name comes from 'the ridge marked by enclosures'. The manor once belonged to the Knights Templar before the order was suppressed in 1308.

▼ **Luckington, The Church c1955** L191002
Dedicated to Our Lady and Ethelbert of Kent, the church has been here for over seven hundred years. It is said that Earl Harold built a hunting lodge nearby at Luckington Court before he became King of England. The village name simply means Luca's settlement.

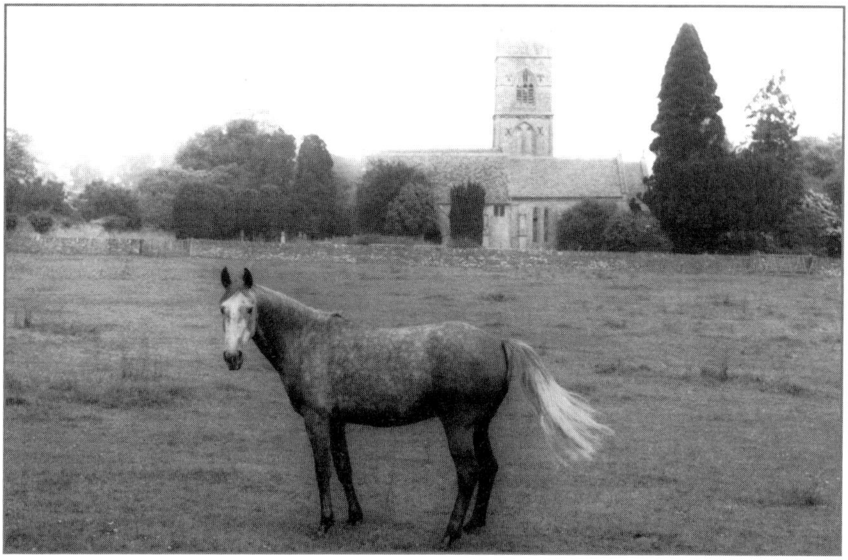

▼ **Ludgershall, High Street c1950** L109009
This place was significant in Saxon times, so much so that the Normans built an impressive castle here; it played an important role in the civil war between Stephen and Matilda. The Crown Hotel is to the left; the army truck beside it is a frequent sight in this part of Wiltshire (Tidworth Camp is nearby).

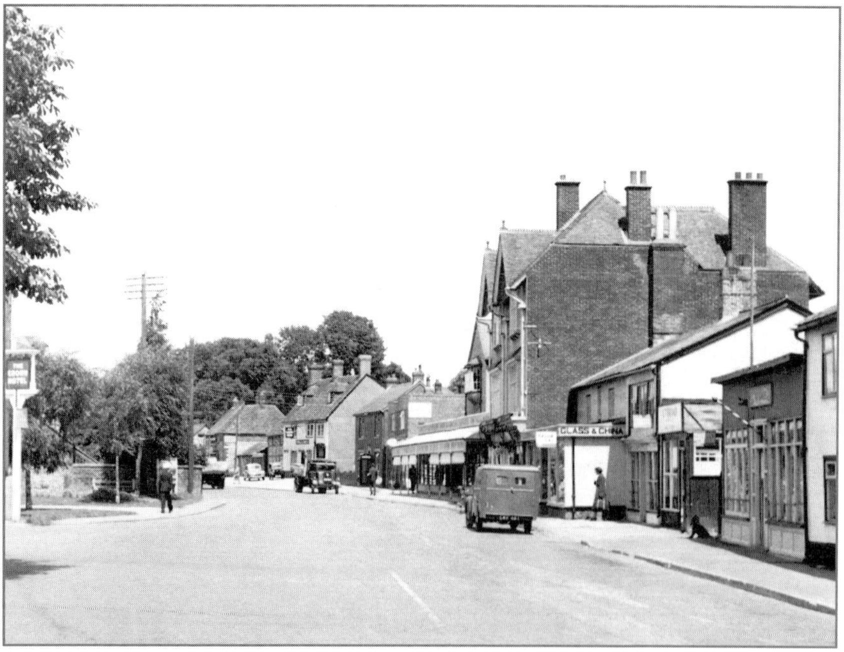

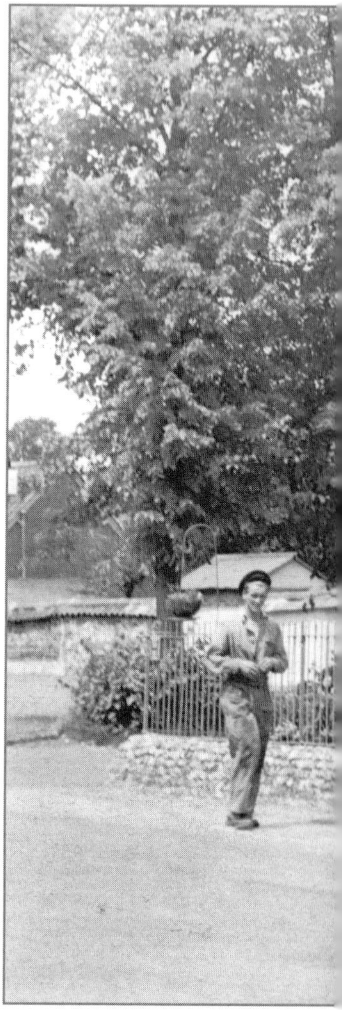

▲ **Ludgershall The War Memorial c1950** L109013
Ludgershall is a former market town dating from Saxon times. Its name may derive from 'Lutegar's gaershealh' (grazing hollow). The Crown Hotel can be seen again behind the Memorial.

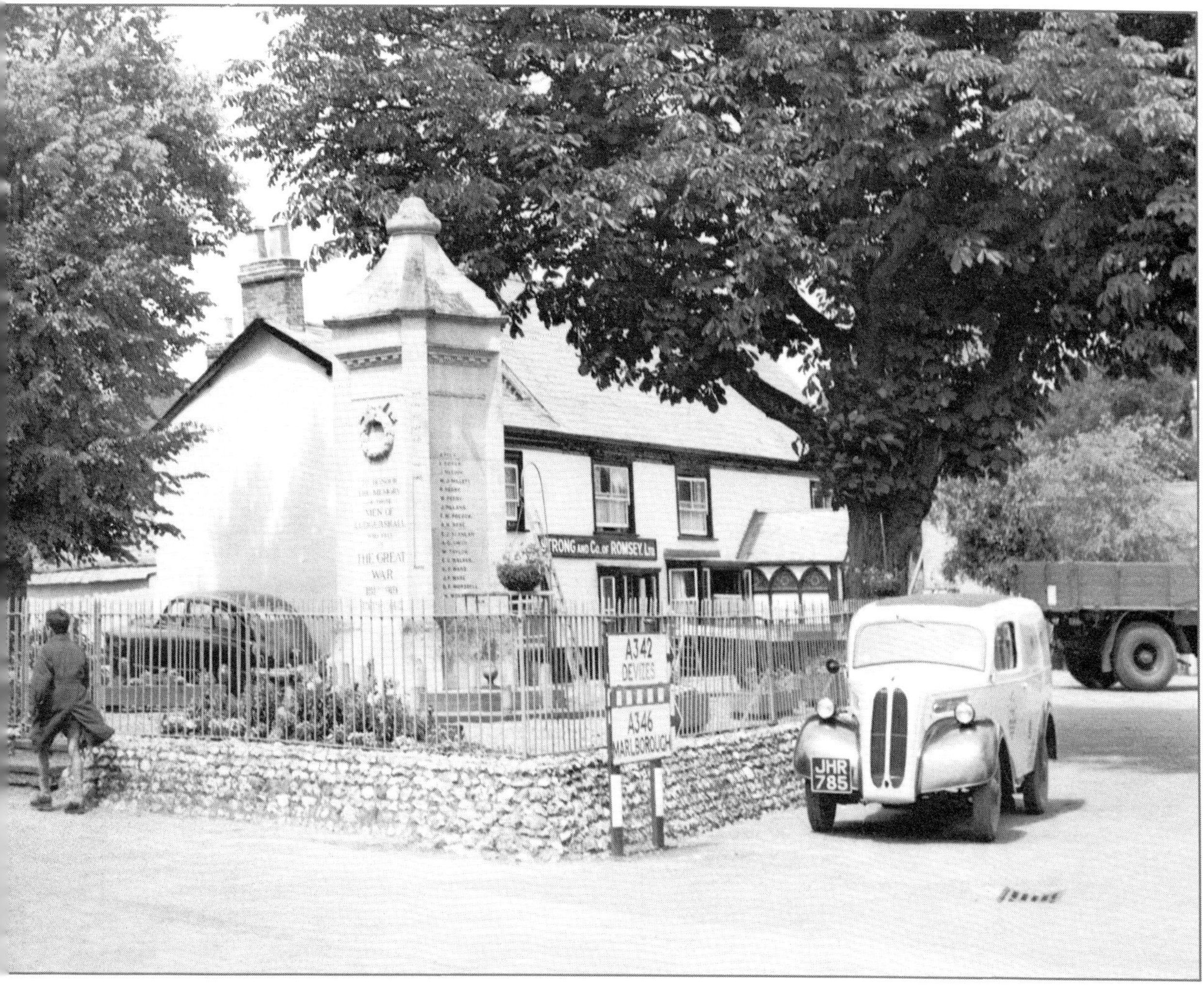

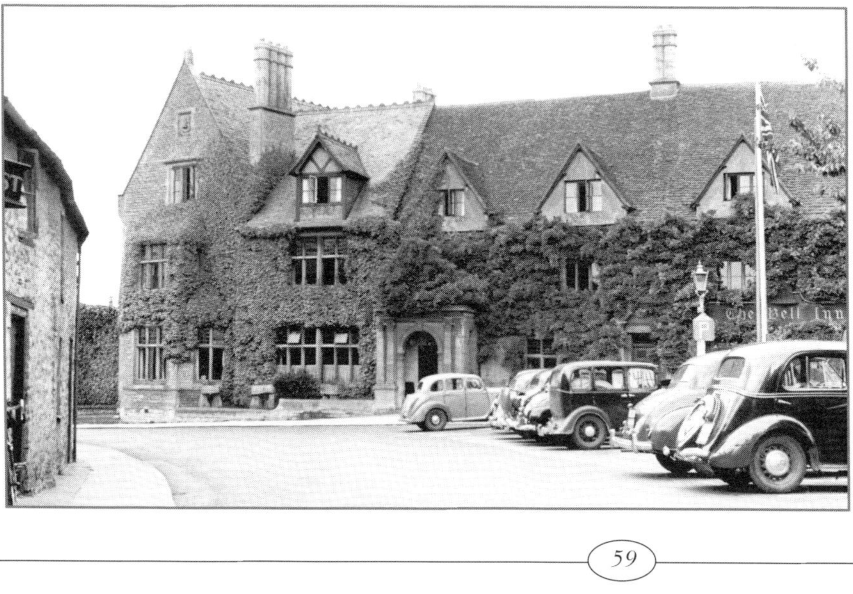

Malmesbury
The Bell Inn c1950

M13010

The Bell Inn was probably once a guest house for the Abbey; it still boasts a 13th-century window. The market town of Malmesbury is the oldest borough in England - it has a charter given by Alfred the Great in 880. King Aethelstan, King Alfred's grandson, rebuilt the abbey in 941, which presupposes the presence of a monastic house even before then. The abbey was closed by Henry VIII in 1539.

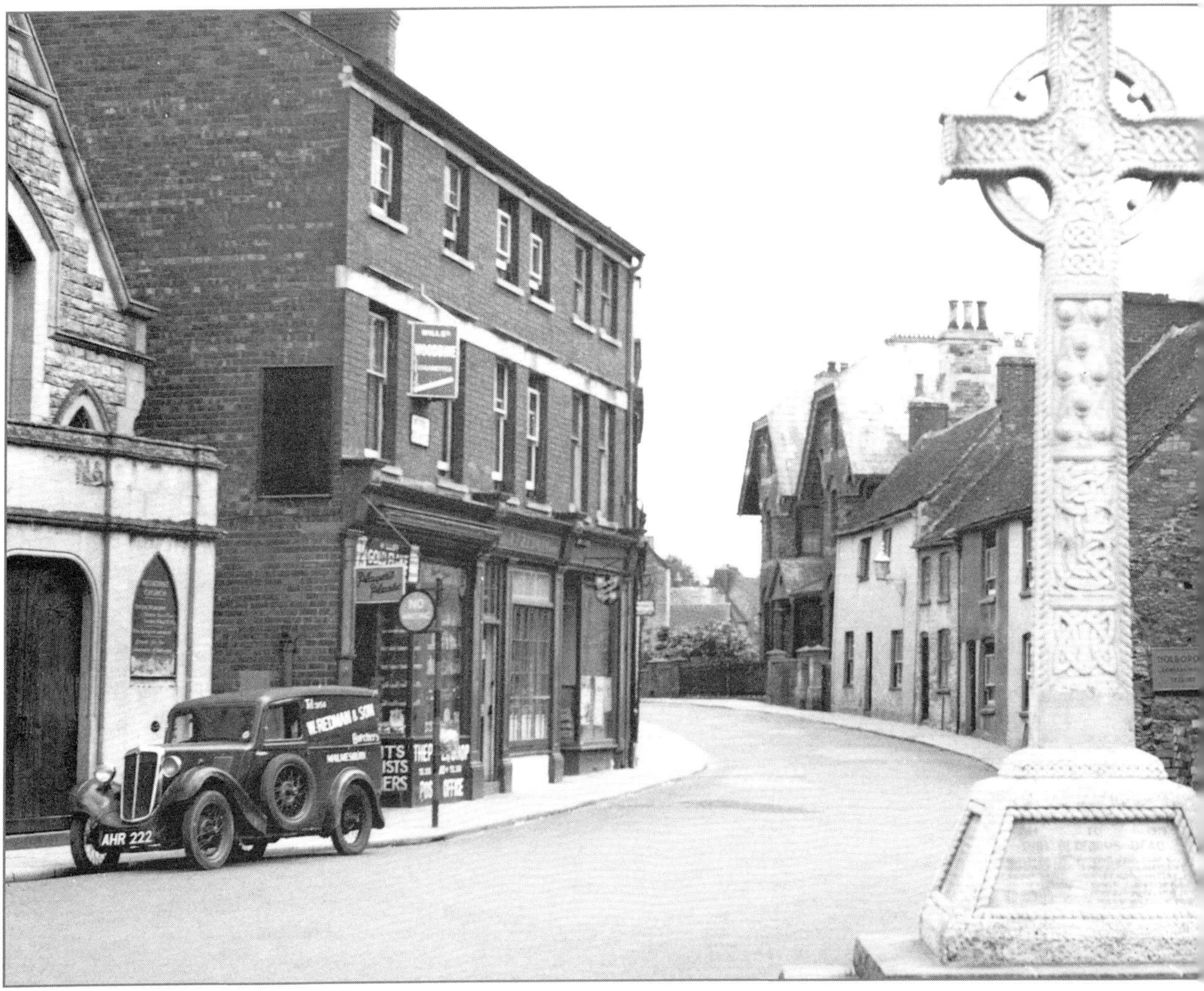

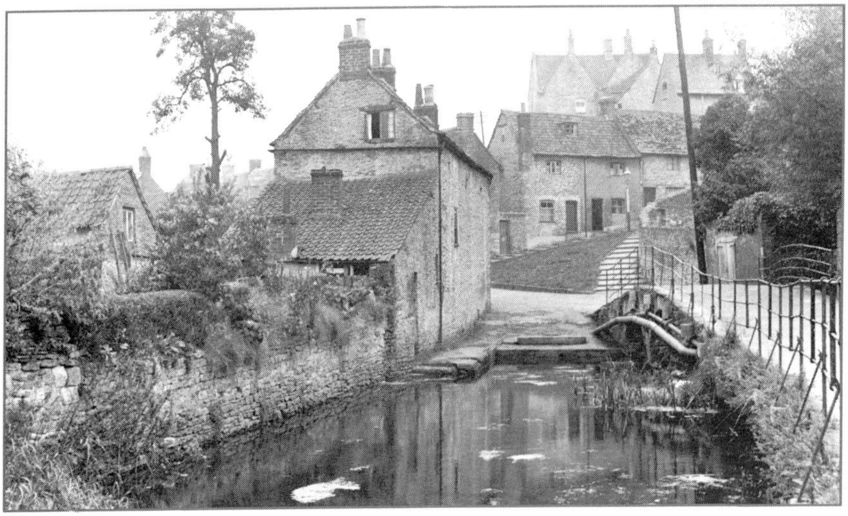

◄ **Malmesbury Baskerville c1955**

M13030

The town's name may come from the names of two missionaries, Maidulph and St Aldhelm, who founded a school here in 596. William of Malmesbury, the famous chronicler of the Arthurian tales, was a monk here in the 12th century.

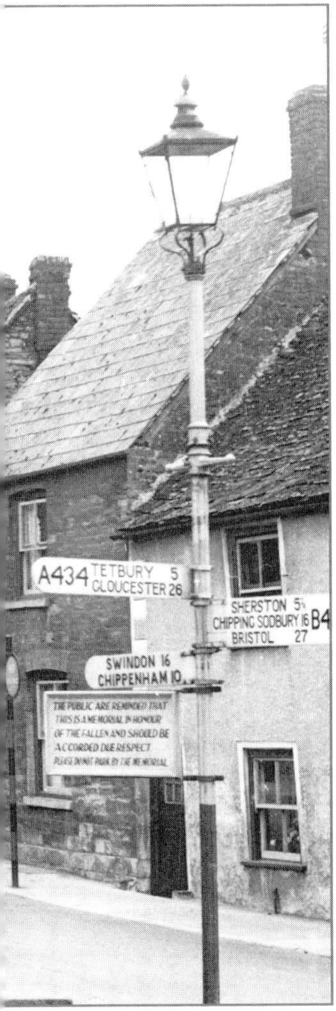

Malmesbury, The War Memorial and Westport Post Office c1950 M13014

Westport is a suburb of Malmesbury, and is renowned for its large monastic barn. The town's history is notable well beyond the medieval period. During the Civil War (1642 to 46), for example, it changed hands between Royalist and Parliamentarian forces not less than five times! The Post Office is behind the W Redman & Son van on the left.

Manningford Bruce The Post Office c1955

M162002

The name means the ford of Manna's people; the Bruce suffix is from Briouze in Normandy. The village is hard to navigate, and it seems it has always been so: Edward Thomas, in his poem 'Lob', wrote: 'Their churches, graveyards, farms and byres, Lurking to one side up the paths and lanes, Seldom well seen except by aeroplanes'.

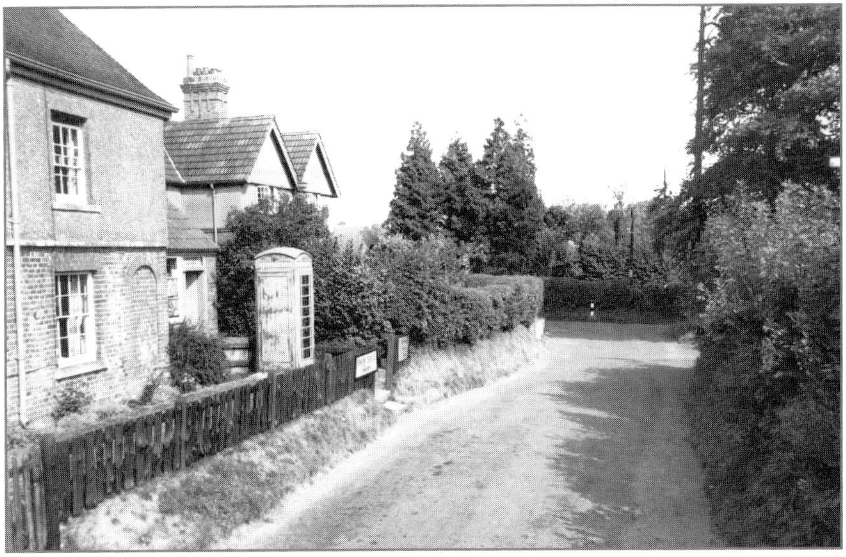

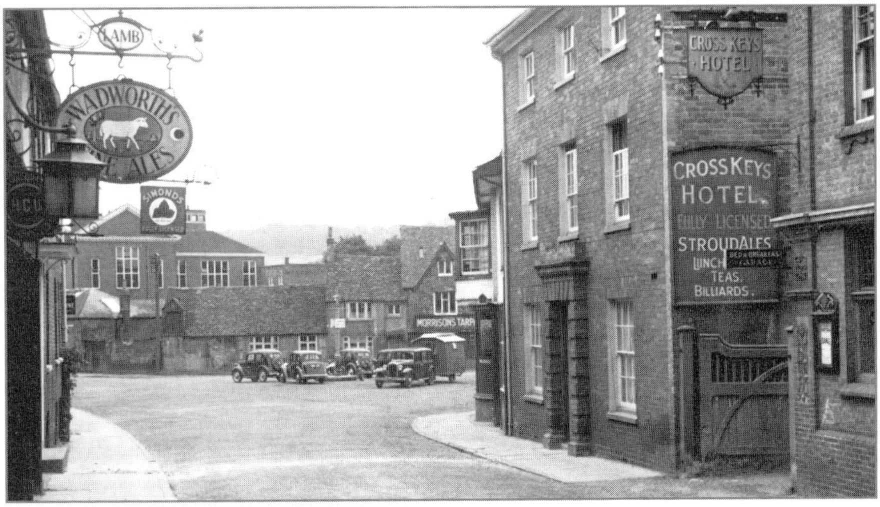

Marlborough The Parade c1950

M34022

The building beyond the parked cars used to be a tannery. Note the Lamb public house on the left, and the Cross Keys Hotel opposite.

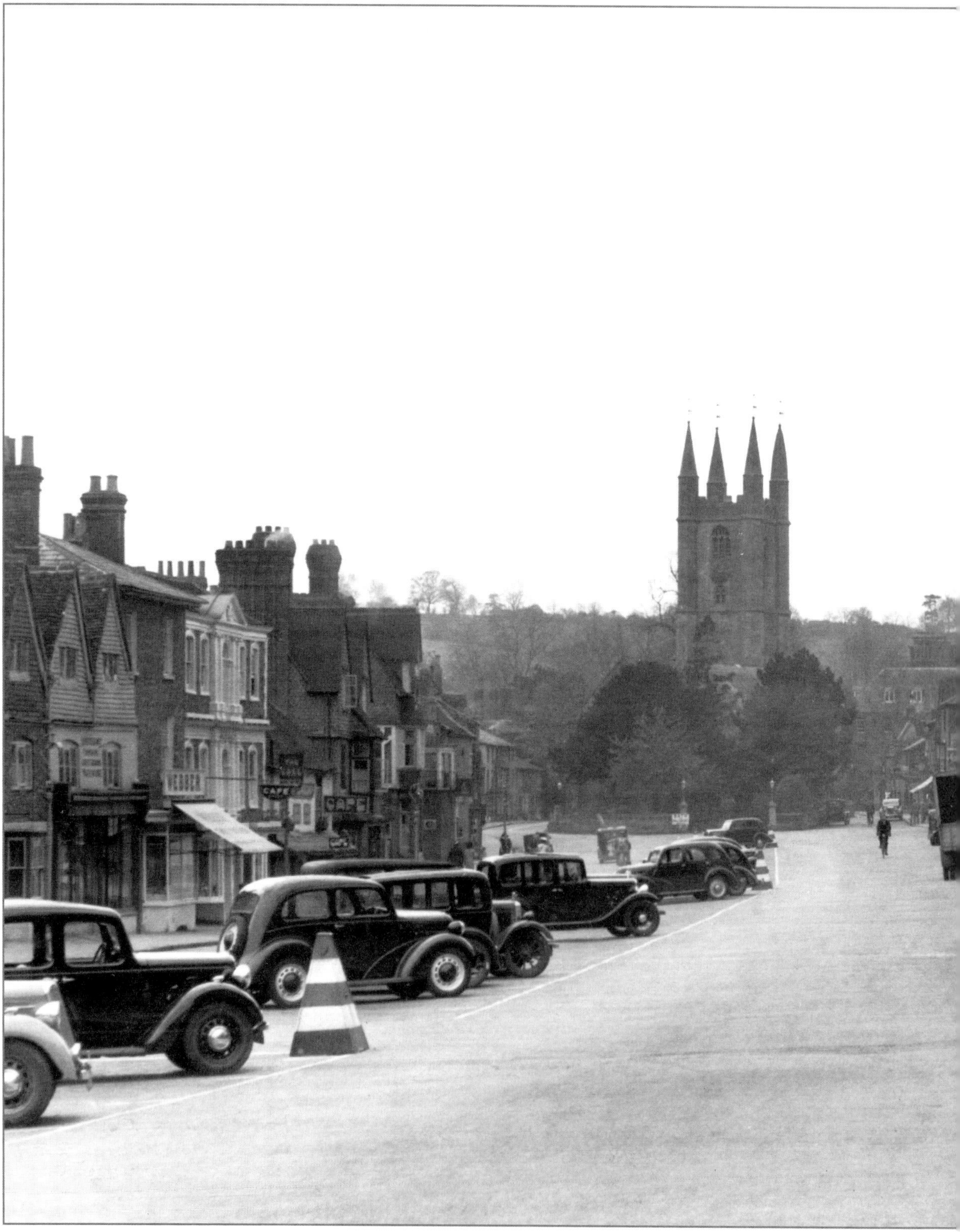
CAFE
CAFE

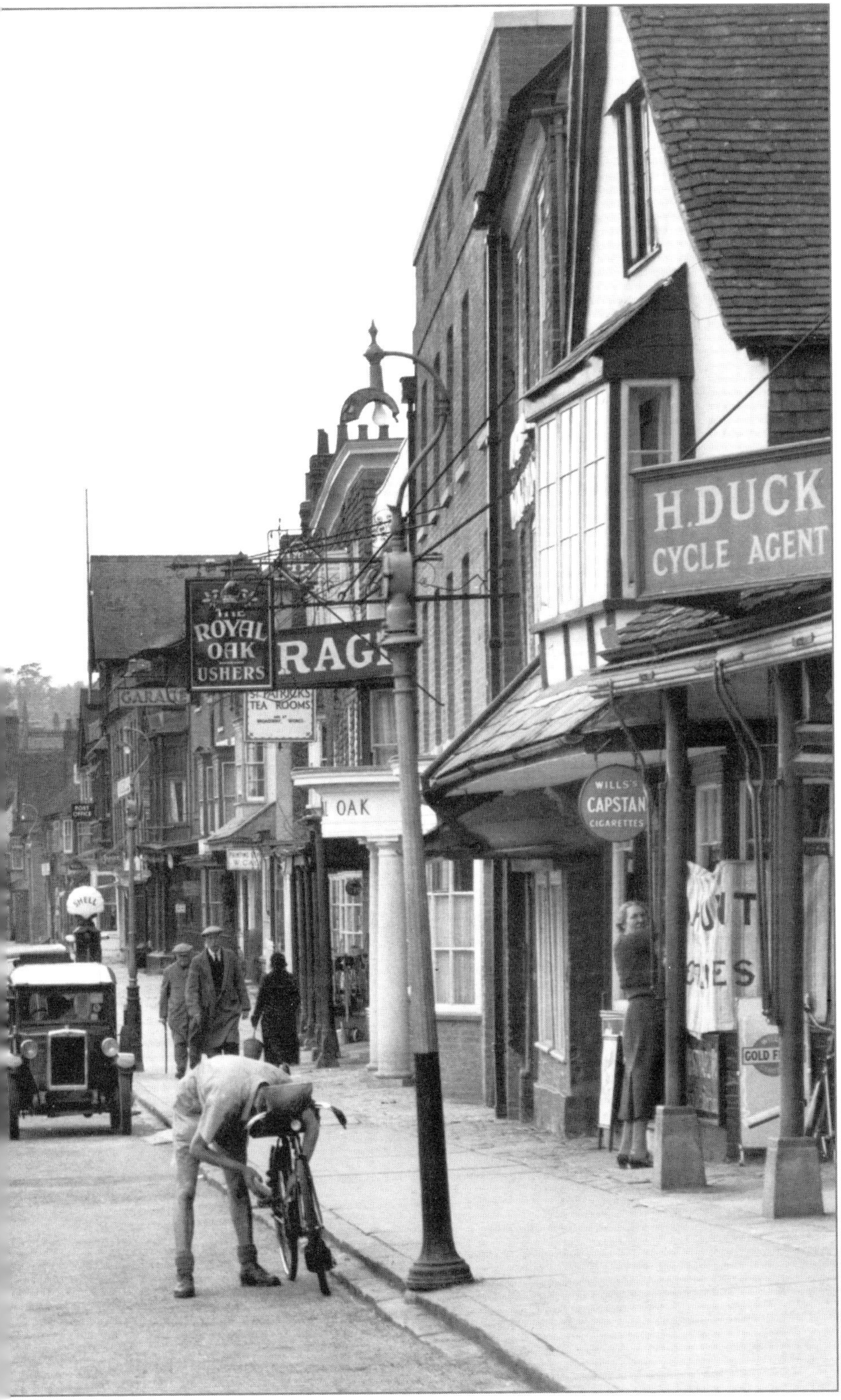

Marlborough High Street c1950

M34011

The town boasts one of the widest high streets in the country. It is thought the town's name came from Maerl's barrow, a burial place, or 'marle burg', meaning chalk town. The church is dedicated to St Peter and St Paul; Thomas Wolsey was ordained here in 1498. Built in 1100, rebuilt in 1450, redundant in 1974, it is now an arts and crafts centre and coffee shop. H Duck Cycle agent is now Duck's Toys.

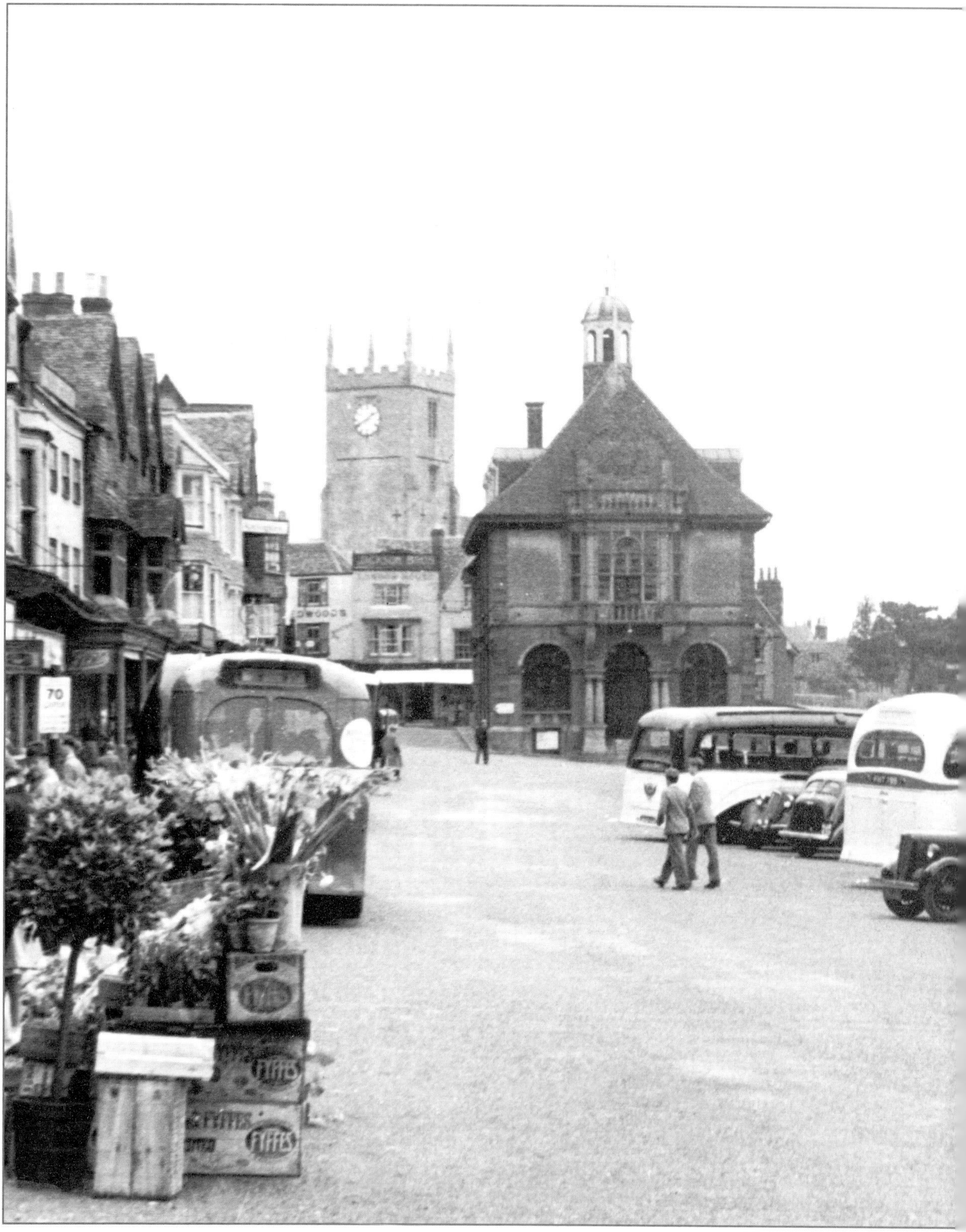
70
FYFFES

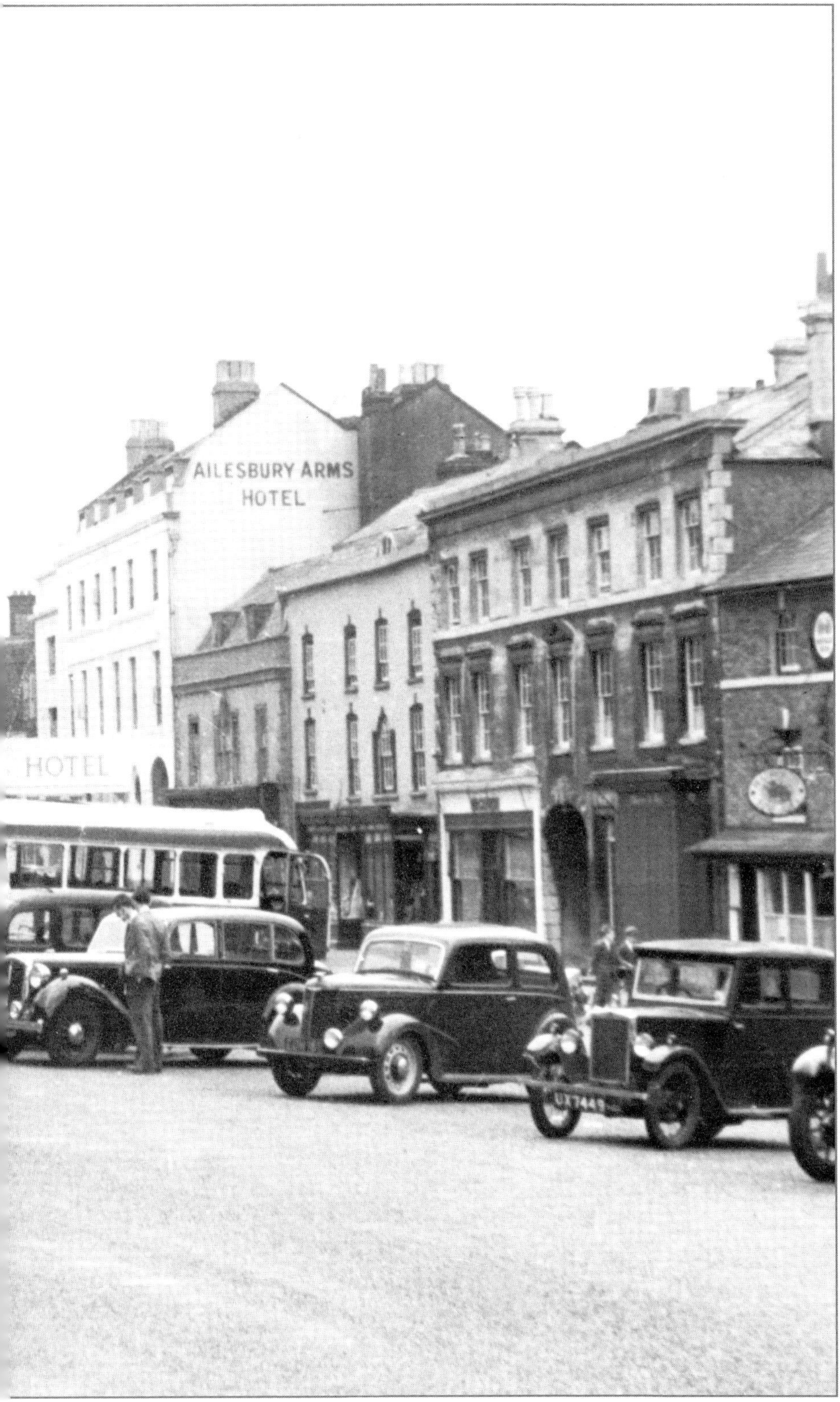

Marlborough
The Town Hall and High Street c1950
M34027

This Town Hall was built on the site of the old market house; it used the pillars of that building and also the door of the lock-up. The Ailsbury Arms Hotel is now renamed the Ailesbury Court Hotel. The Jackson Brothers shop in front of the church of St Mary the Virgin is no longer trading.

▼ **Marlborough, Polly Tea Rooms c1955** M34103
This popular haunt was once destroyed by fire; you can nevertheless drink tea here today - albeit in a now flat-roofed building.

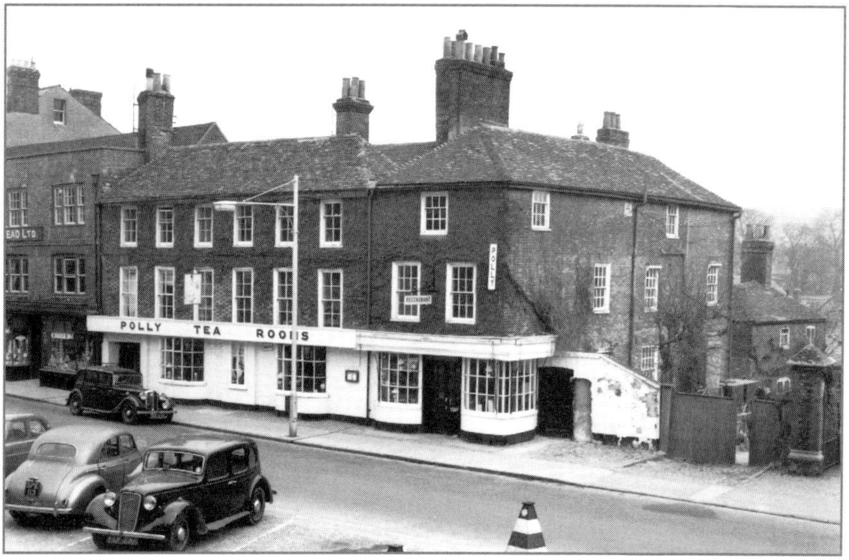

▼ **Marlborough, Passage Way to High Street c1965** M34125
Ralph Sayle and Son is now the Oxfam shop, and W T Calvert is now an Indian restaurant. Part of the facade of a fascinating and well-stocked second-hand book shop can just be seen on the left.

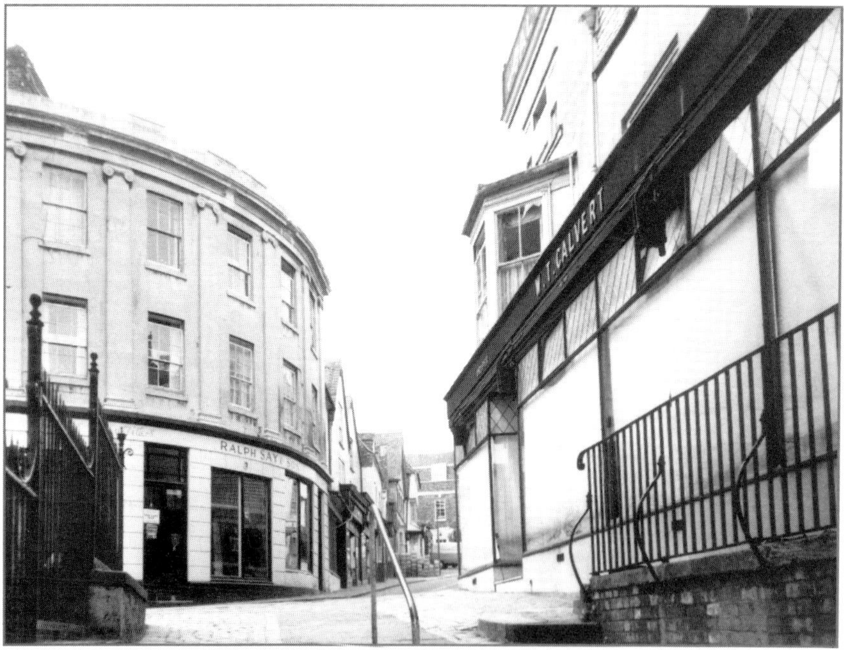

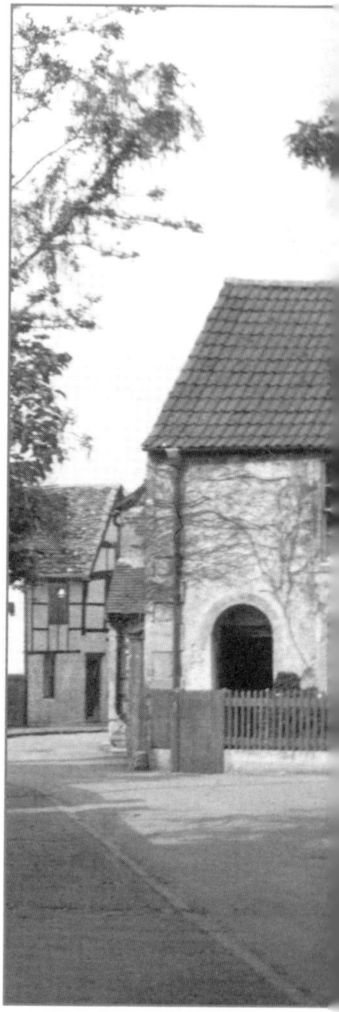

▲ **Melksham Canon Square and the War Memorial c1955**
M164004
Originally a forest village, Melksham prospered in the medieval period as a wool town. The name derives from the Saxon 'meolchamm', meaning land in the bend of a river where milk is produced.

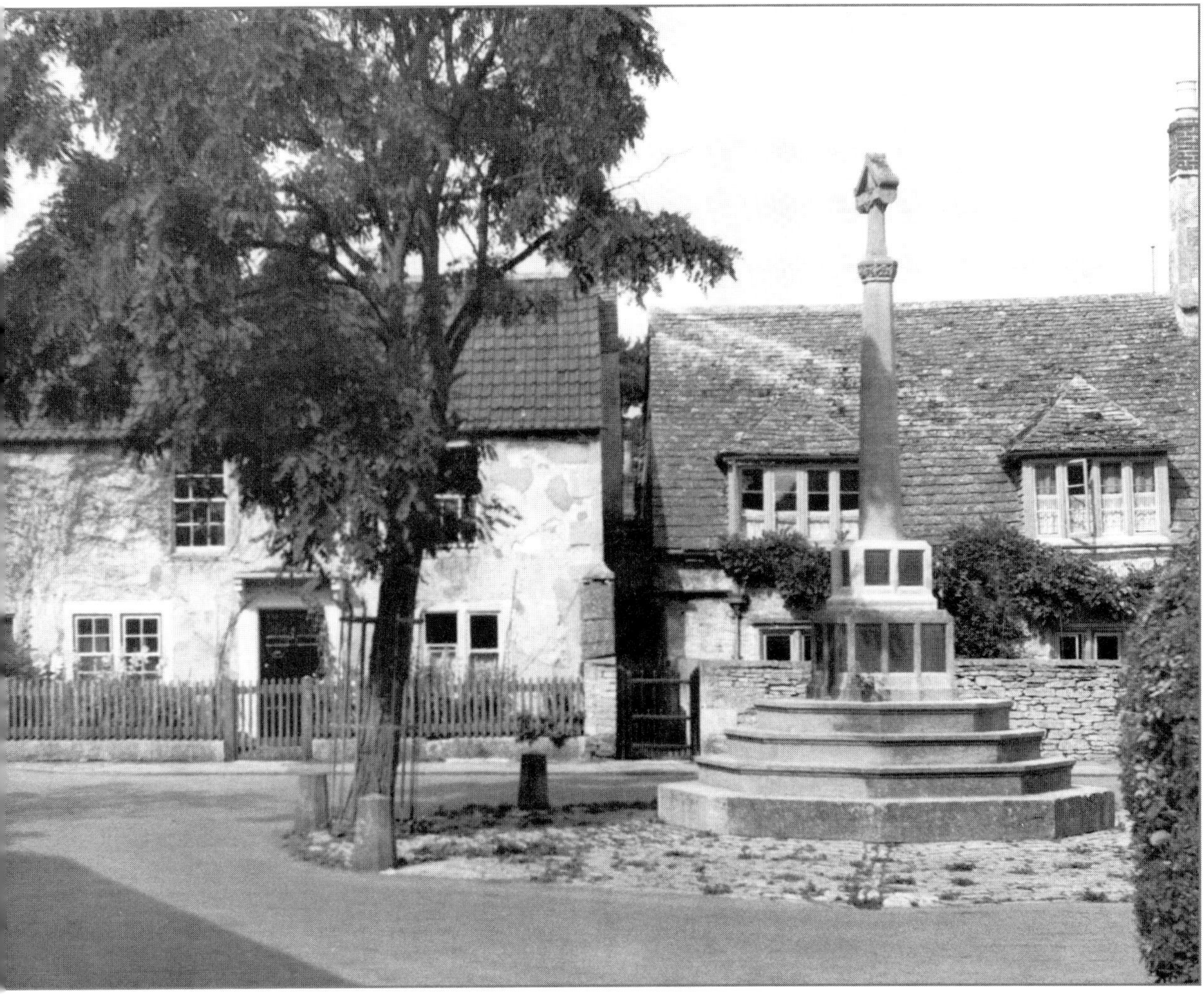

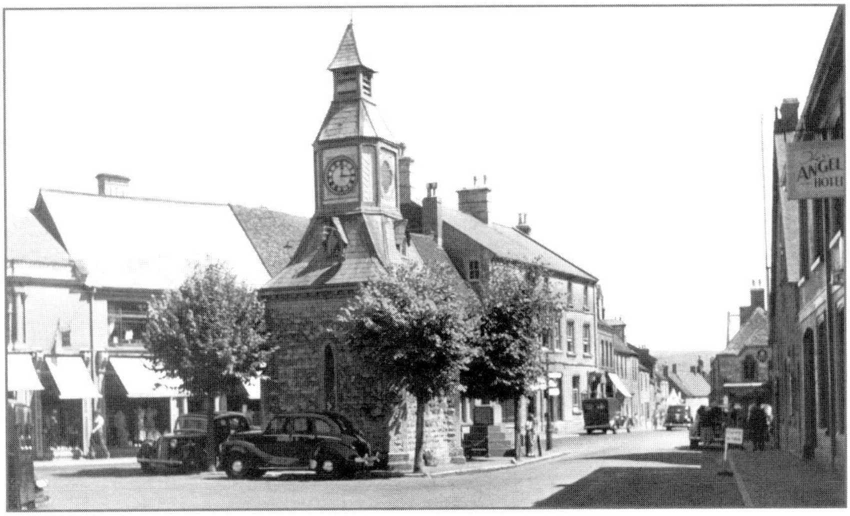

◄ **Mere, The Clock Tower c1950** M166002
Erected in 1866, this interesting building, the old market house, once also housed a school established by William Barnes in the Cross Loft, where he also wrote his poems about the Blackmore Vale. The Angel Hotel on the right no longer exists, except in name - Angel Corner is a row of shops and a tea-room on Angel Lane.

▼ **Mere, Salisbury Street c1950** M166015

The Youth Club on the right no longer exists. Note the Hovis sign above the grocer's shop on the left, and the three-wheeler on the right.

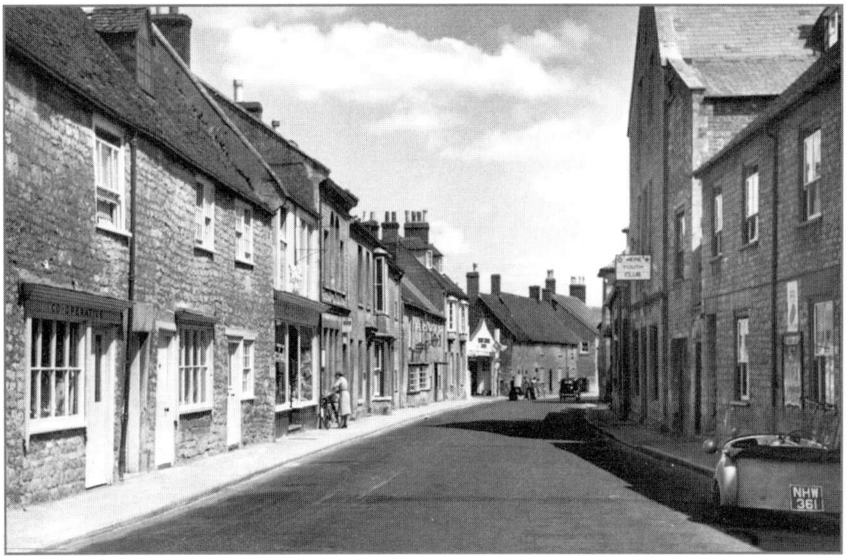

▼ **Mere, The Talbot and the Old Ship Hotels c1955** M166023

The Ship Inn, once known as the Sign of the Ship, was converted from the 17th-century mansion of Sir John Coventry. The wrought-iron 18th-century sign is the work of Kingston Avery, and shows the sailing ship badge of John Mere (founder of the chantry in the town in the 14th century). The Talbot was formerly the George Inn; Charles II apparently dined here while on his way to Heale on 6 October 1651.

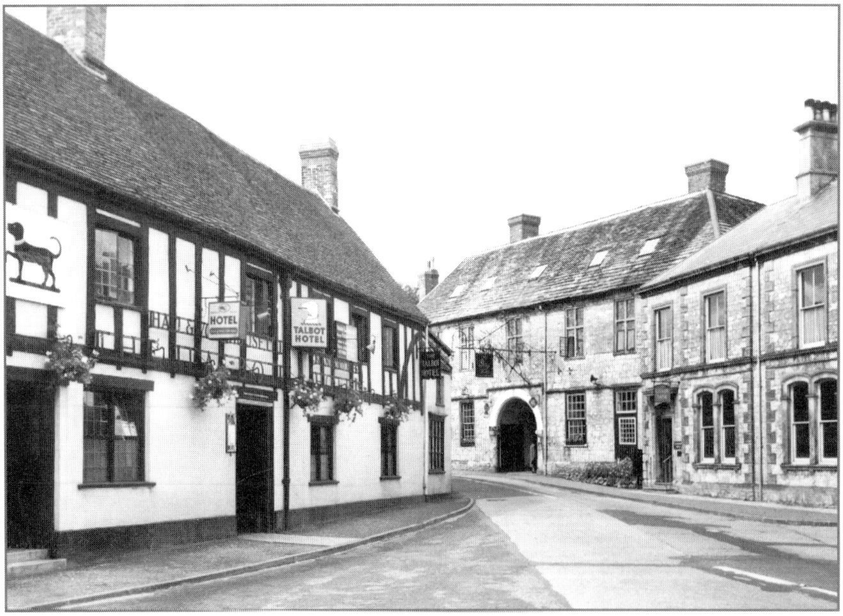

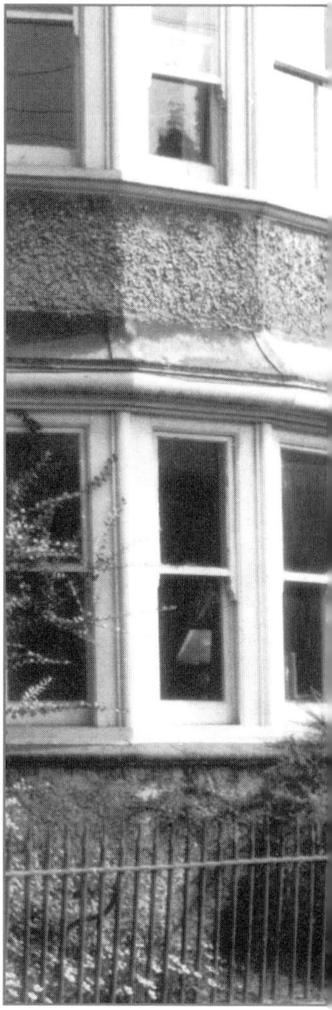

▲ **Milton Lilbourne The Village c1955**

M165002

Milton derives from the Saxon for middle farm, and Lilbourne from Walter de Lillebon, who owned the manor in 1242. The village exists today almost exactly as pictured here; even the pavements are the same. The bay window to the left belongs to Westering House.

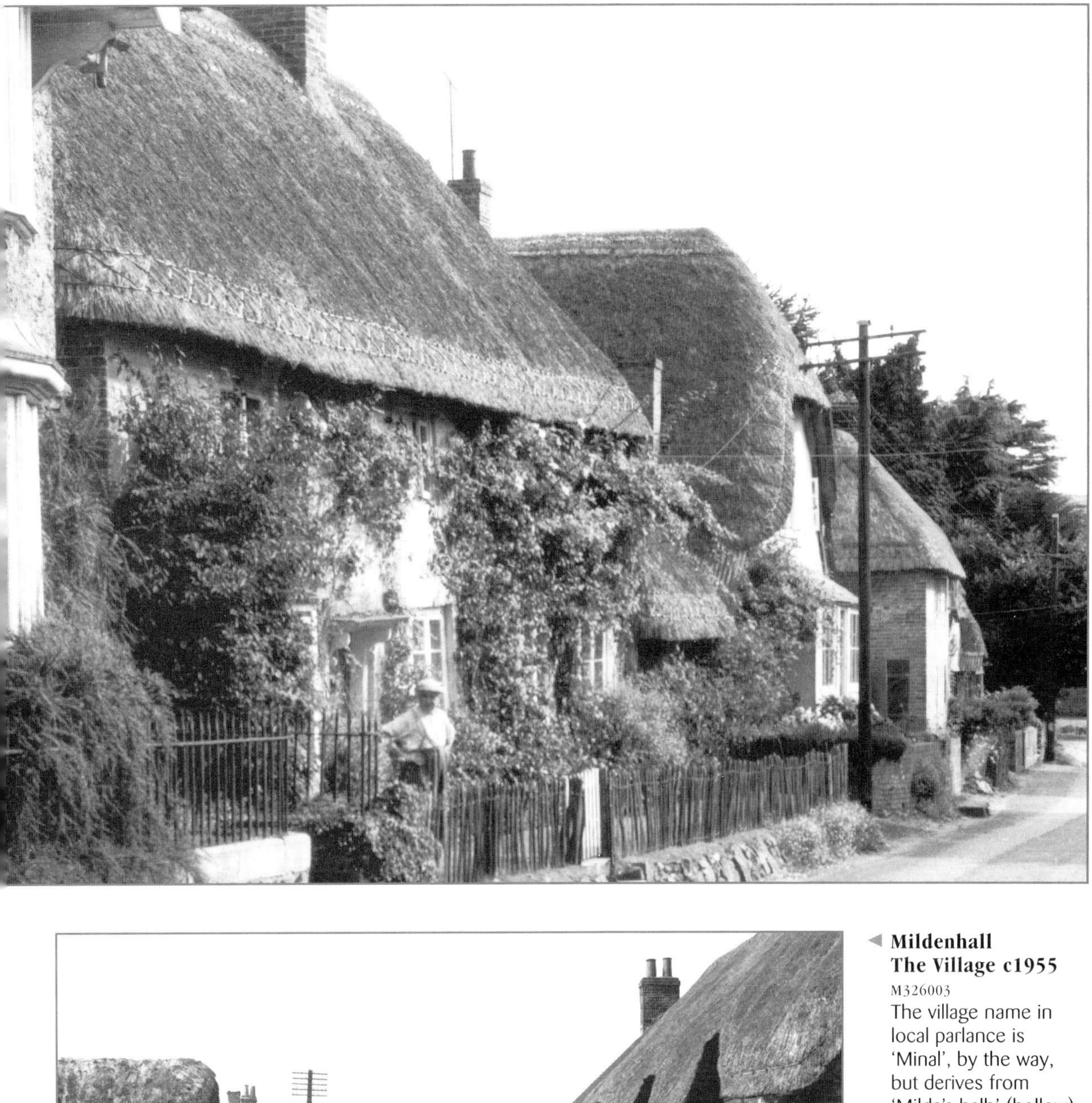

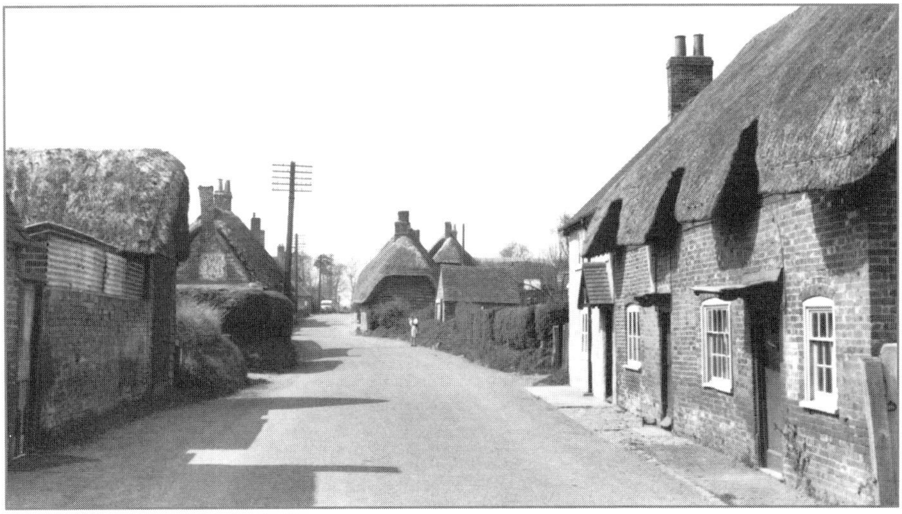

Mildenhall
The Village c1955

M326003

The village name in local parlance is 'Minal', by the way, but derives from 'Milda's halh' (hollow). The village is built on the site of the Roman settlement of Cunetio.

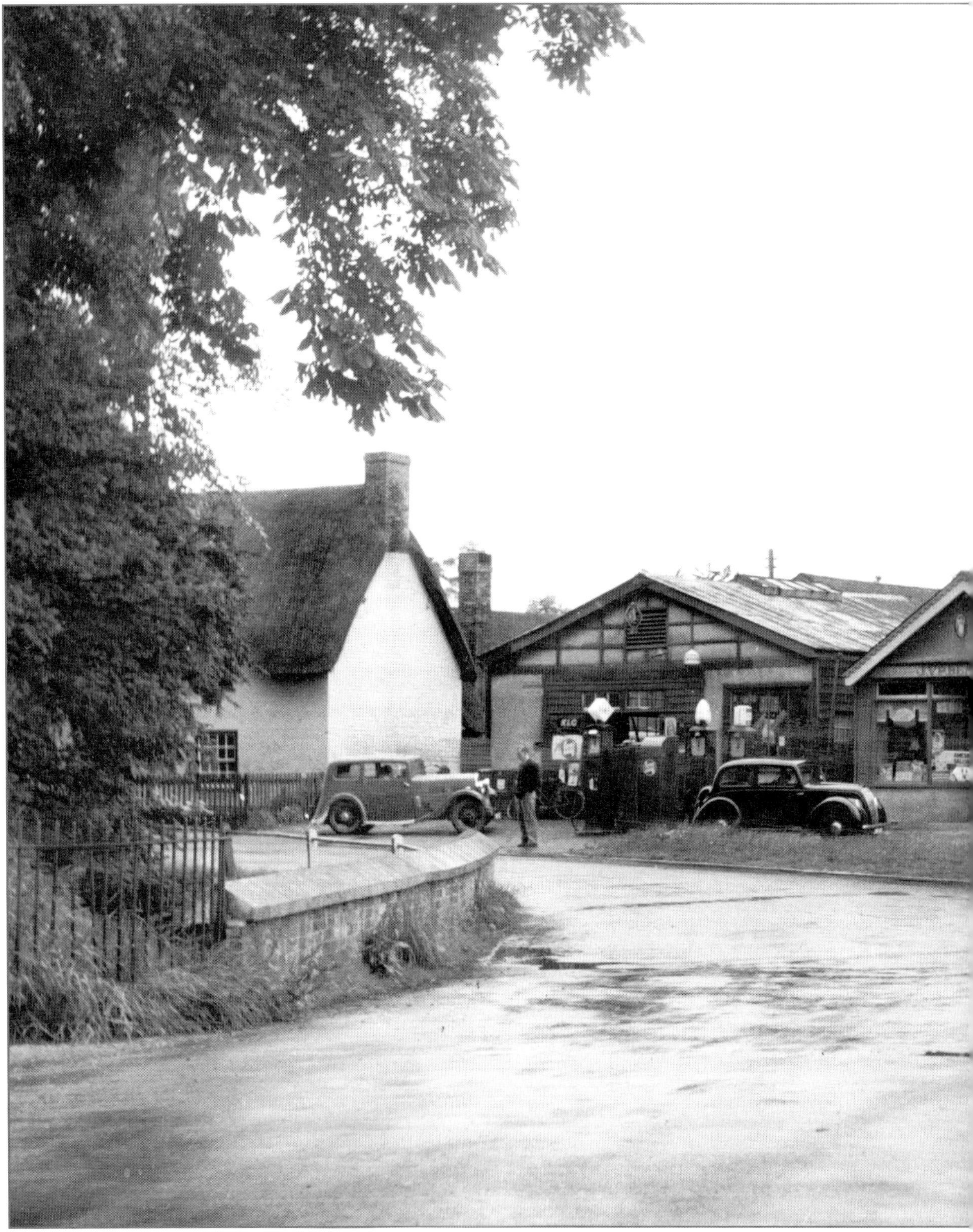

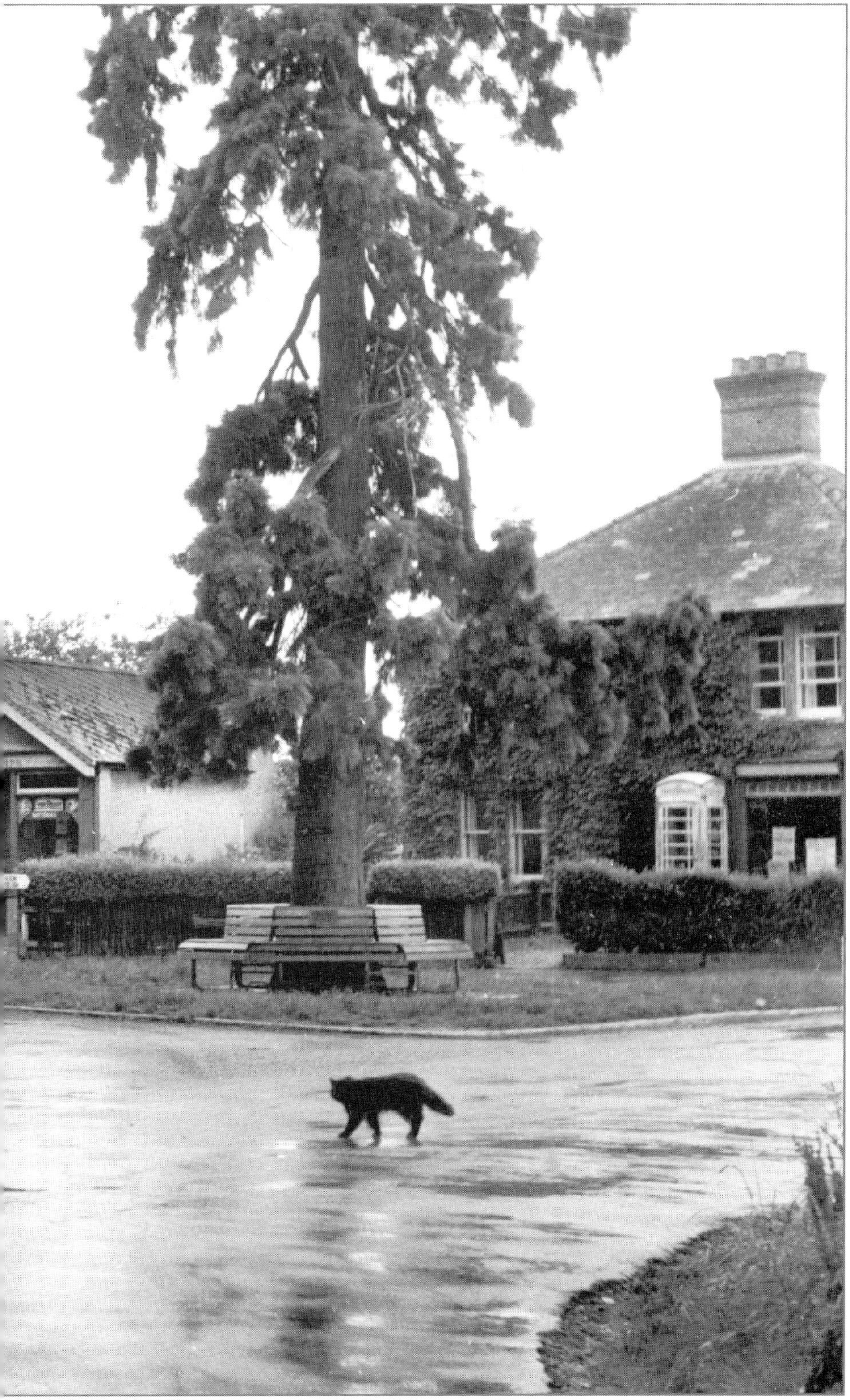

Netheravon Post office Corner c1950 N80003

As with so many Wiltshire towns and villages, the military presence is a considerable influence on the village. Parts of the parish were bought by the War Department in 1898, and in 1904 a cavalry training school was established in Netheravon House. Note the sign proclaiming JVP Bennett as the proprietor of the chemist next door to the garage.

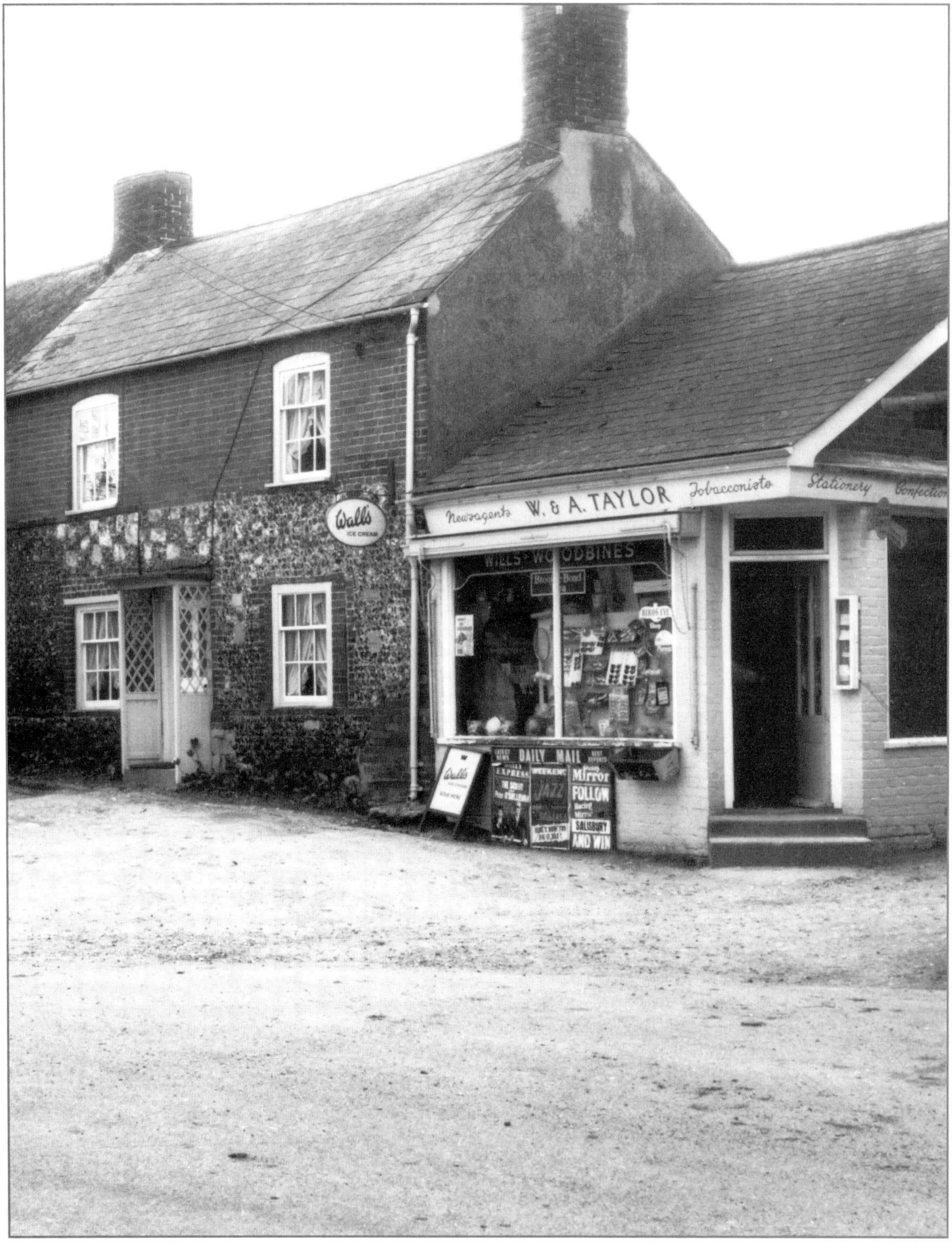

Netheravon, The Village c1965 N80042

Nether simply means lower, and avon derives from the Welsh word for river - 'afon'. The W & A Taylor newsagents is now a fish and chip shop.

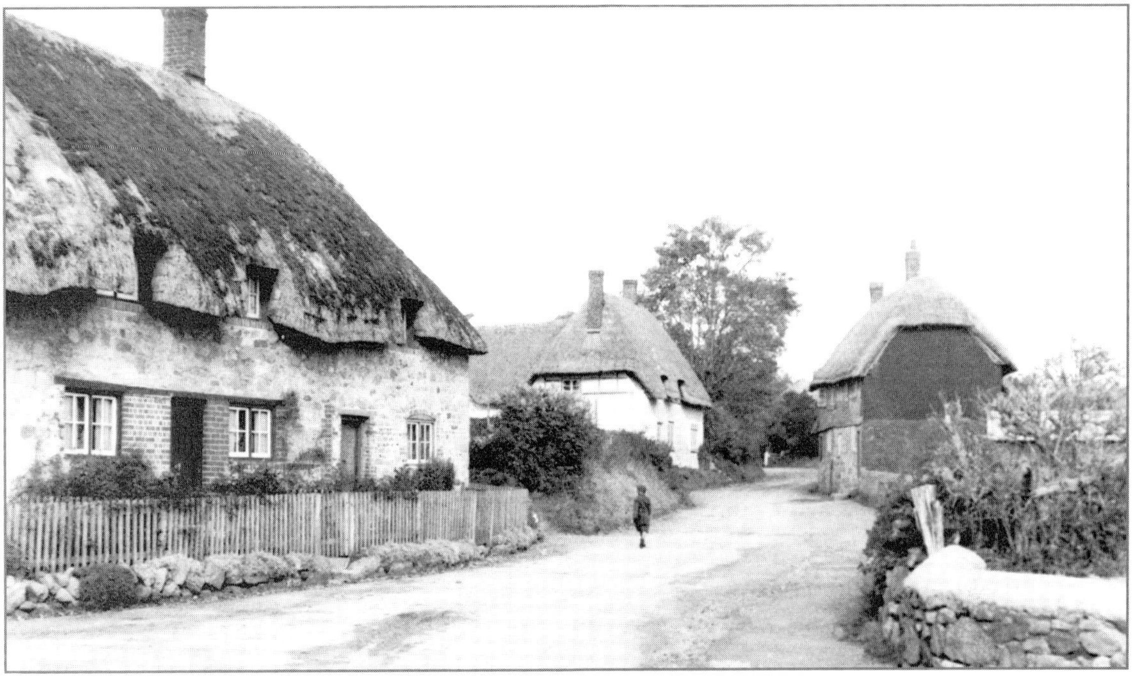

Ogbourne St Andrew, The Village c1955 056001
The name derives from the Saxon for Occa's stream ('Occa's burna'). This Ogbourne was previously Ocheburna parva (Little Ogbourne).

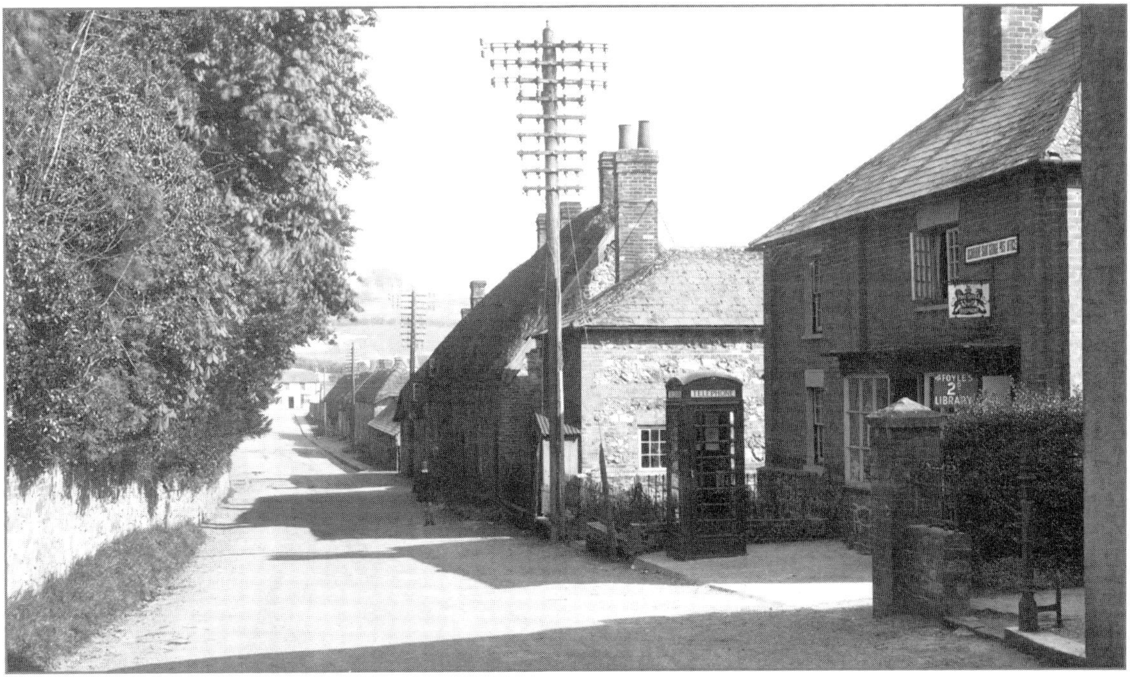

Ogbourne St George, The Post Office c1955 057005
Set on one of the highest points of the Marlborough hills, this, the largest of the three Ogbournes, was once Ocheburna magna (Great Ogbourne).

▼ **Old Sarum, The Old Castle Inn c1965** O58001
The site of the original settlement which moved from here to become Salisbury, Old Sarum has a fabulous history. It was an impressive Iron Age hill fort, and the site of a Norman castle from which the inn in the picture presumably derives its name, but after the settlement moved it was gradually reclaimed by nature - it was used as pasture land in c1500. This did not stop it sending a representative to Parliament until 1832!

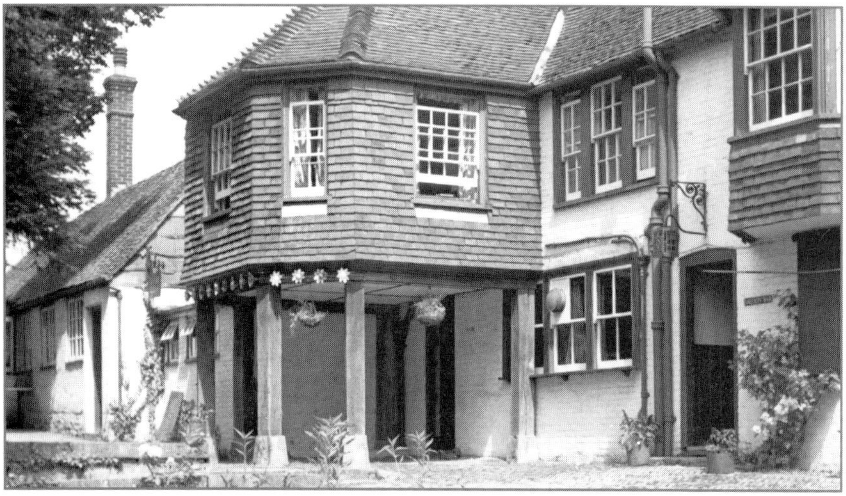

▼ **Pewsey, The King Alfred Statue and Market Place c1950** P51002
King Alfred once owned land here; this statue was erected to commemorate the 1911 coronation of George V on 25 June 1913. Note the Nicol Cash Drapery Stores on the right.

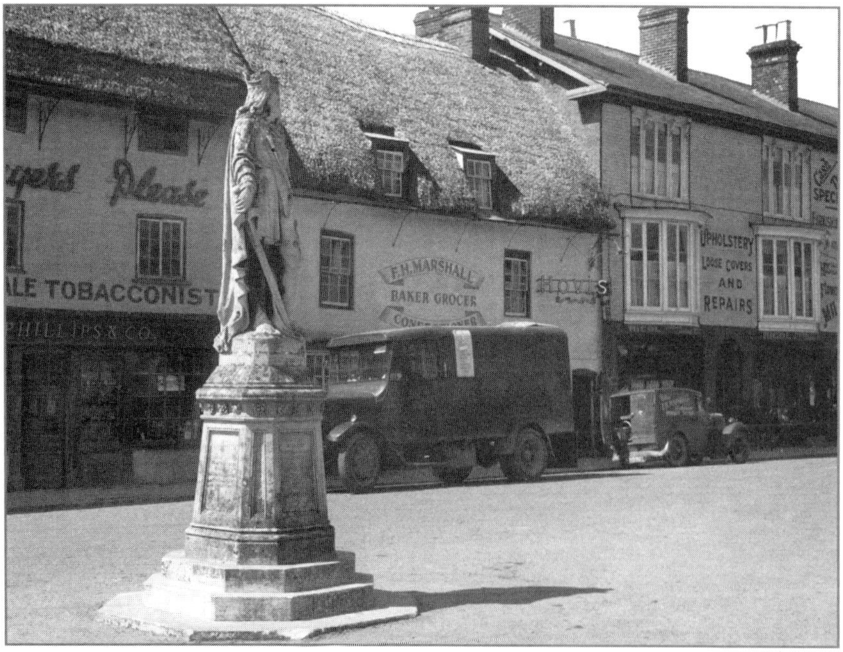

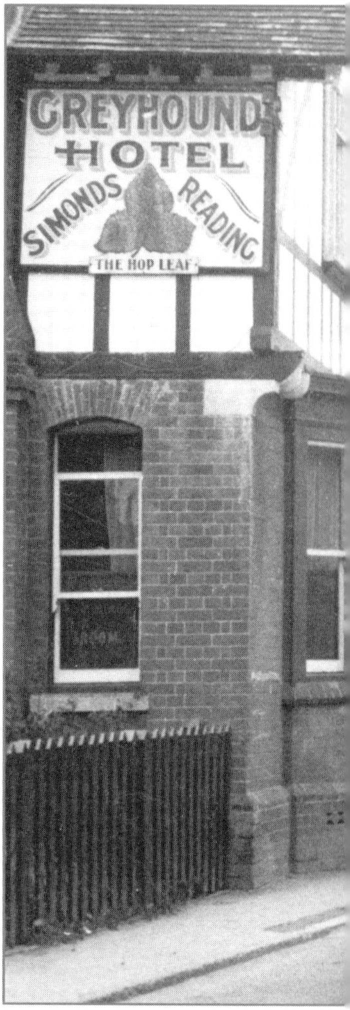

▲ **Pewsey, North Street c1950** P51012
Note the Royal Oak pub beyond the Greyhound Hotel on the left.

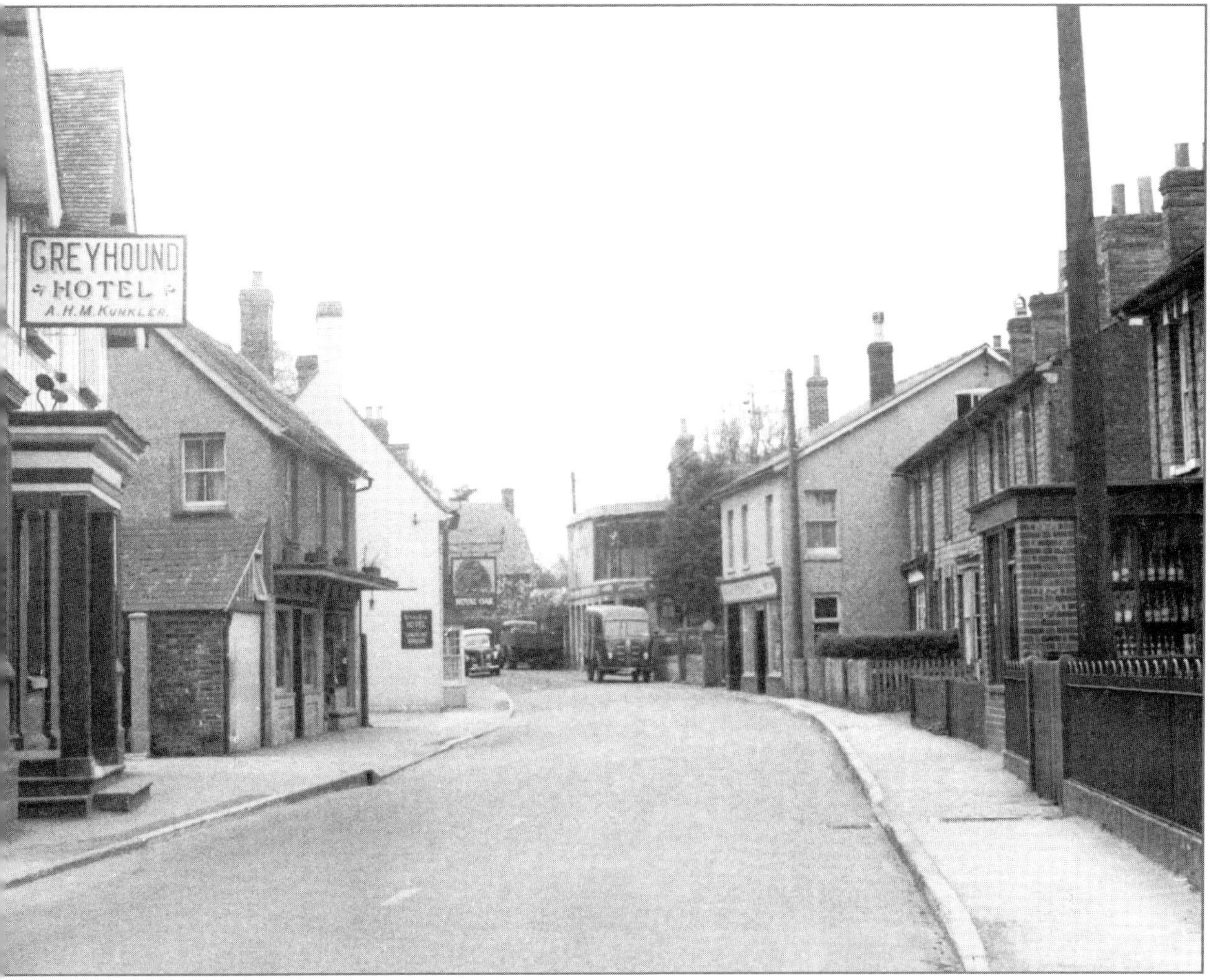

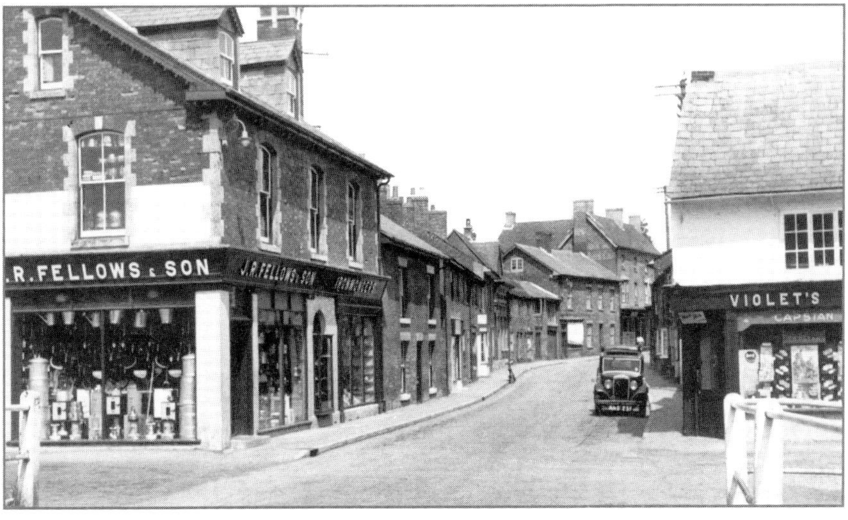

◄ **Pewsey, High Street c1950** P51019
The name derives from the Saxon 'Pefe's eg' (island) and was Pefesigge in 880, Pevesie in the Domesday Book and Pewse in 1524.

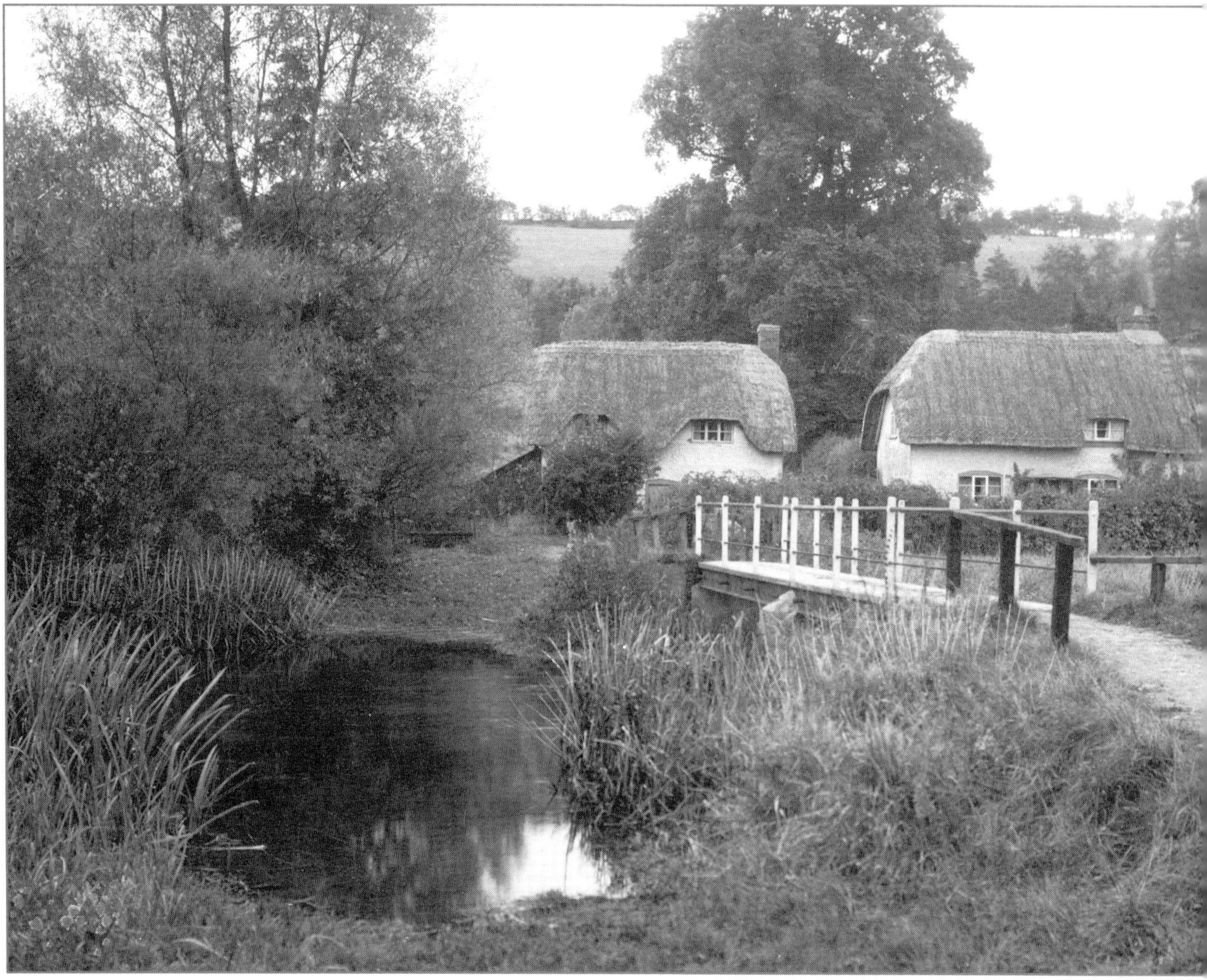

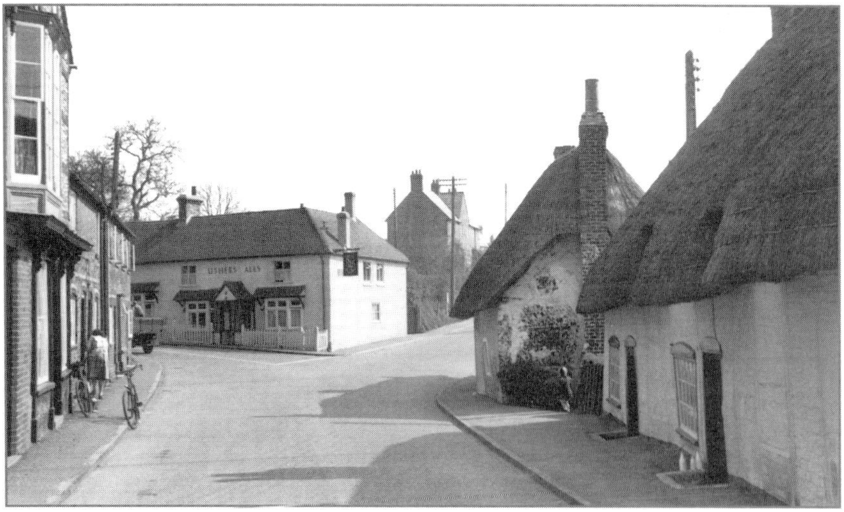

Ramsbury, Oxford Street c1955 R6012
Listed as Oxenfordstrete in 1331, the village name derives from the 947 reference to Rammesburi, giving raven's fort.

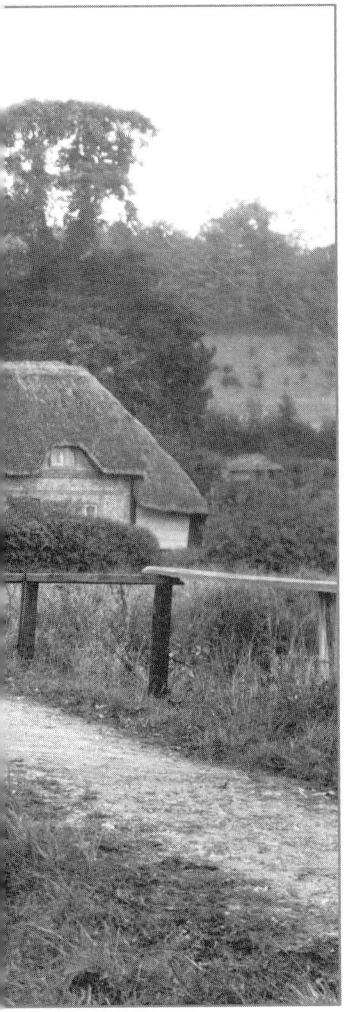

Ramsbury, Riverside c1955 R6010

The River Kennet has always played a significant role in the life of the village. Known for its trout since the 17th century, it also gave rise to productive water meadows. Watercress was grown here from the 1890s.

Rushall, The Village c1965 R256001

Note the thatching being carried out on the second cottage.

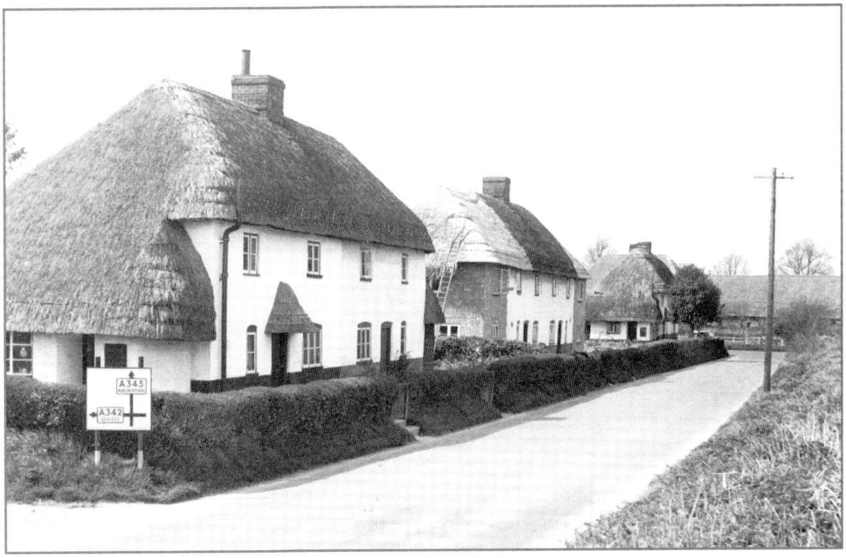

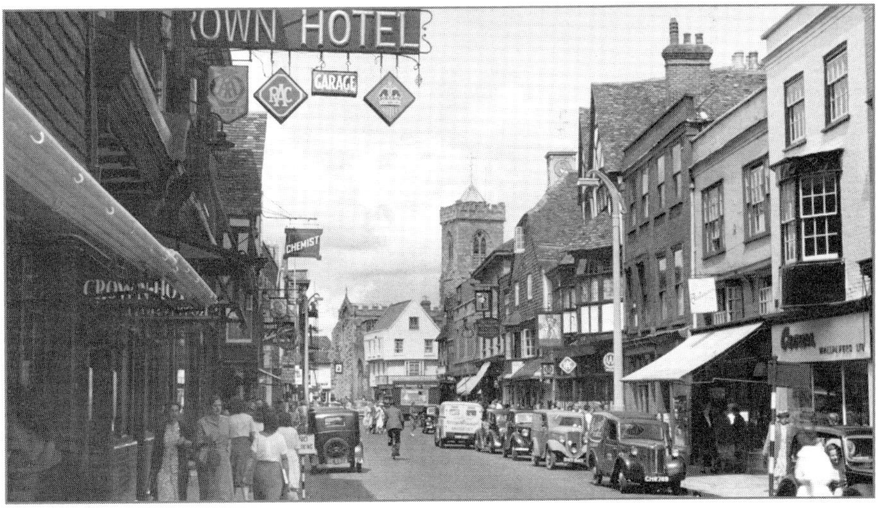

Salisbury, High Street c1950 S48088

New Sarum is Wiltshire's only city, but smaller than Swindon! Its story began once Old Sarum's was drawing to its close - it was decided to abandon Old Sarum in 1220 owing to its exposed position, a shortage of water and disputes with the local authorities, and relocate to the Saxon settlement of 'searaburg' (armour fort).

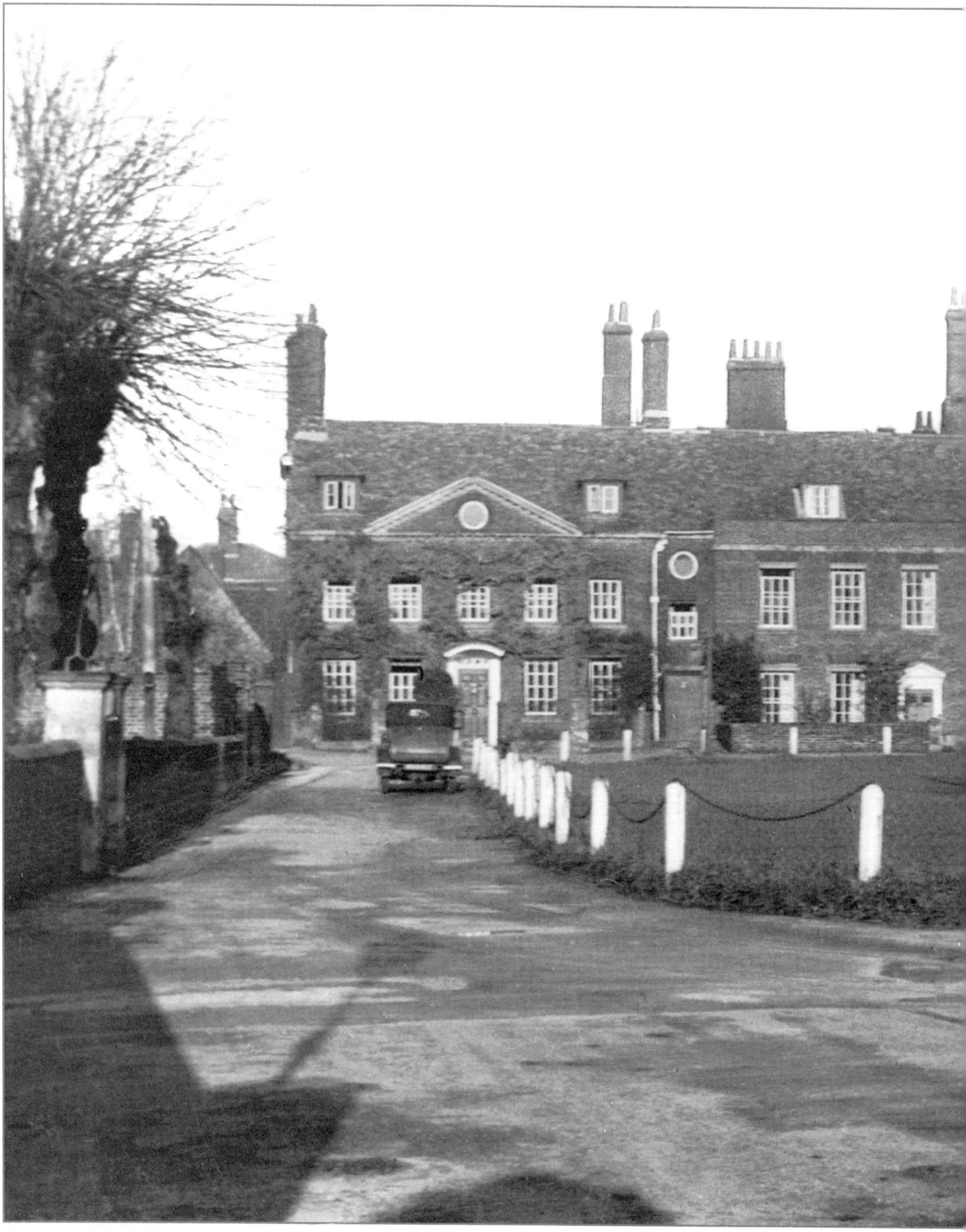

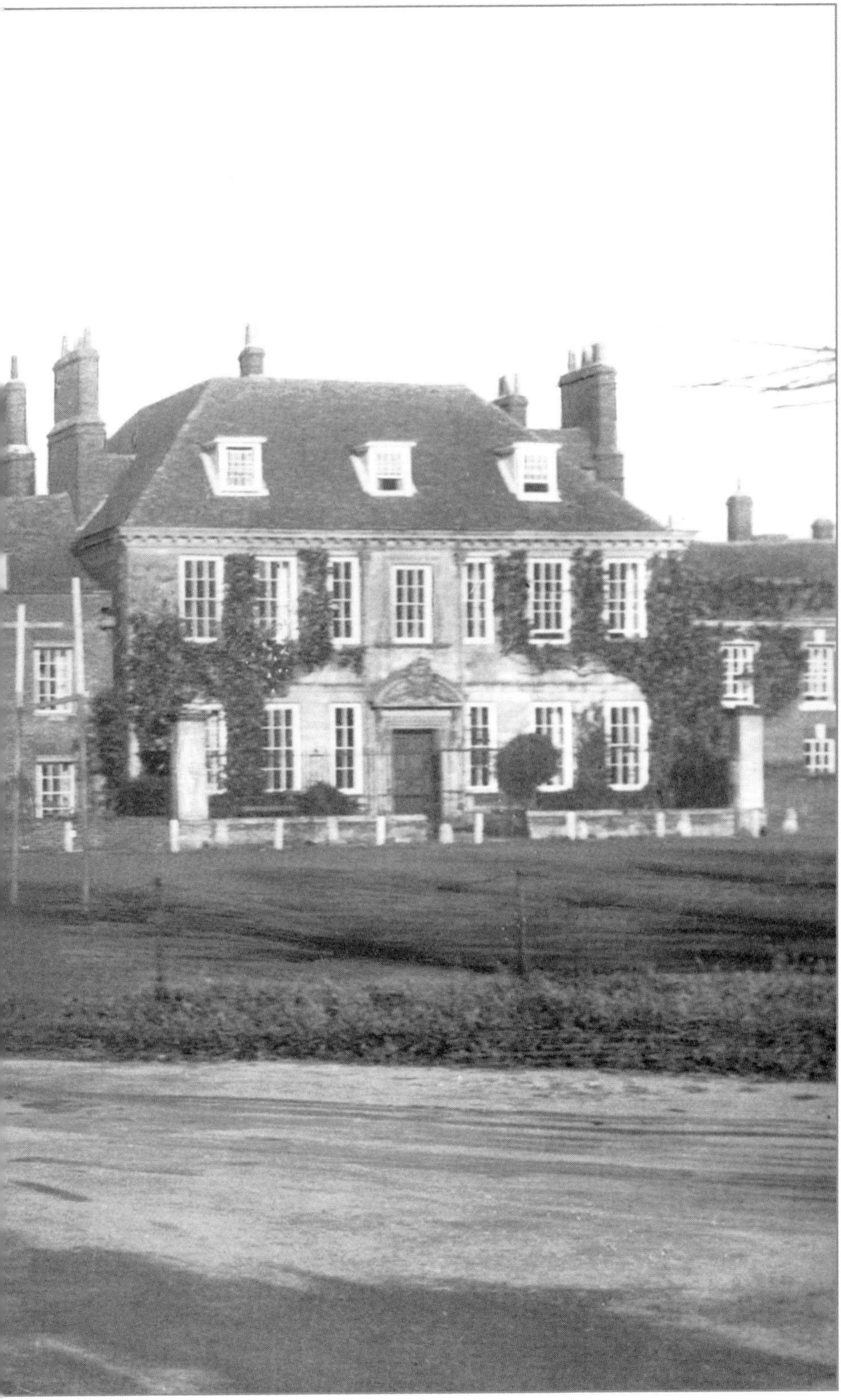

Salisbury, The Close c1950 S48079
Still locked up at 9pm, the Close is a contrast to the bustling shopping areas, and has always been so. Walled in 1331, it is the largest Cathedral Close in England, and has many fine buildings within its precinct.

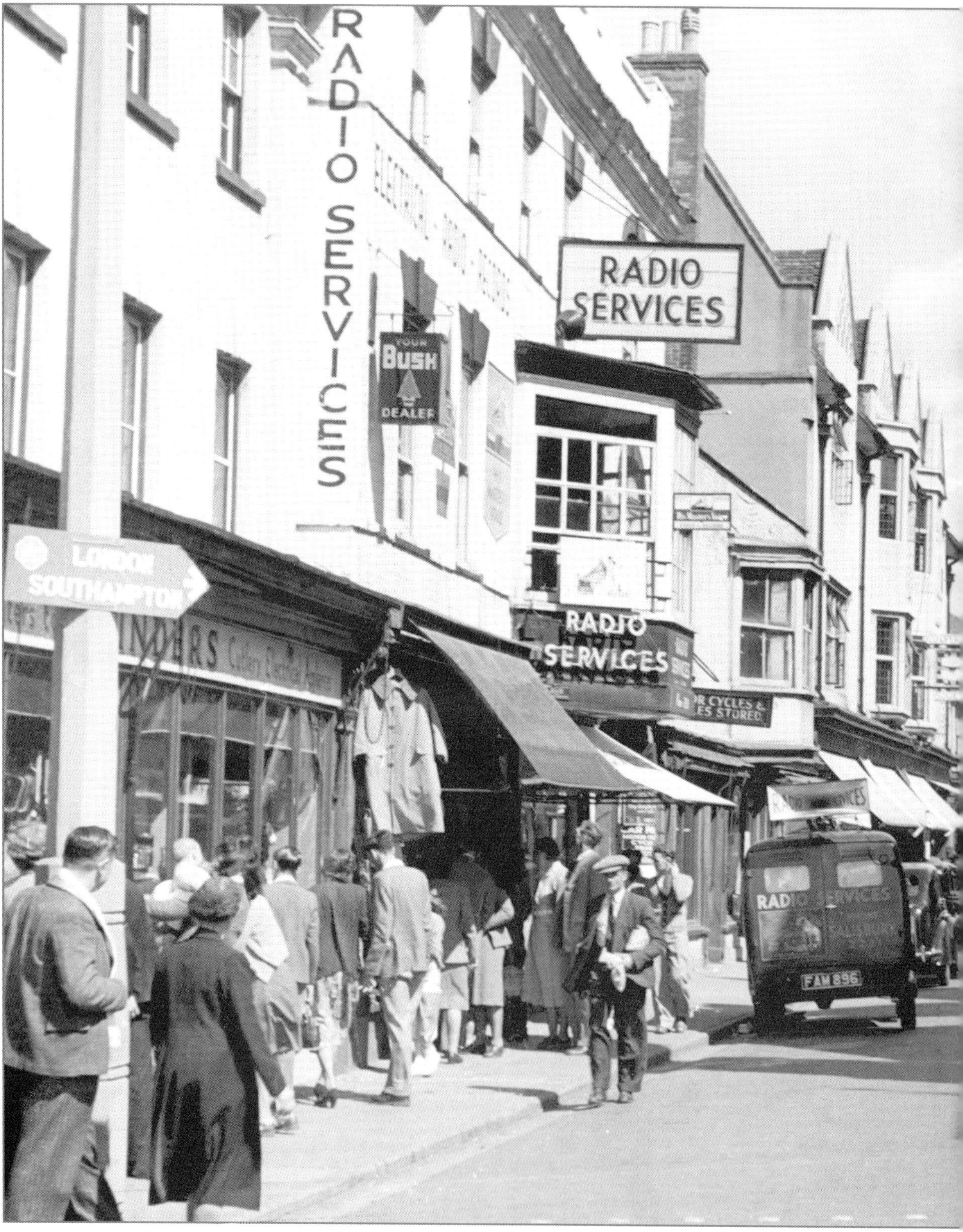
RADIO SERVICES
YOUR BUSH DEALER
RADIO SERVICES
LONDON
SOUTHAMPTON
RADIO SERVICES
RADIO SERVICES
FAM 896

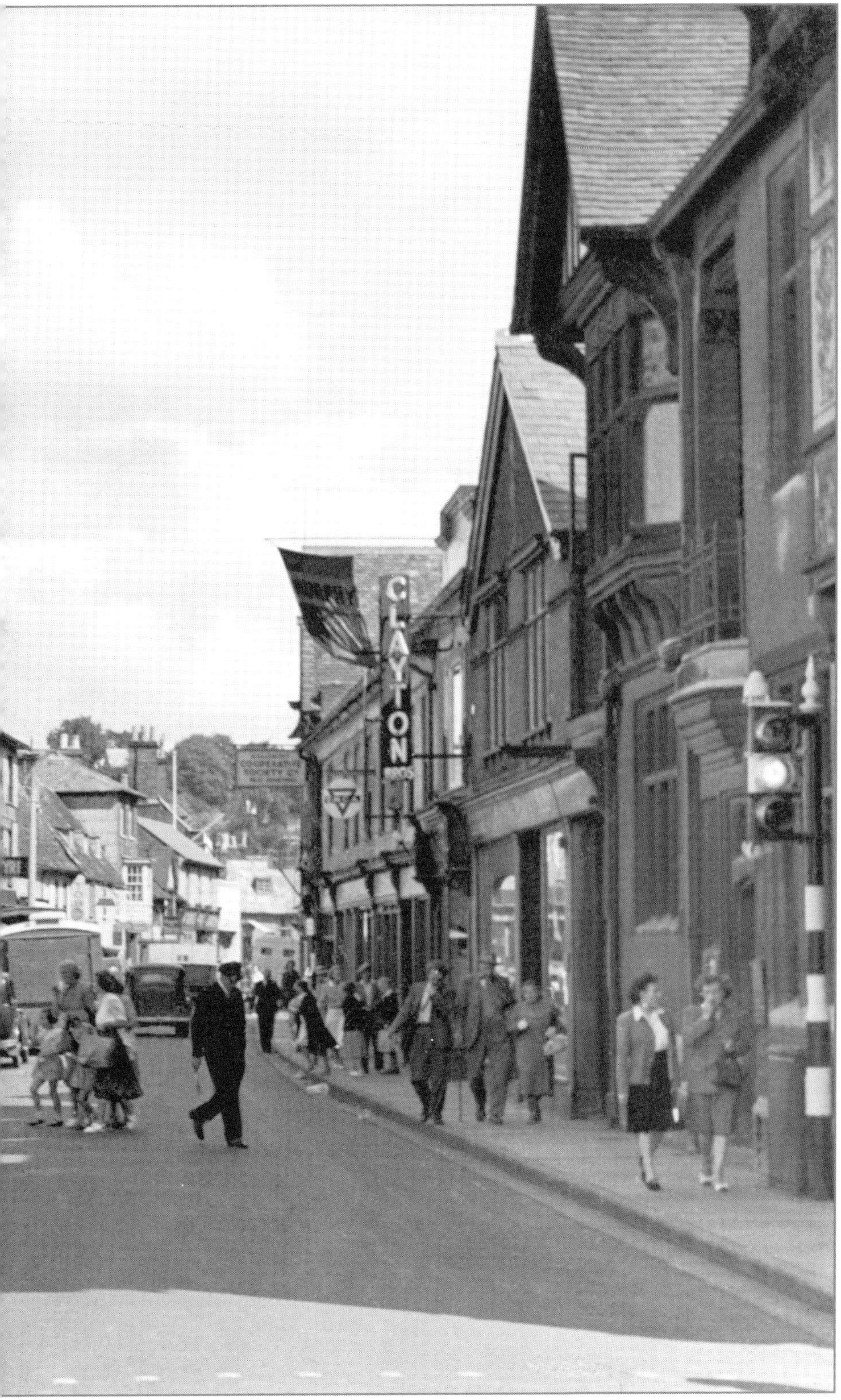

Salisbury, Winchester Street c1950 S48097
Note the Radio Services van parked outside the shop of the same name.

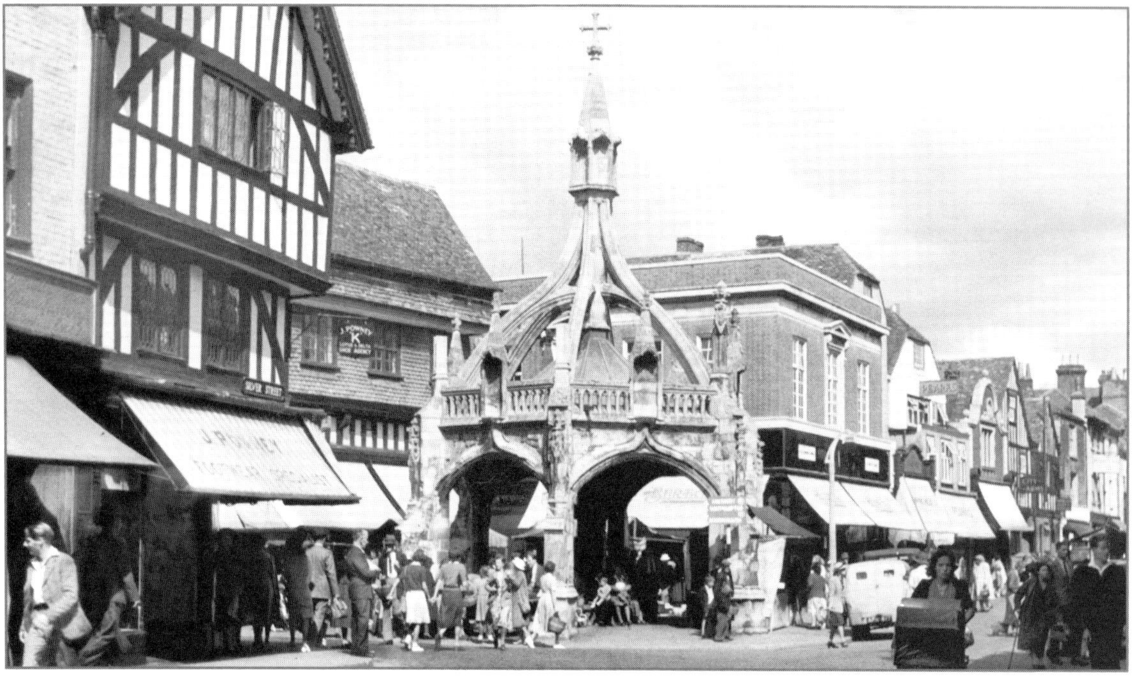

Salisbury, The Cross c1950 S48102
The hexagonal Poultry Cross was built in the 15th century. Its open ogee arches, and the flying buttresses supporting the spirelet, are a notable landmark in the city.

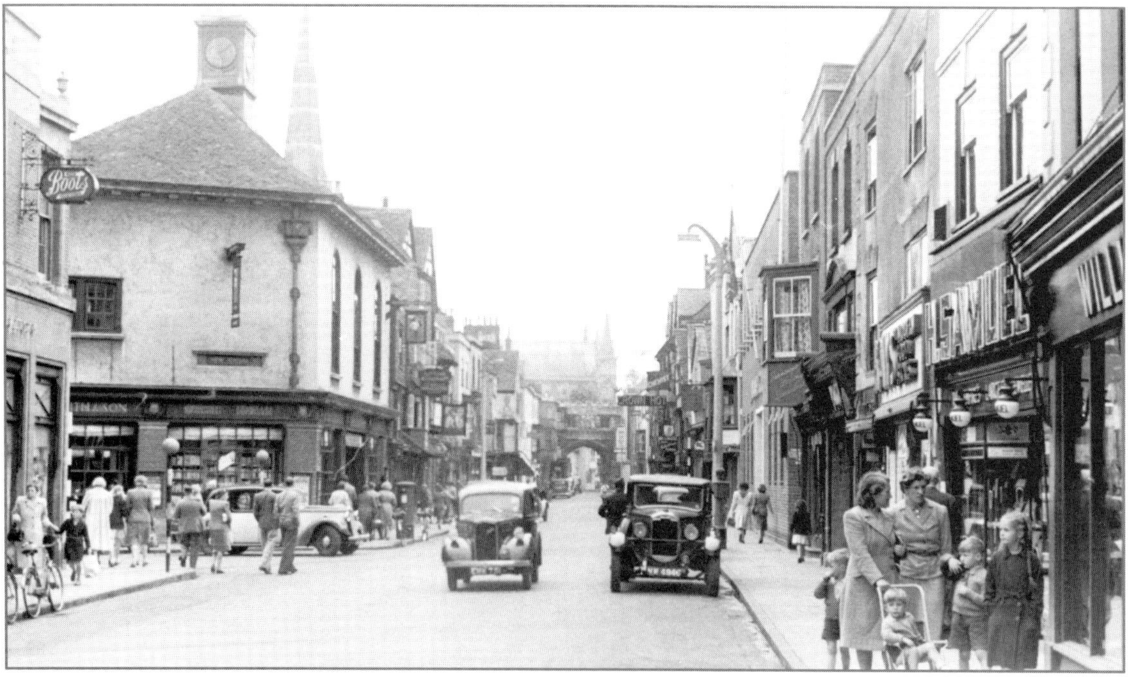

Salisbury, High Street c1950 S48133
The city was planned as an entity from the very outset, and the layout of its streets reflect this. The Crown Hotel is on the left.

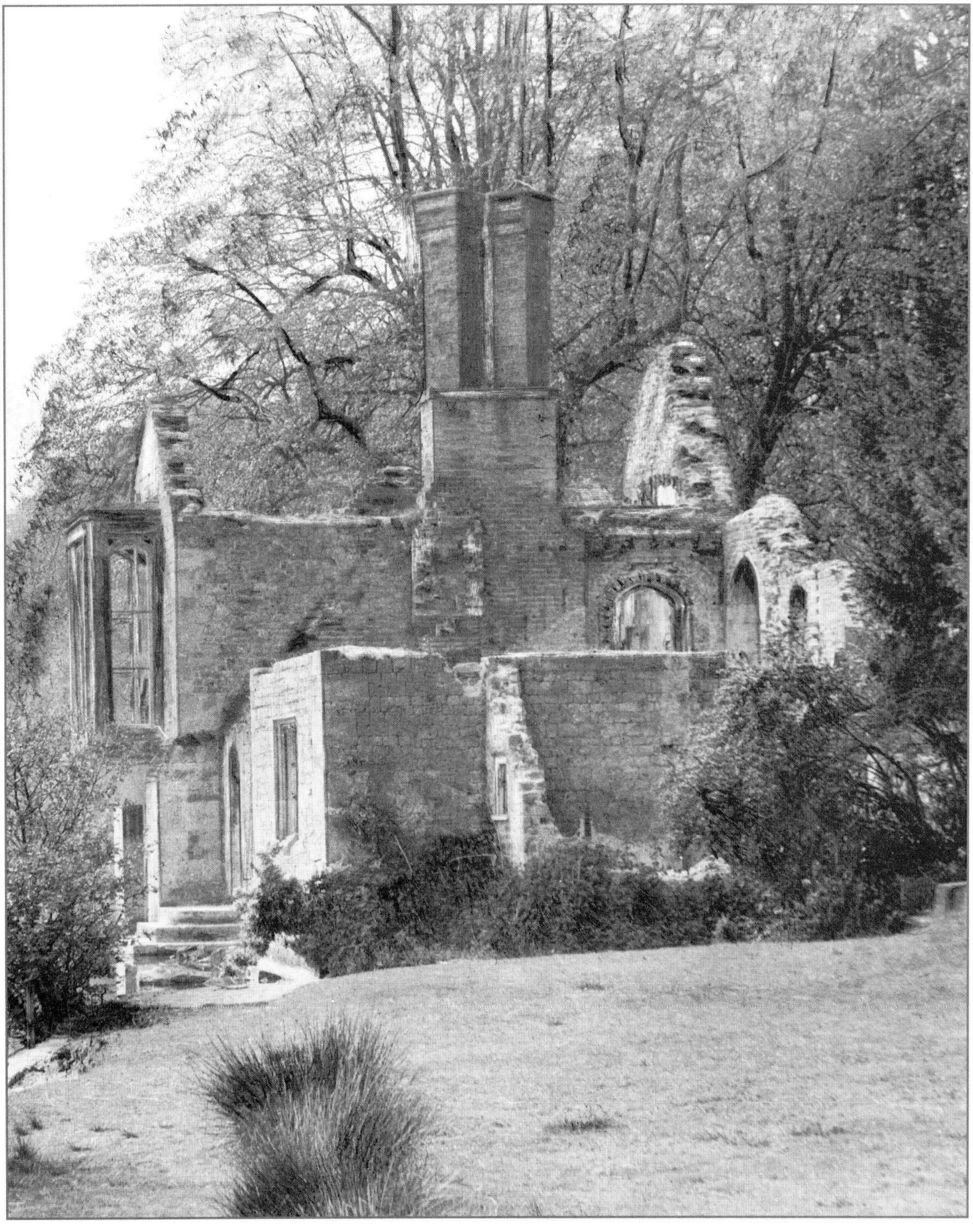

Longleat, Shearwater c1960 L190005

This thirty-eight-acre lake, part of the Longleat estate, was man-made in 1791 to the design of Francis, Duke of Bridgewater. The task was conducted by estate tenants, who constructed the weir and this building - a venue for the entertainment of the lord's guests. There is a flourishing sailing club on the lake today, and the starting gun is discharged from the bay window you can see in the picture.

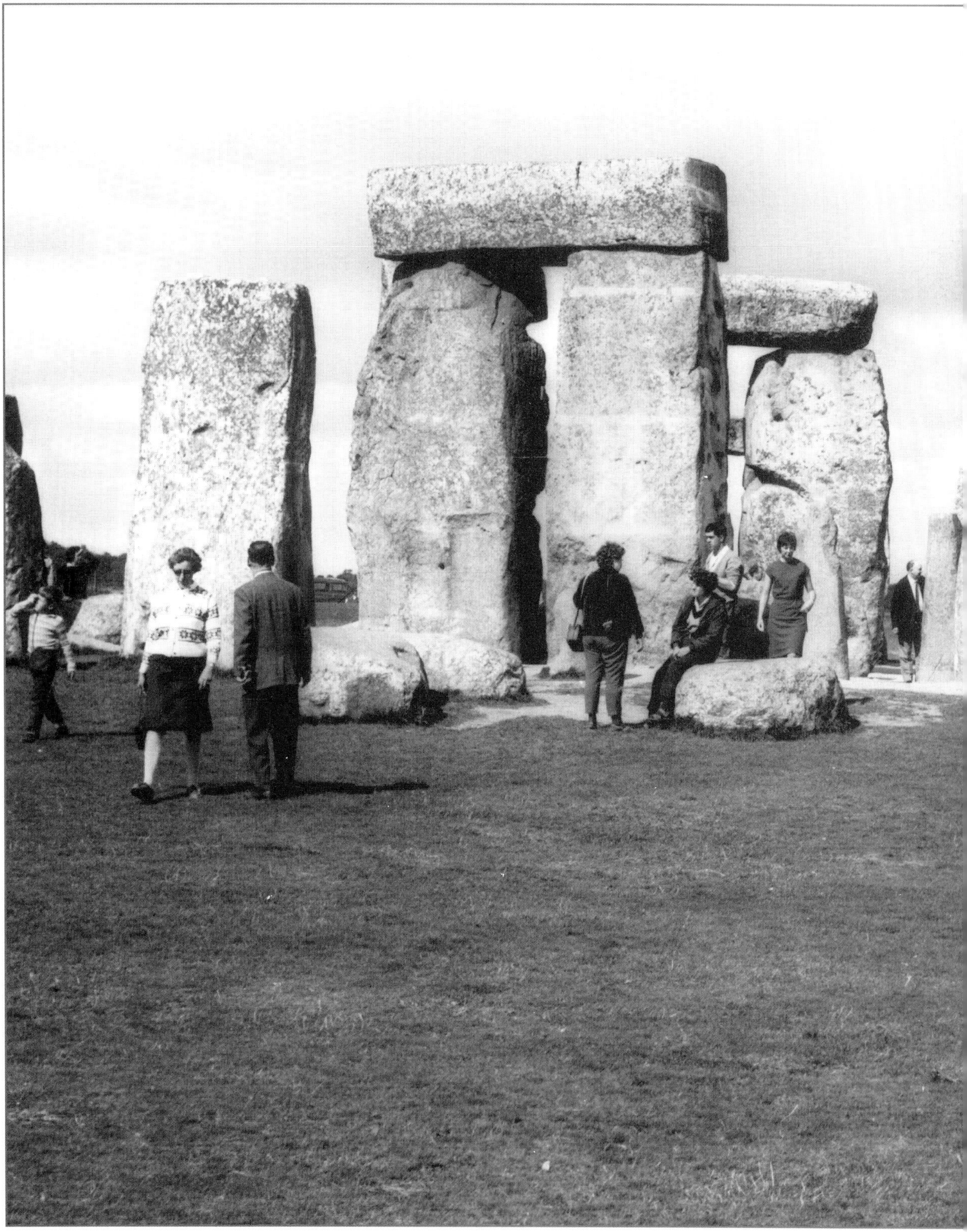

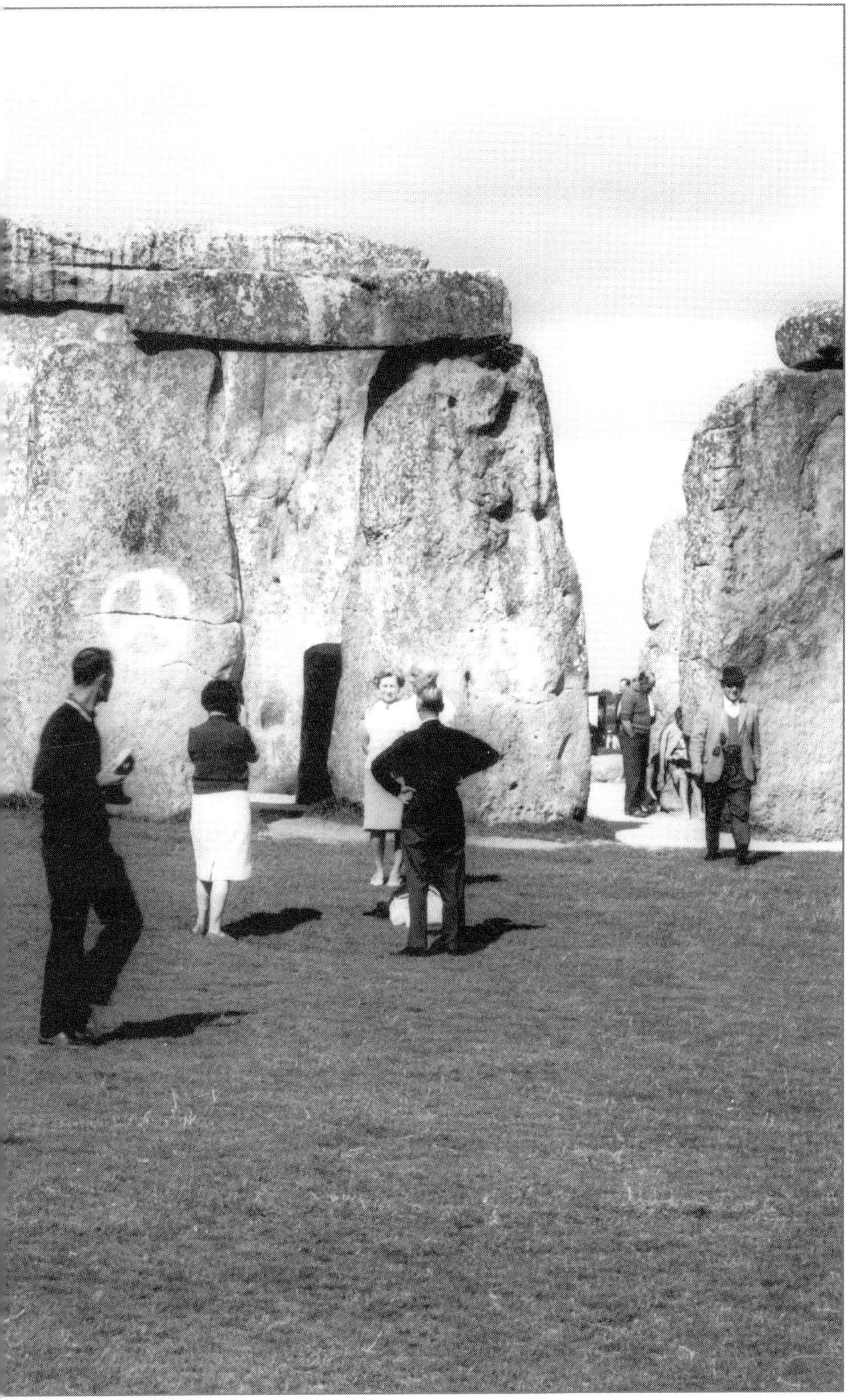

Stonehenge c1960

S205108

This place needs little introduction! It is thought that its construction started some 5,000 years ago, although its purpose still remains something of a mystery today. What is clear is that its principal axis aligns with the midwinter and midsummer sunrises. Note the CND symbol painted onto one of the stones.

▼ **Stourhead, Stourton Church and the Green c1965** S741084

This delightful village sits by the grounds of Stourhead House, the home of Henry Hoare II, who had acquired the place in 1717. The original owners, the Stourton family, made the mistake of being both Royalist and Catholic during the Civil War; by 1704 they had to sell the estate.

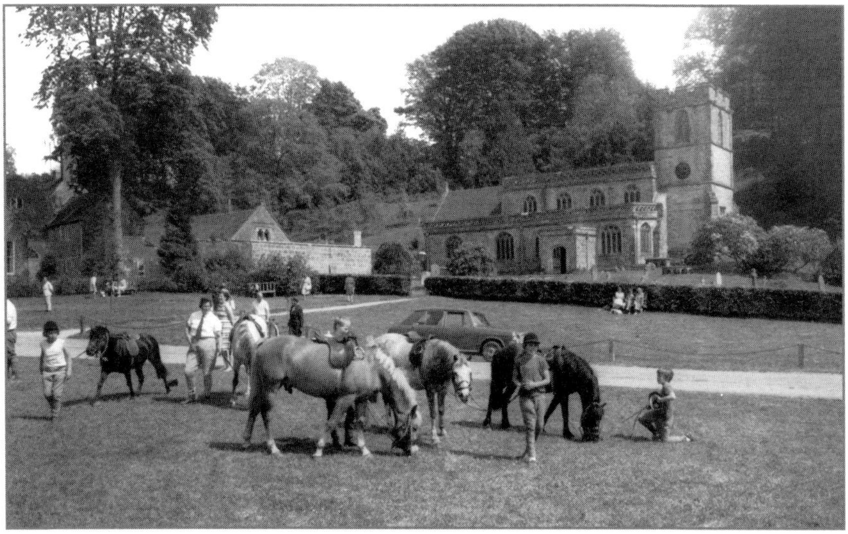

▼ **Swindon, Regent Street c1950** S254021

The largest town in the county, Swindon was a simple hilltop community until the 1840s. What was once a thriving cattle, horse and sheep market was transformed by the arrival of the railway works.

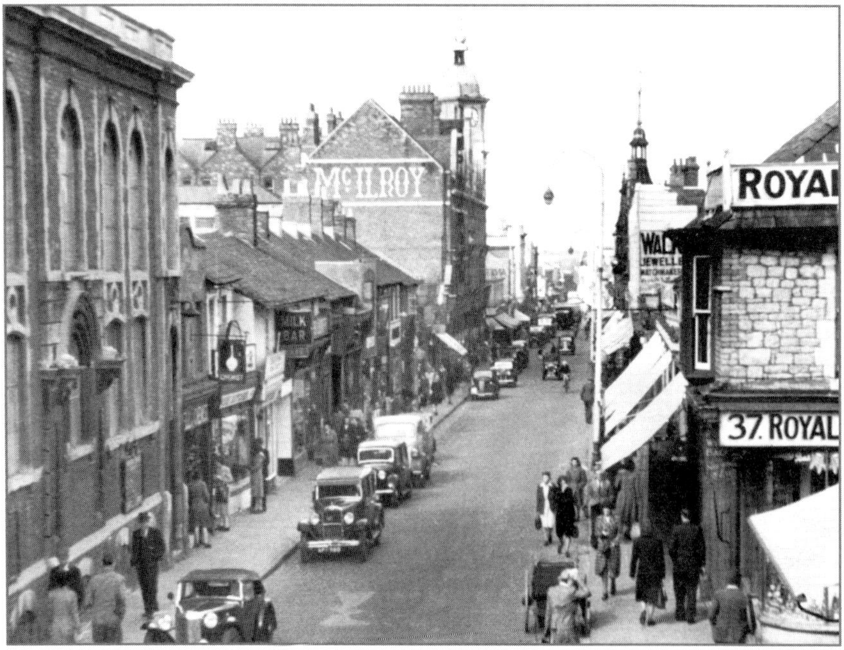

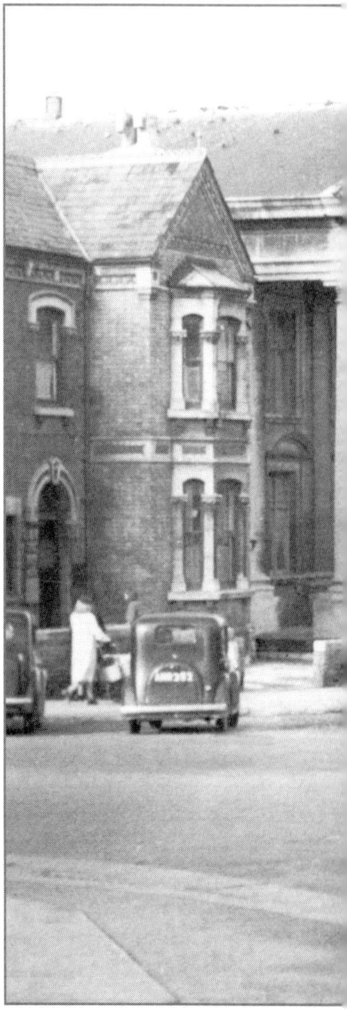

▲ **Swindon, Regent Circus and Regent Street 1948** S254009

Note the Baptist Tabernacle on the left, and Bell Bros advertising their knitwear and 'reliable repairs'. The town's name comes from 'swin dun' - swine down, perhaps referring to the hill which provided pasture for pigs.

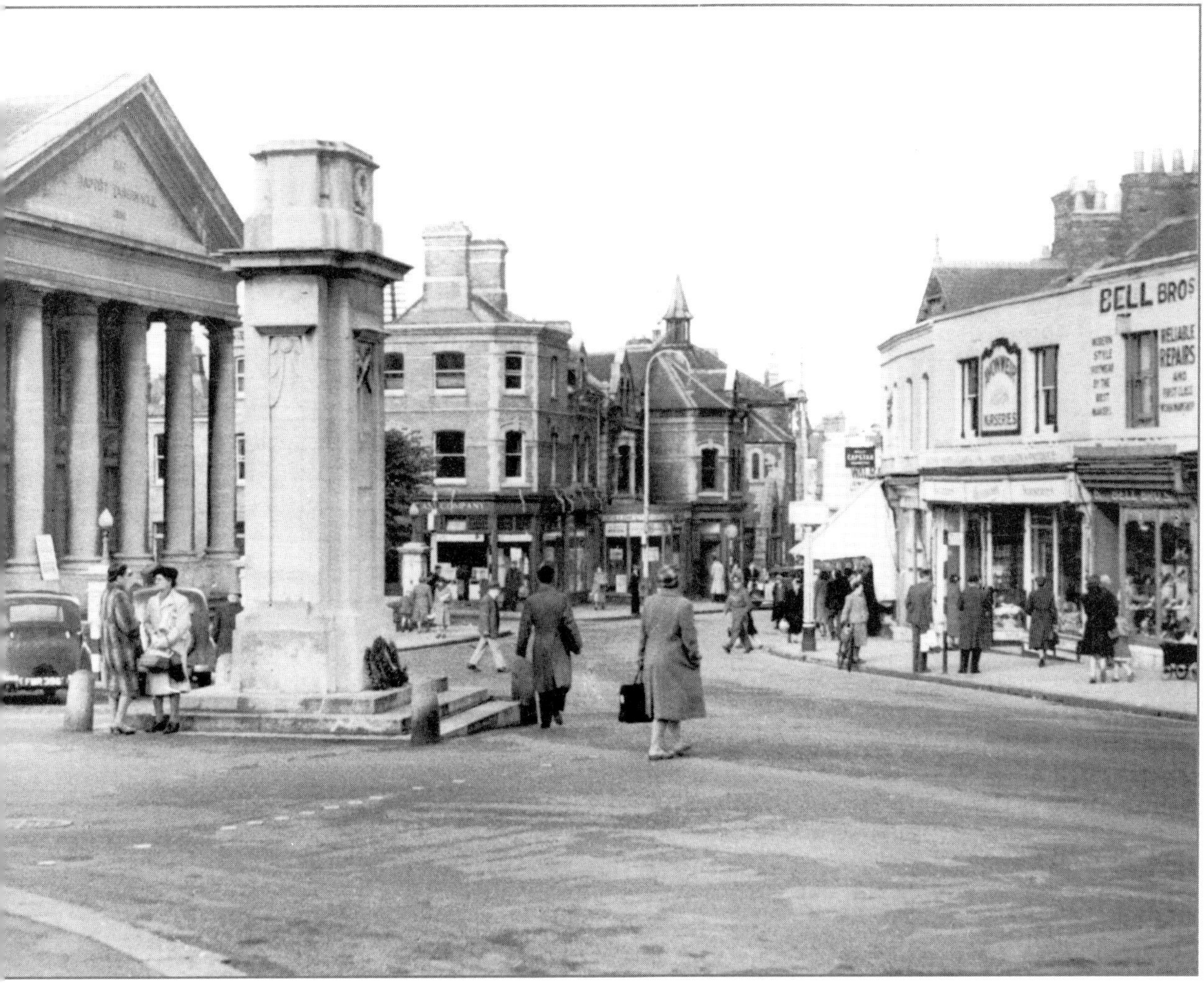

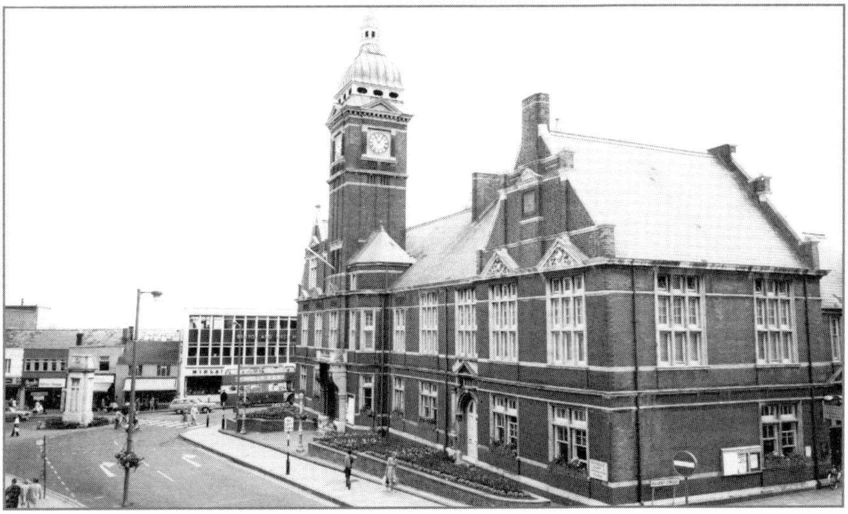

Swindon, The Town Hall c1965 S254098

The new, redbrick houses of New Swindon, generated by the prosperity of the railway works, spread up the hill, threatening to envelop the grey limestone buildings of Old Swindon. The two 'halves' of Swindon were united in 1900.

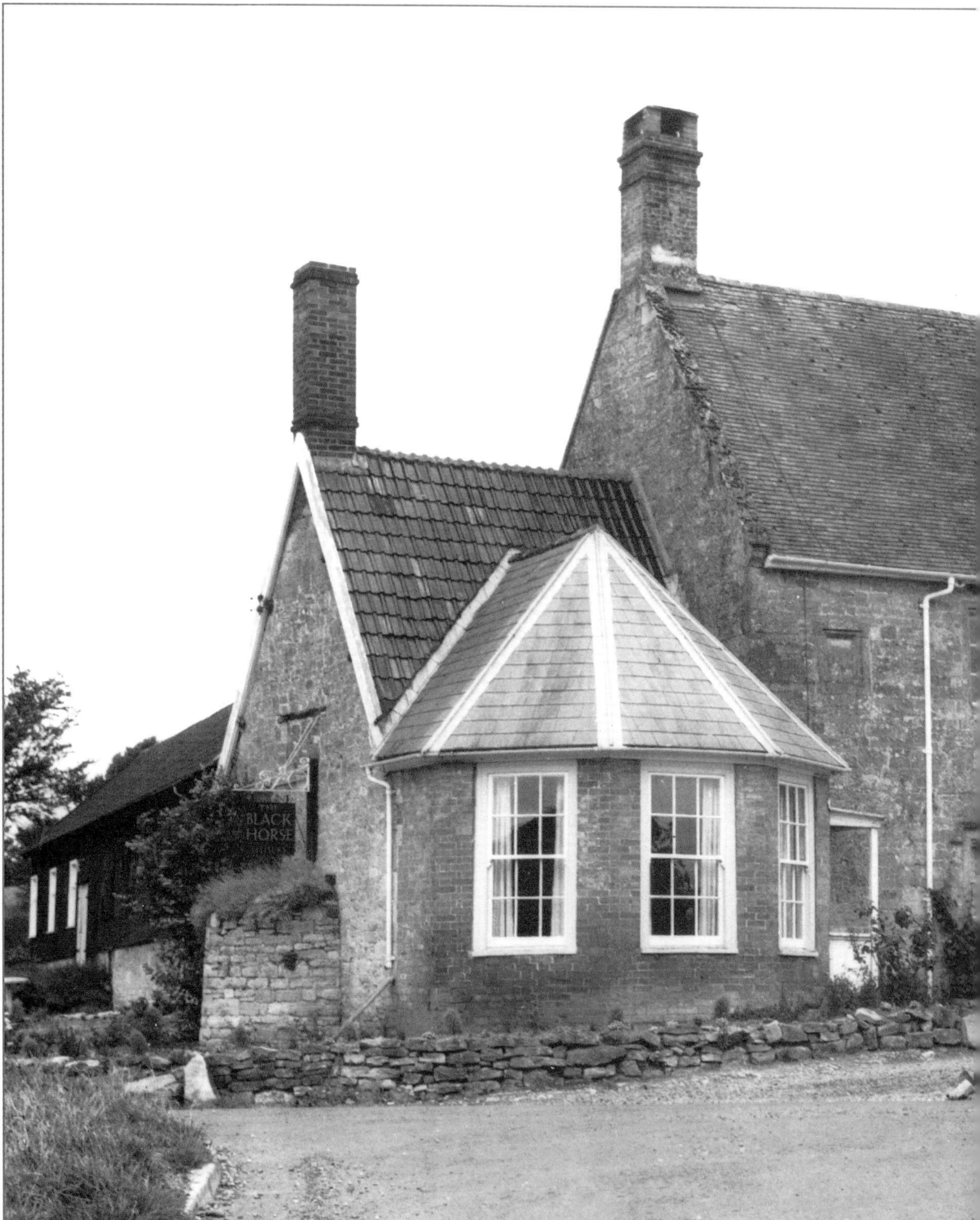
BLACK
HORSE

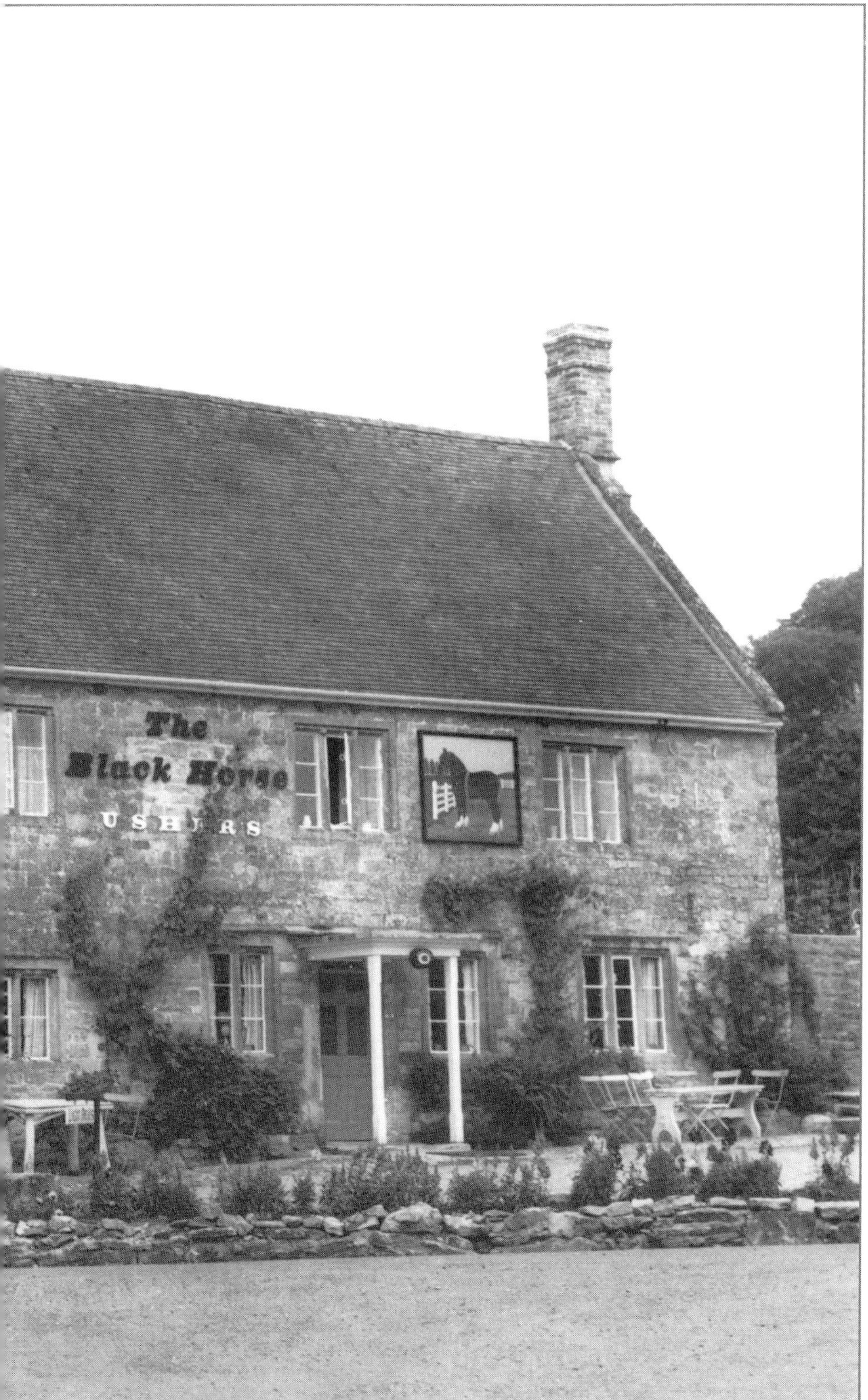

Teffont Magna
The Black Horse
c1960 T147009
The Black Horse was once an 18th-century farmhouse, but it became a pub when the turnpike road through here was opened in 1820. It has now returned to residential use, whilst to the rear of it we can see the new offices of the Francis Frith Collection in the now-converted barn.

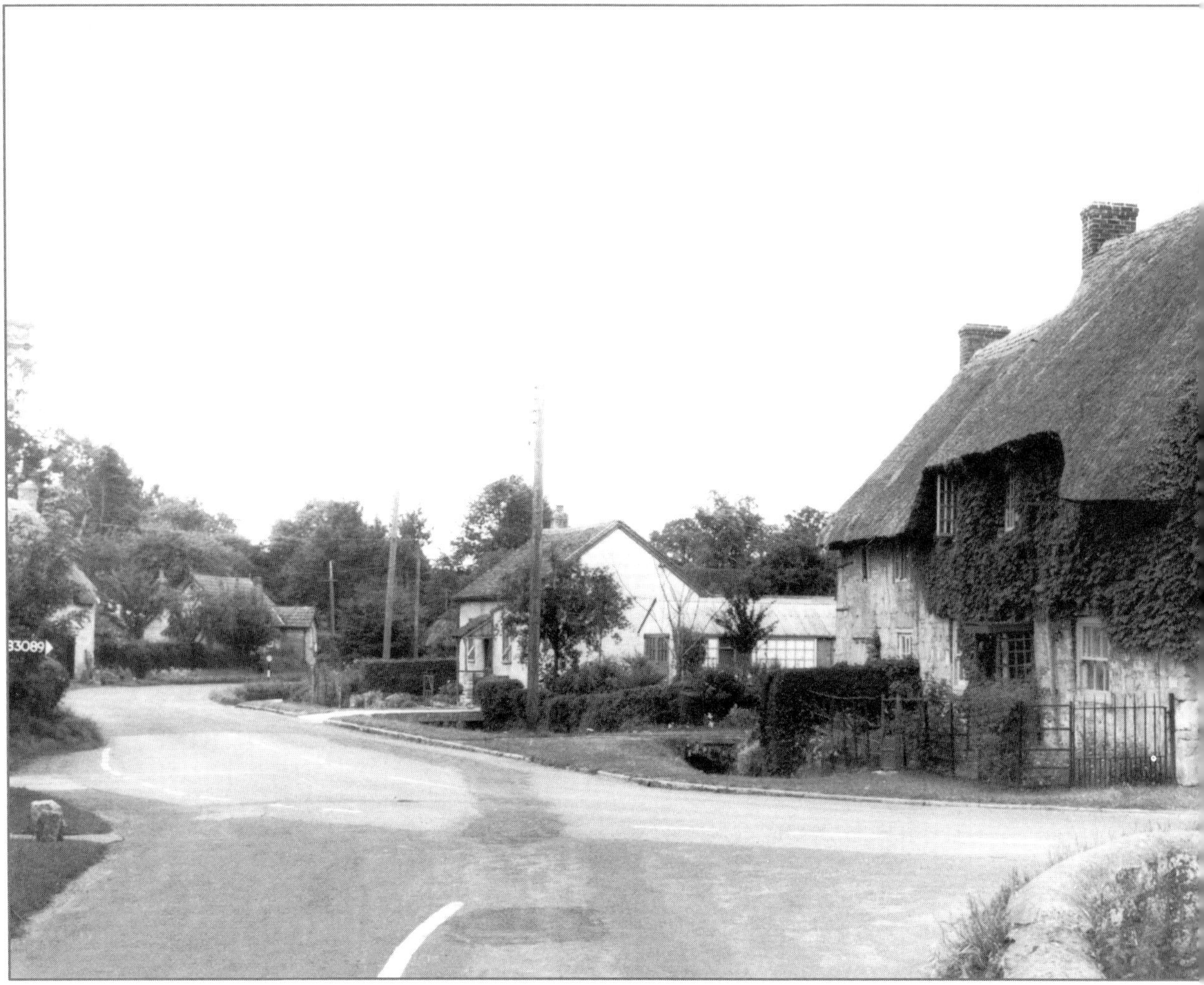

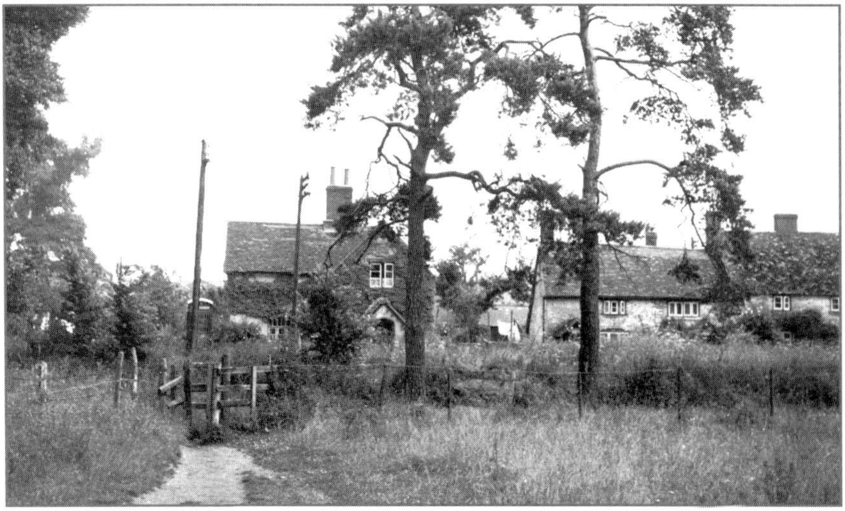

◄ **North Tidworth The Footpath c1955**
N81002 Tidworth is very much a military town. As the son of a soldier, I spent some years in Furze Hill Close in the town.

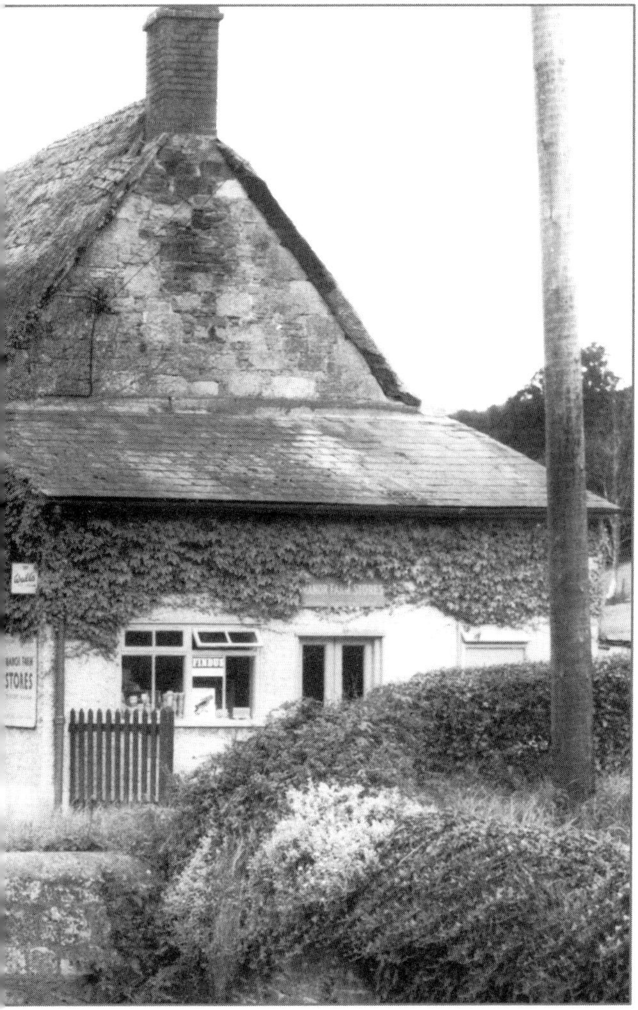

◄ **Teffont Magna Manor Farm Stores c1960** T147004
This is one of the few villages in Wiltshire that still retains a name with Celtic rather than Saxon origins.

▼ **North Tidworth Station Road c1960** N81021
The village name simply means Toda's homestead.

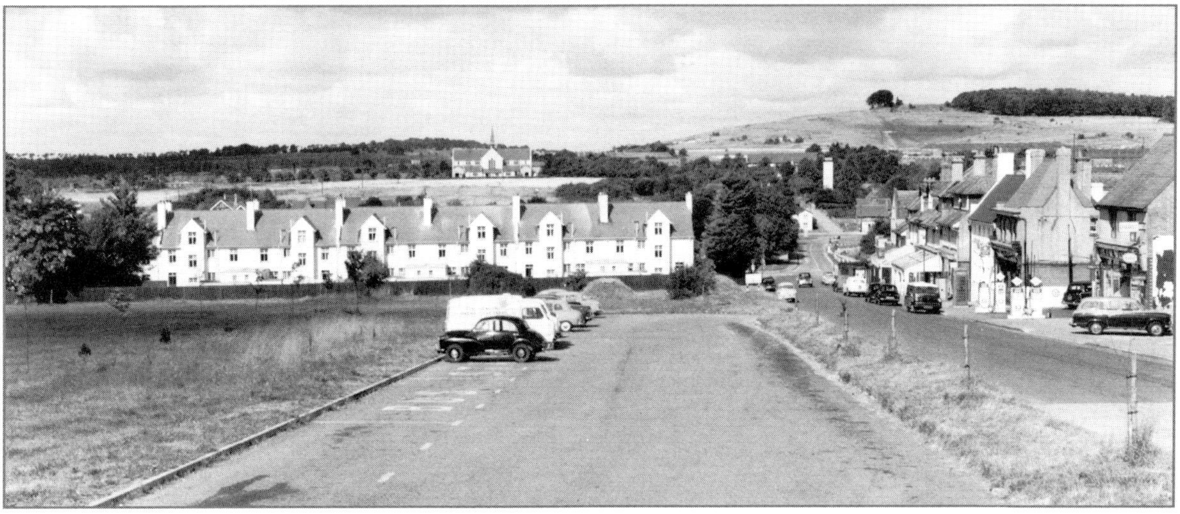

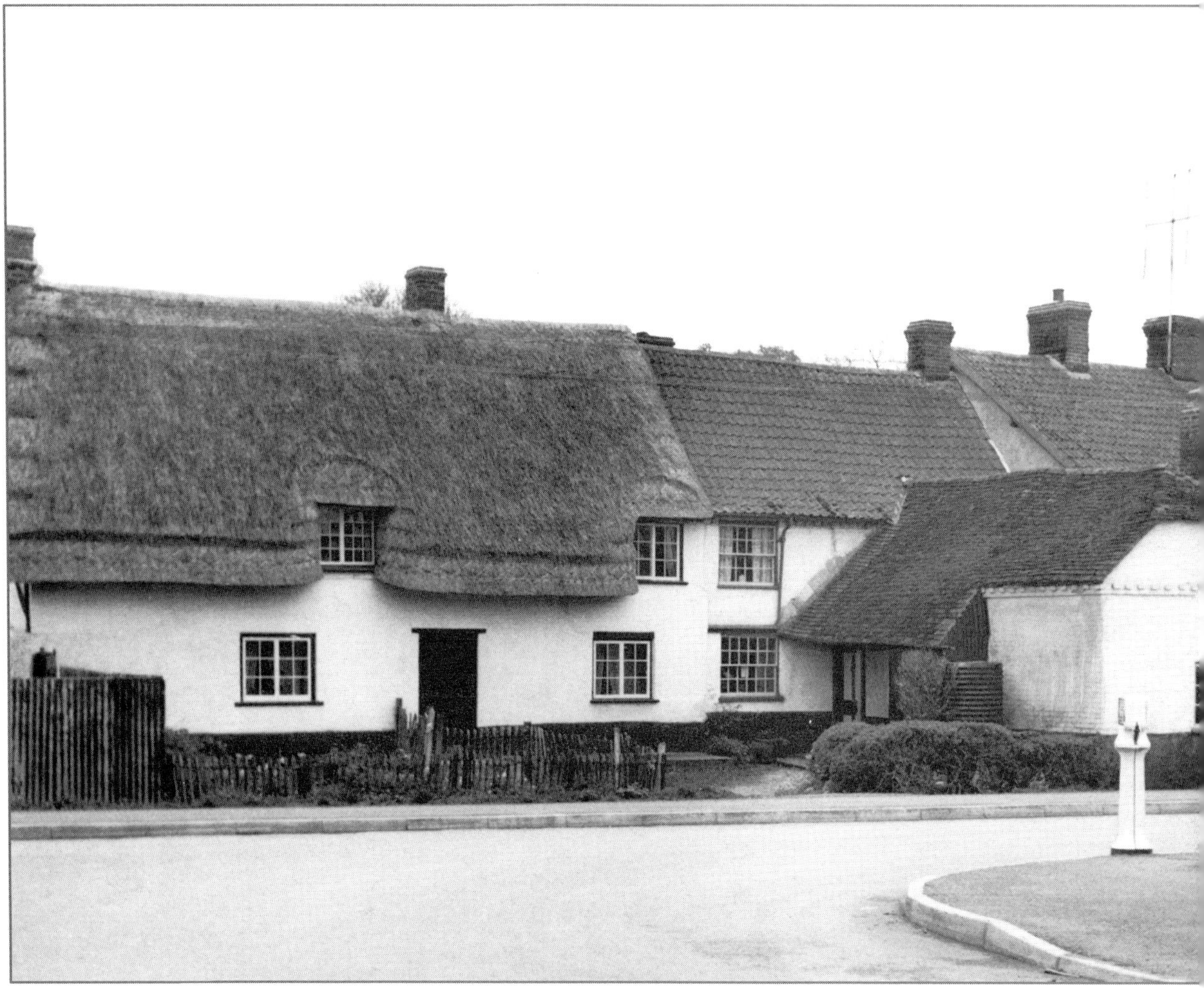

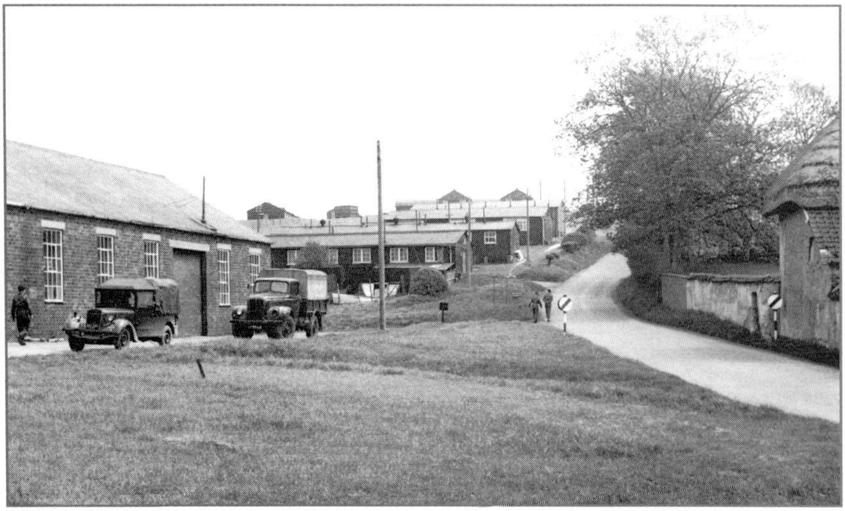

◄ **Tilshead Westdown Camp c1960** T149010
The army is never far away in this part of Wiltshire.

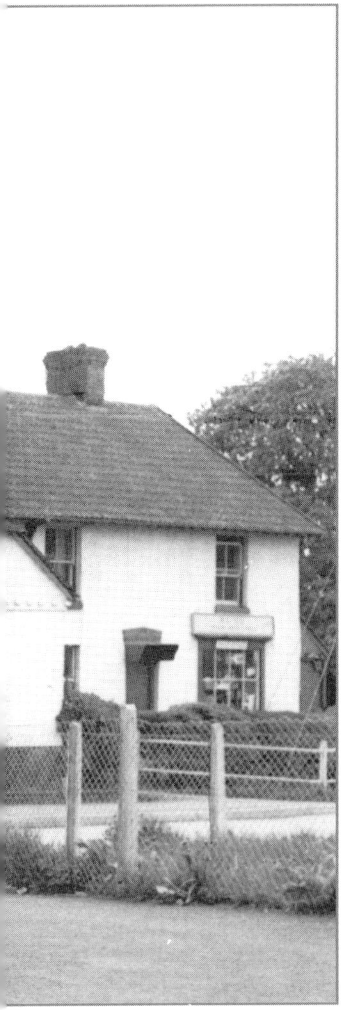

Tilshead
The Post Office c1960
T149006

Tilshead
The Post Office c1965
T149027
The village name derives from the Saxon, and means Tidwulf's hide. In 1086 the Domesday Book lists this as a prosperous town with no less than sixty-six burgesses.

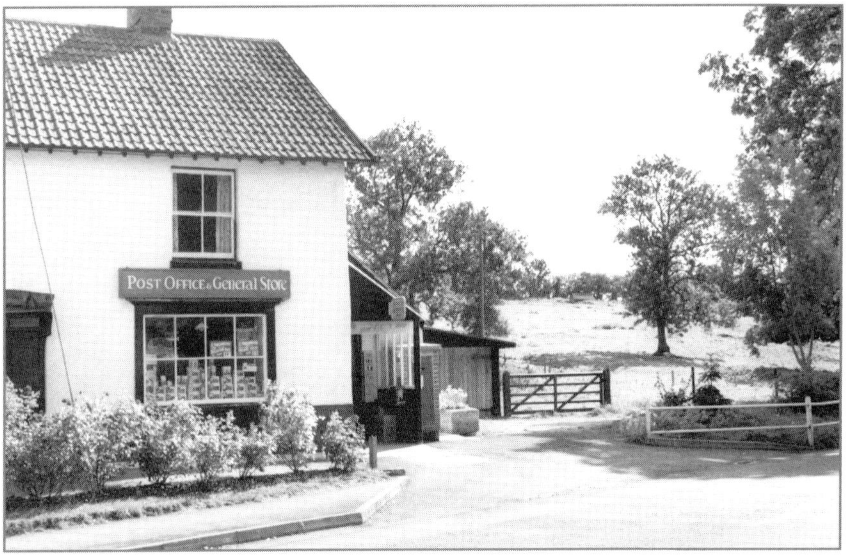

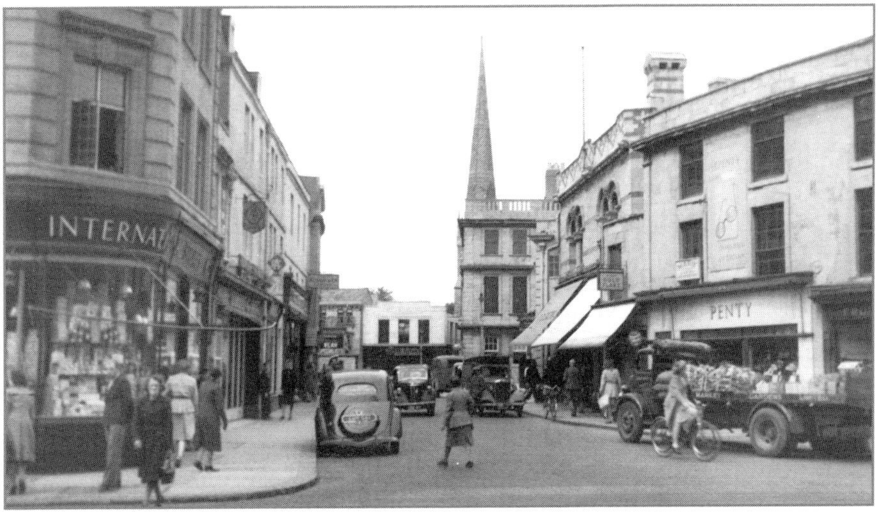

Trowbridge c1950
T84003
From its beginnings as a simple settlement, Trowbridge was catapulted into a new age with the building of de Bohun's castle in the 12th century. Much of its prosperity was subsequently built on its weaving mills. Note the International Stores on the left, and Penty's optician's shop on the right.

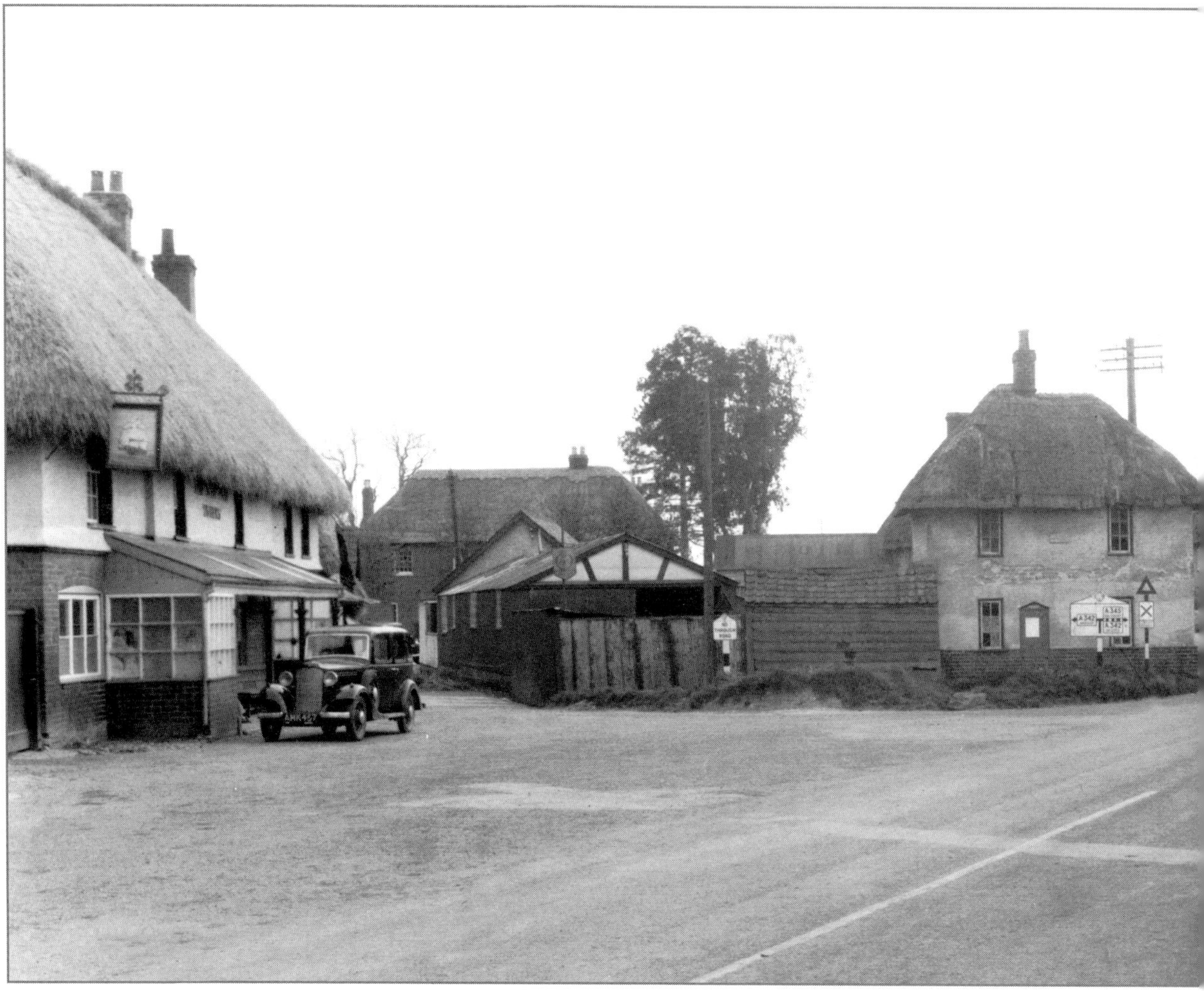

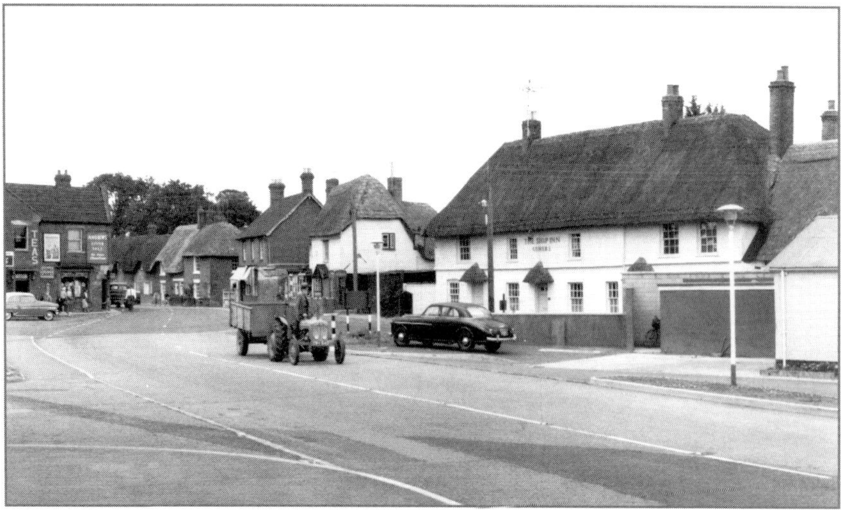

◄ **Upavon, The Village c1960** U25007
The Central Flying School of the Royal Flying Corps was established here in 1912; after World War I, the base was home to fighter squadrons. Perhaps the village's most famous son was Henry 'Orator' Hunt, MP (1773-1835).

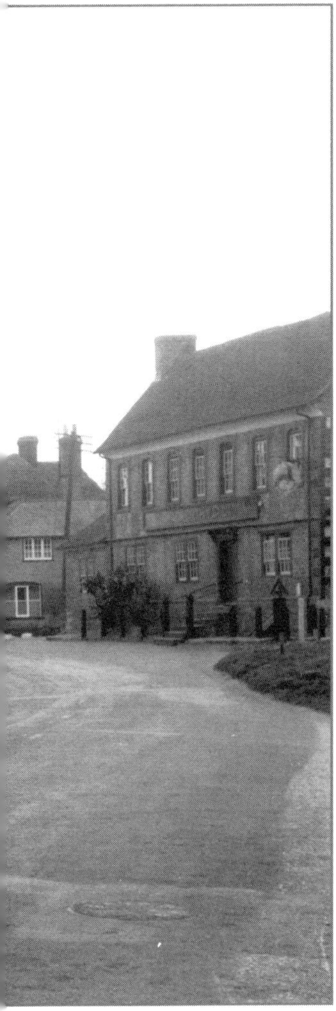

◄ **Upavon, The Green and the Ship Inn c1950** U25005

The 17th-century John Newman, minister of Upavon, once petitioned the magistrates, saying: 'God Almighty is greatly dishonoured, his sabbaths profaned, good laws condemned and the infinite of youth extremely corrupted'. Clearly, Upavon has not always been the peaceful village pictured here.

▼ **Wanborough High Street c1960**

W260003

The Harrow Inn can be seen in the centre, and note the Dominion and Regent petrol pumps.

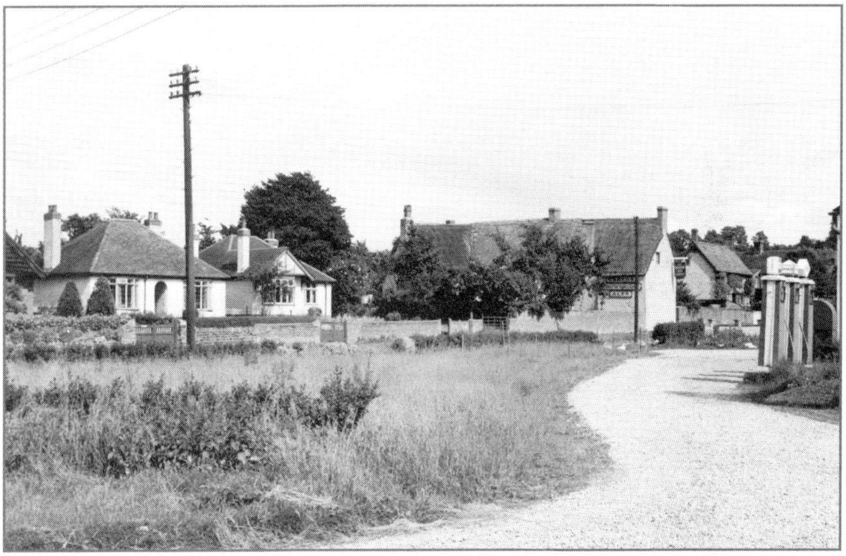

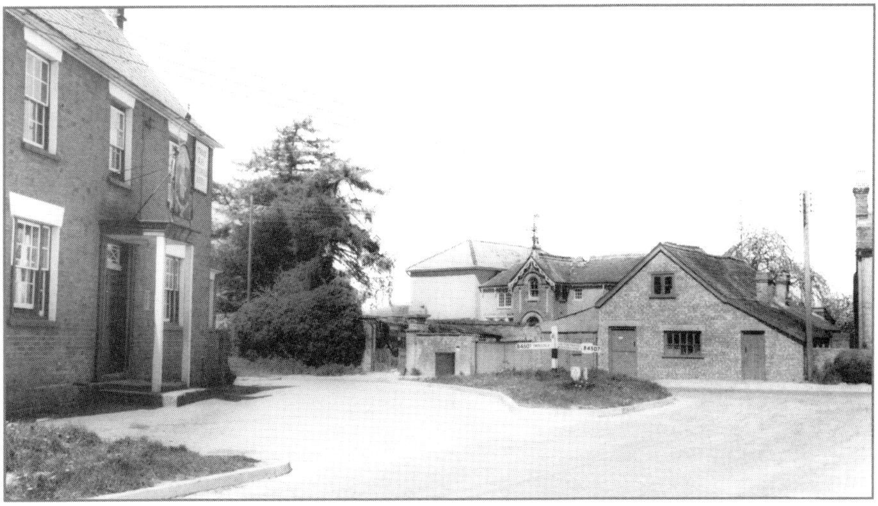

◄ **Wanborough The Village c1960**

W260013

The village name derives from the Saxon 'waegn' (waggon) and 'beorg' (hill), which reminds us that it was a resting place for drovers taking their cattle to London, sometimes upwards of 800 per week. The Roman Ermine Street is close by.

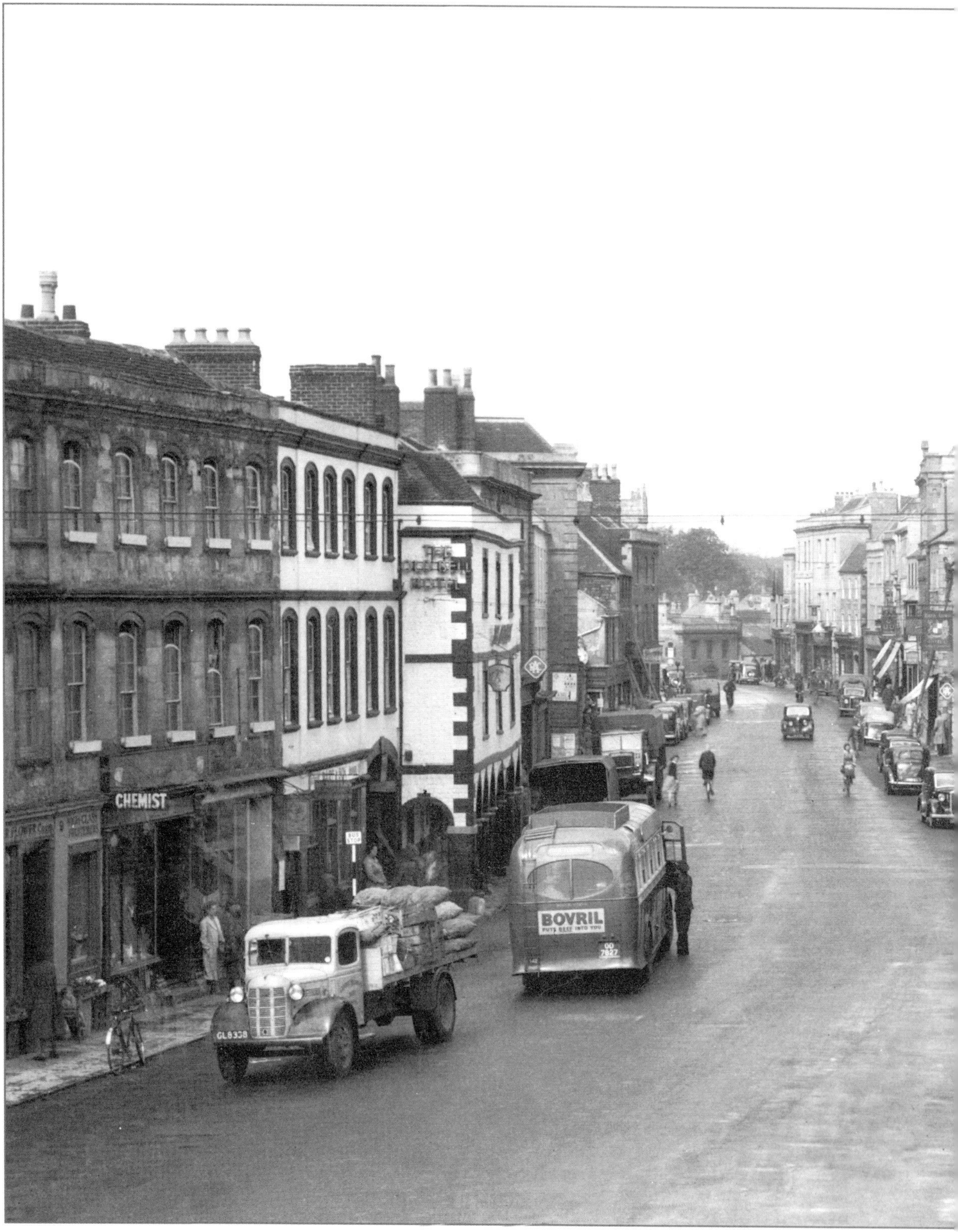
CHEMIST
BOVRIL

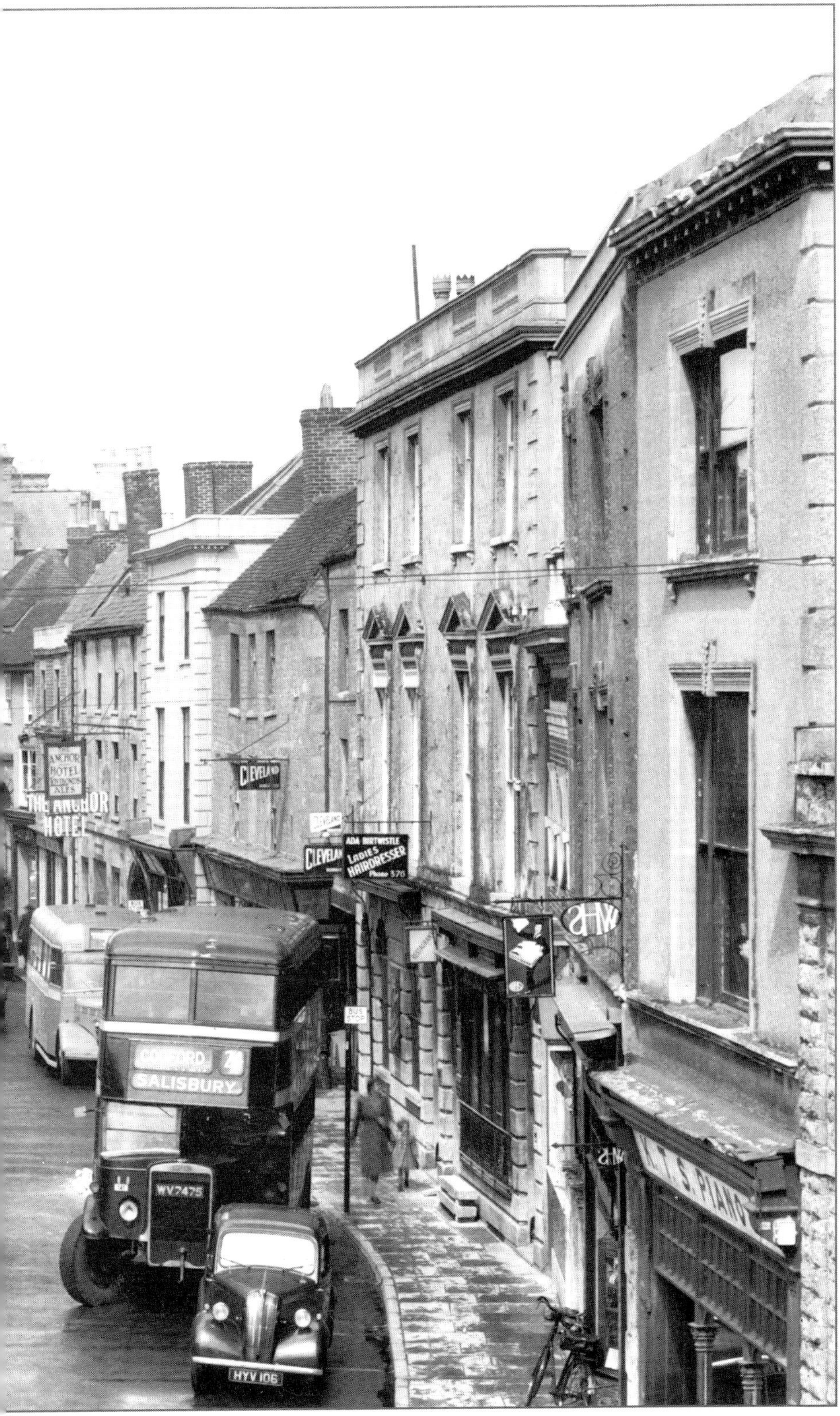

Warminster
The Market Place
c1950 W261009

Built of local stone on the edge of the Wylye Valley, Warminster is closely connected with its military establishments. Note the Old Bell Hotel on the left (now the Old Bell Inn), the Anchor Hotel on the right (still in existence) and the bus advertising Bovril. The photograph is taken from an upper storey of the old Post Office.

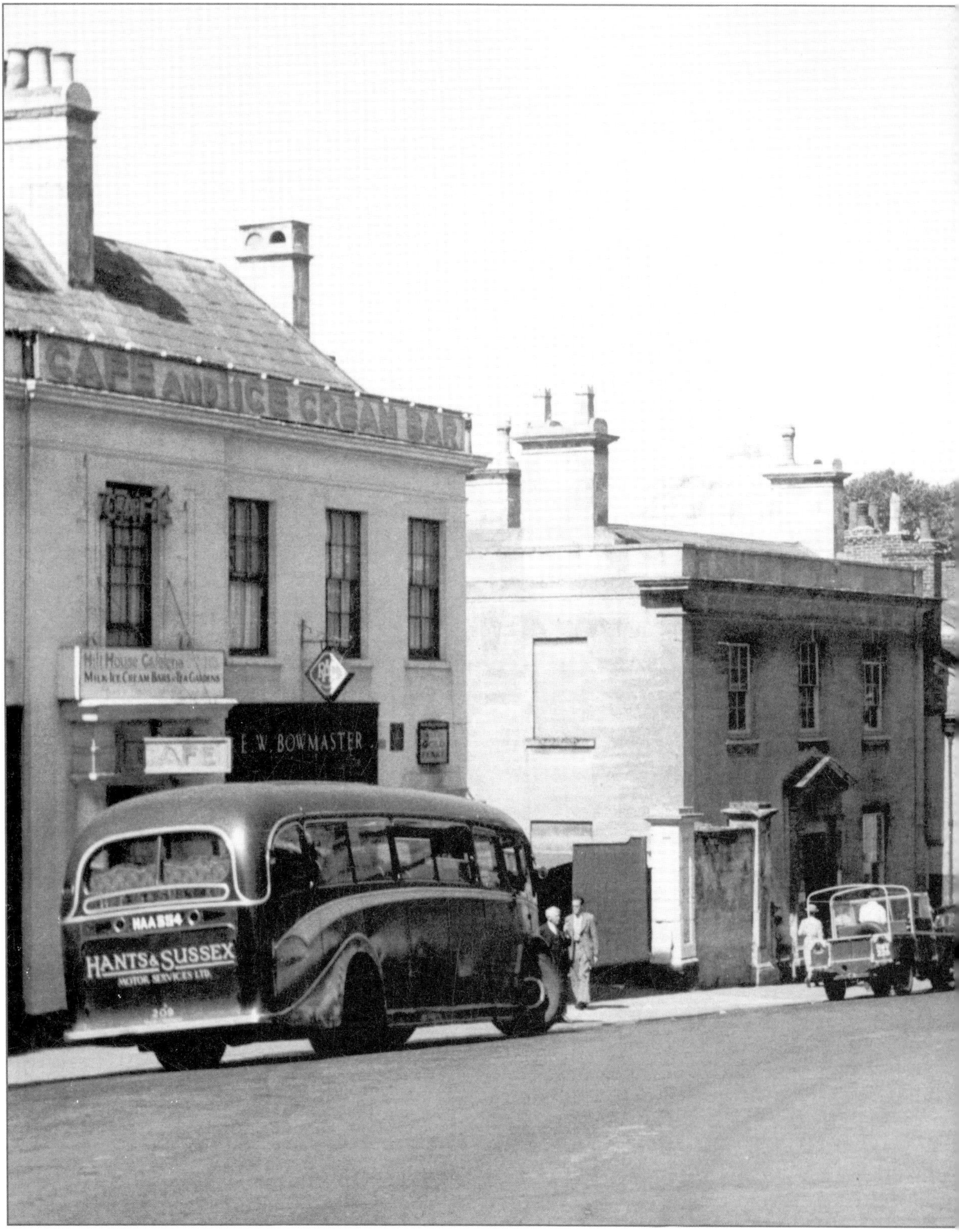
CAFE AND ICE CREAM BAR
Hill House Galleria
MILK ICE CREAM BARS & TEA GARDENS
CAFE
E. W. BOWMASTER
NAA 894
HANTS & SUSSEX
MOTOR SERVICES LTD

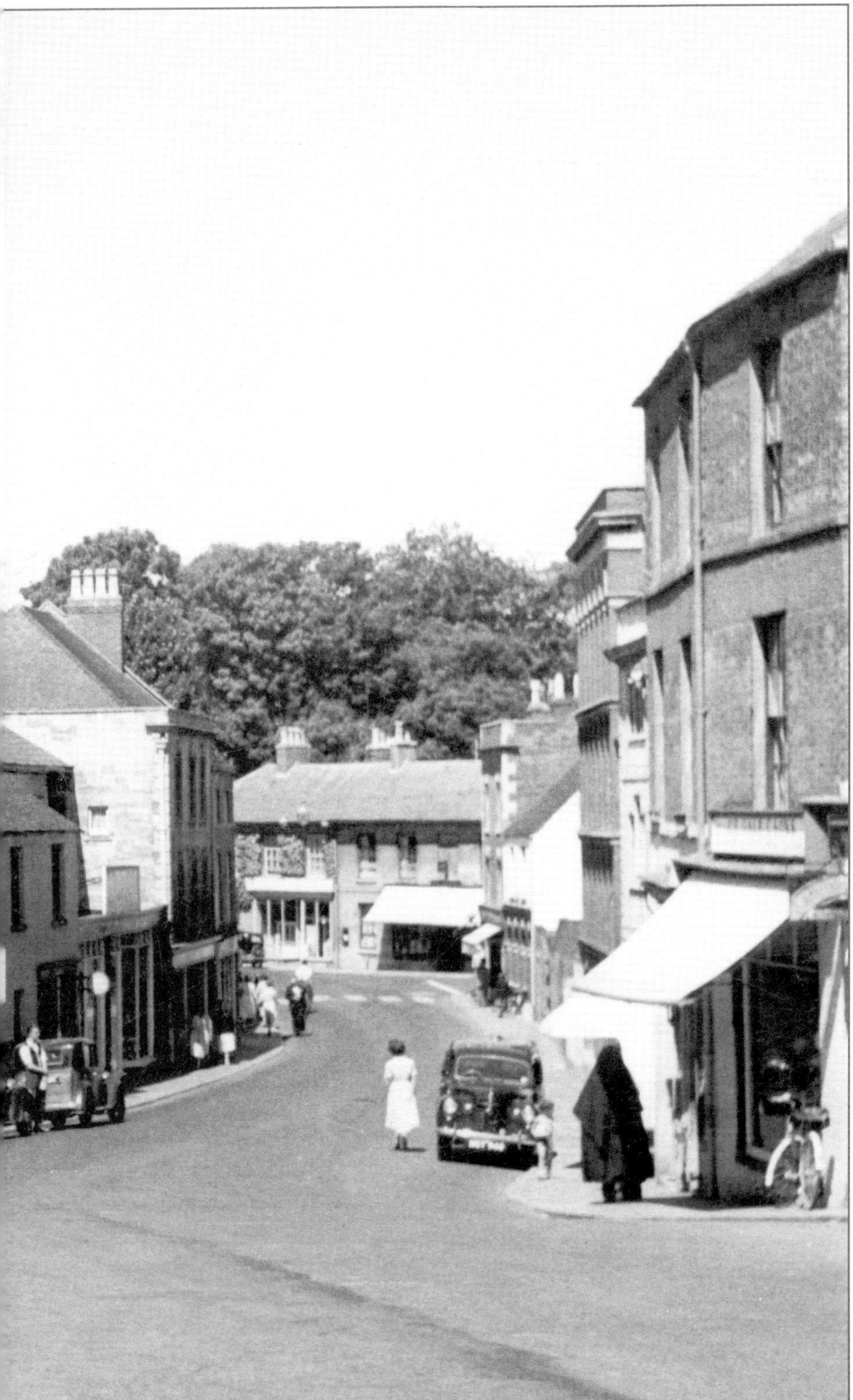

Warminster High Street c1950

W261024

Warminster has been a market town for many years; Daniel Defoe referred to it as 'without exception the greatest market for wheat in England'. This view looks down the High Street; note the Hill House Cafeteria on the left. The two-storey F W Bowmaster Motor services on the left is now a rather disappointing flat-roofed Woolworths.

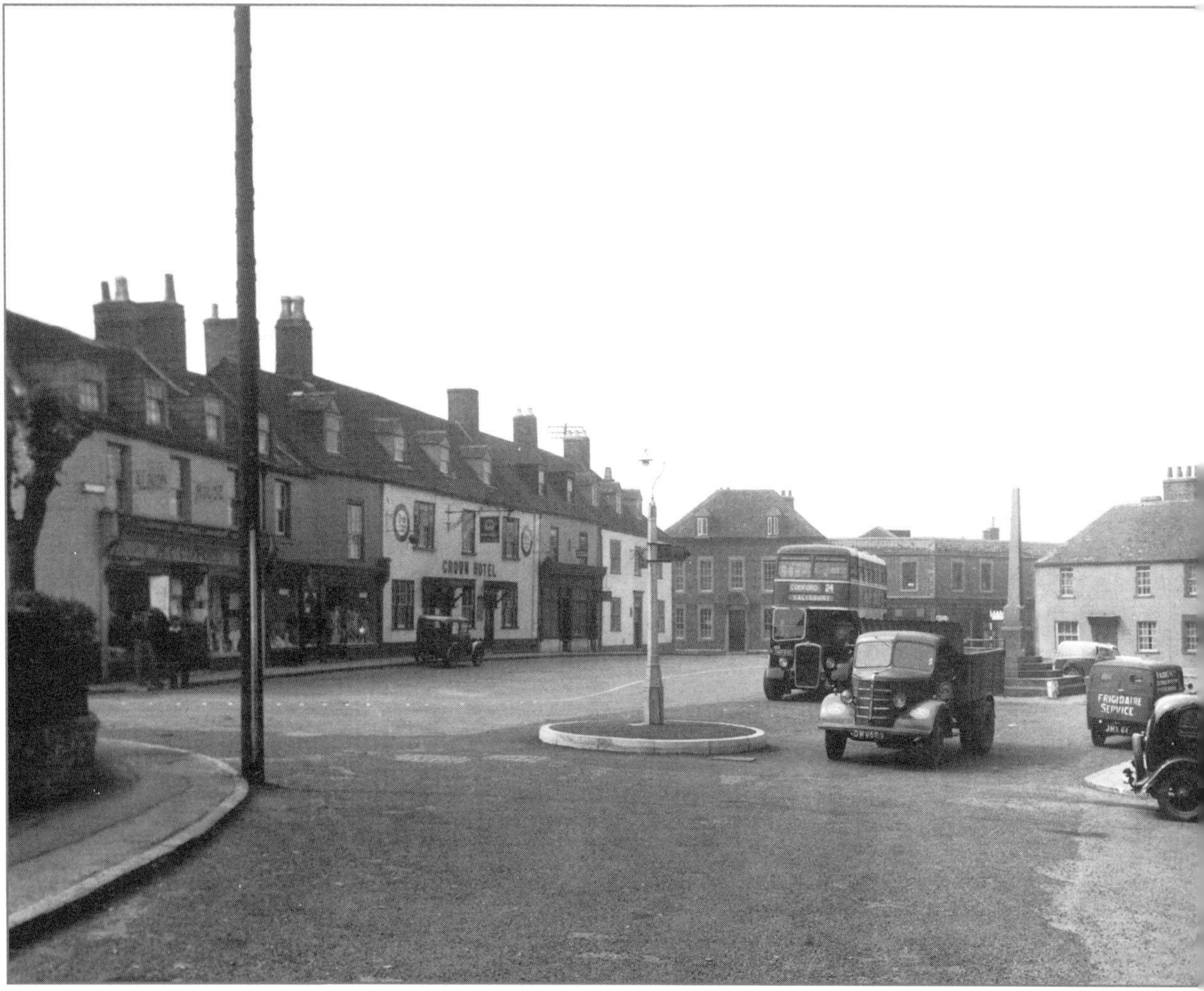

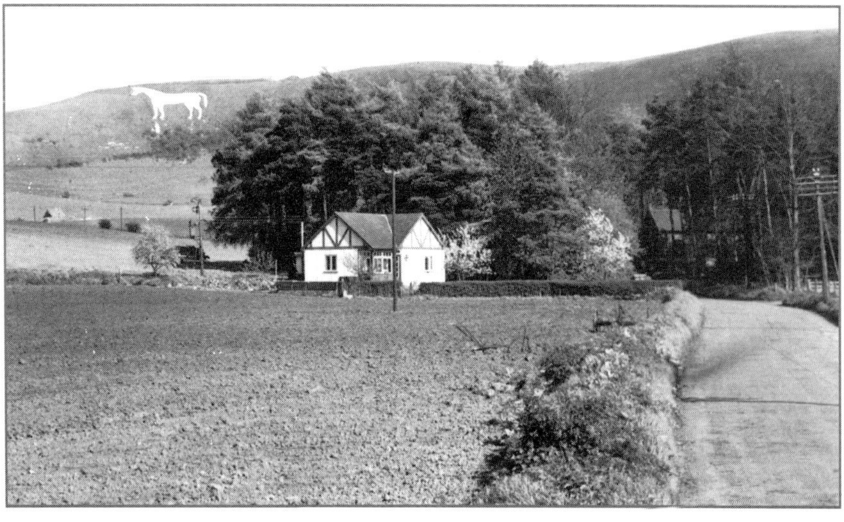

◄ **Westbury, The White Horse c1955** W263013
With parents living in Bratton, I have to be sensitive to a local controversy: is the Westbury White Horse really the Bratton White Horse? Charles Tennyson Turner (1808-1879) wrote: 'As from the Dorset shore I travell'd home, I saw the charger of the Wiltshire wold; A far-seen figure, stately to behold, Whose groom the shepherd is, the hoe his comb'.

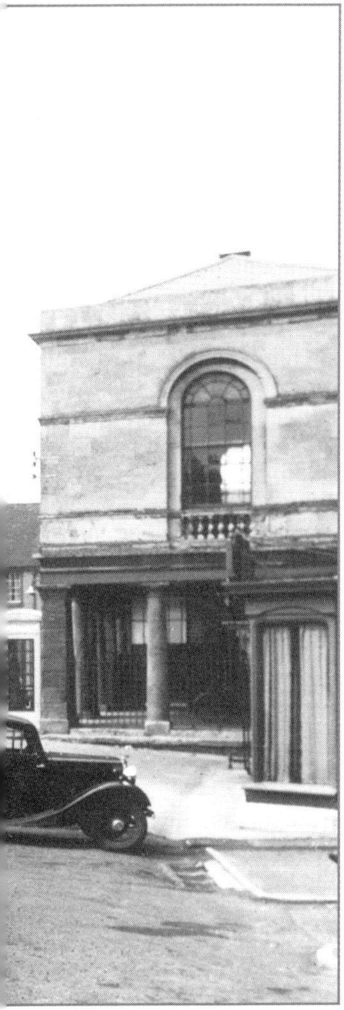

Westbury, The Market Place c1950 W263004
Note the Crown Hotel on the left, and the No 24 bus to Codford and Salisbury - this area is now car parking. This picture is taken from Canon Green, once the site of a magnificent artillery piece melted down to aid the World War I war effort. The Town Hall on the right was built by Sir Massey Lopes. The monument by the bus has mysteriously disappeared.

Westbury Leigh The Village c1950
W264002
The village takes its name from the Saxon 'leah' (wood or clearing) added to the name of Westbury.

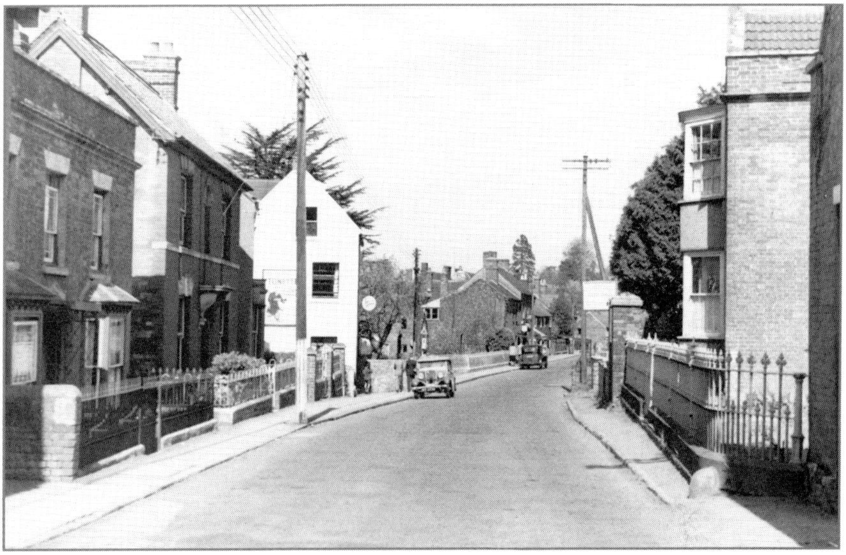

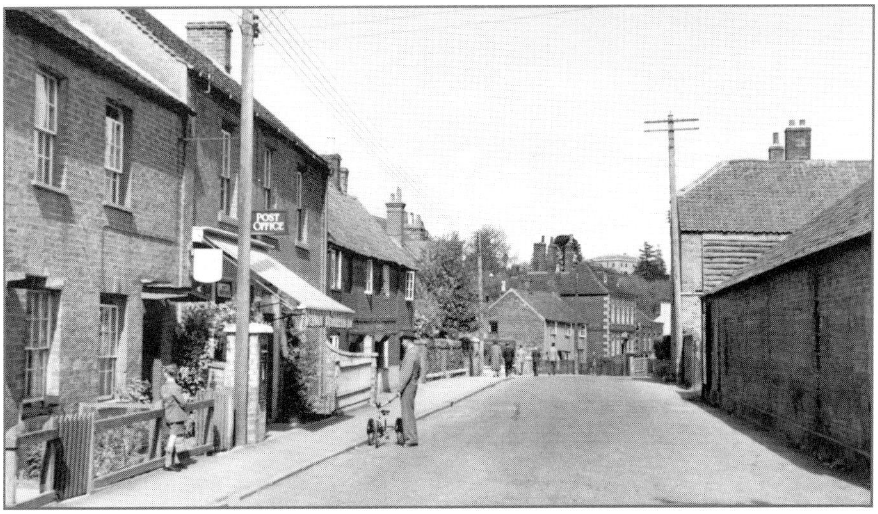

Westbury Leigh The Village c1950
W264005
This photograph is taken from further down the street, and shows the Post Office on the left-hand side, which is still in existence. The white-painted house also still exists, now minus the advertising board.

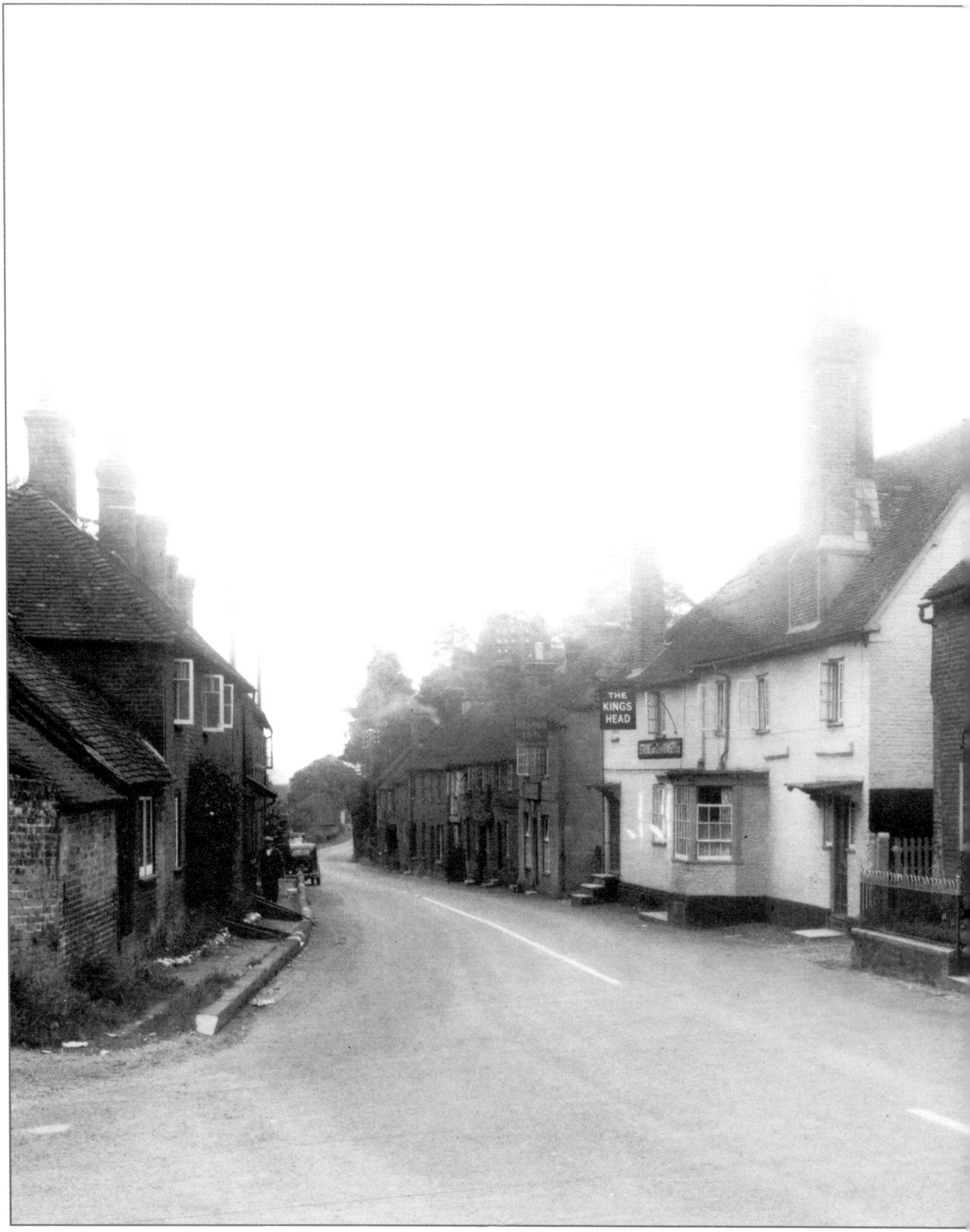
THE
KINGS
HEAD

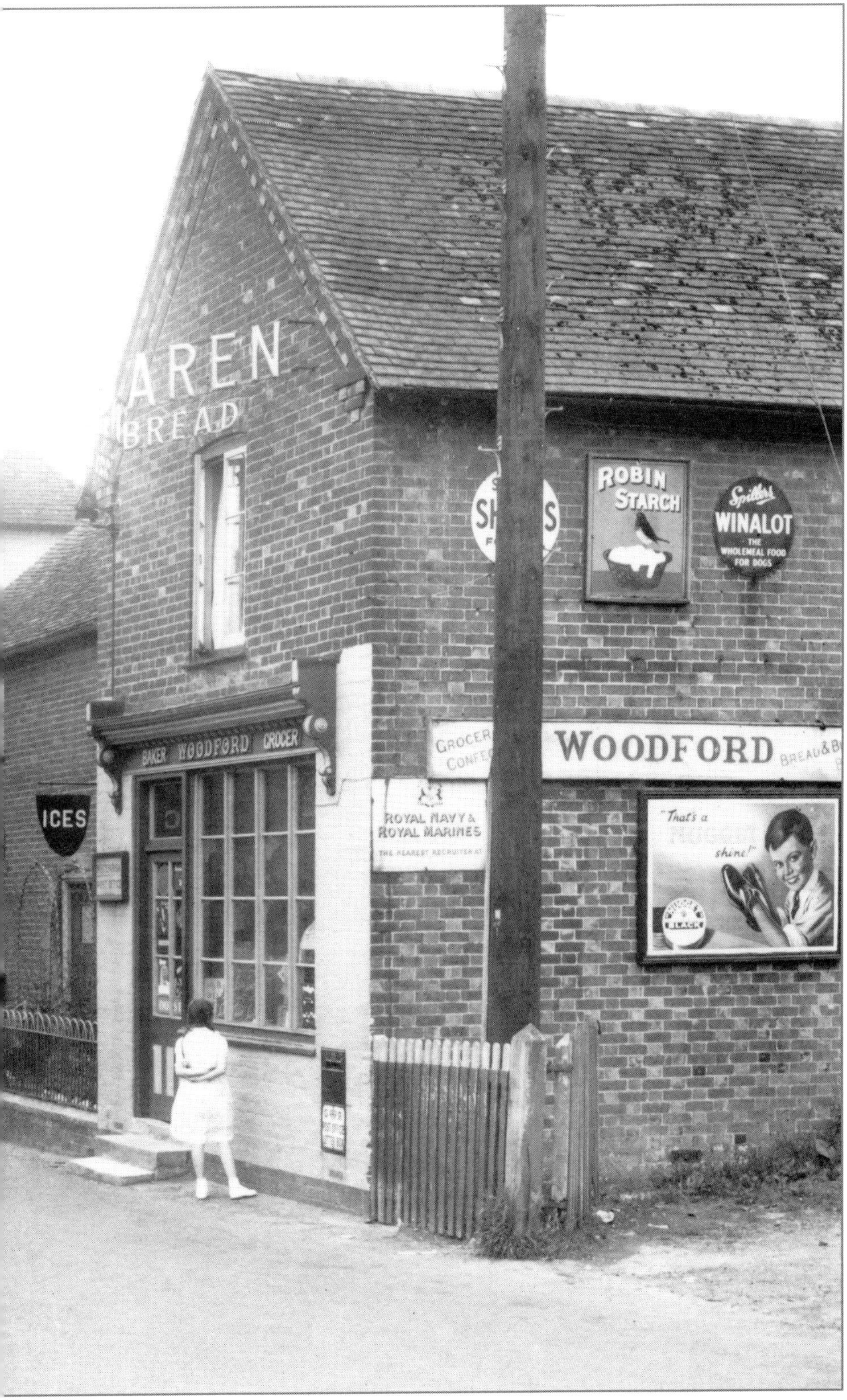

Whiteparish
The Street c1945

W265008

Note the Royal Navy & Royal Marine recruitment, Nugget Butter, Winalot and Robin Starch posters outside the grocer's shop on the right. The King's Head is further up on the right.

▼ **Whiteparish, Bunkers Hill c1945** W265002

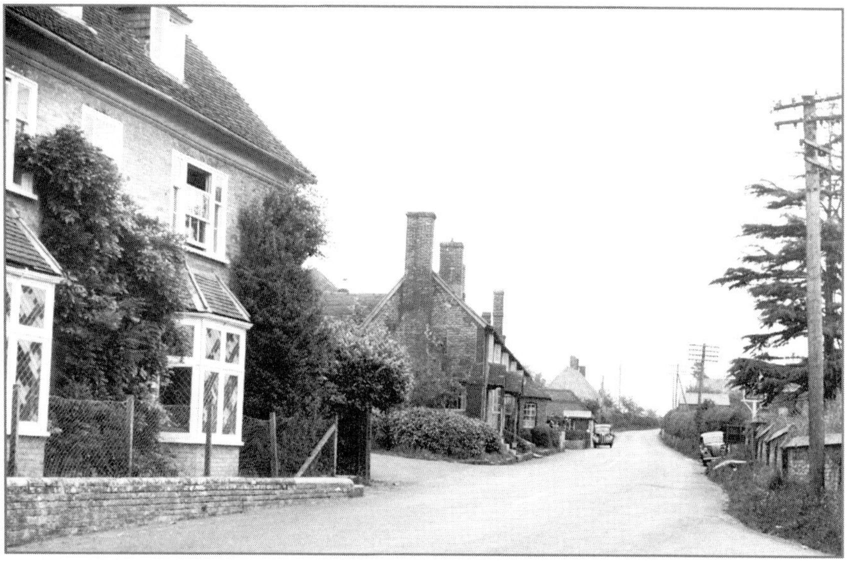

▼ **Whiteparish, The Village c1955** W265020

The White Hart pub is on the left. An inhabitant of the village, Sir Giles Eyre, found himself in hot water and was 'plundered by soldiers' for refusing to make forced loans to Charles I. His memorial in Whiteparish church says he was 'a man much oppressed by publick power'.

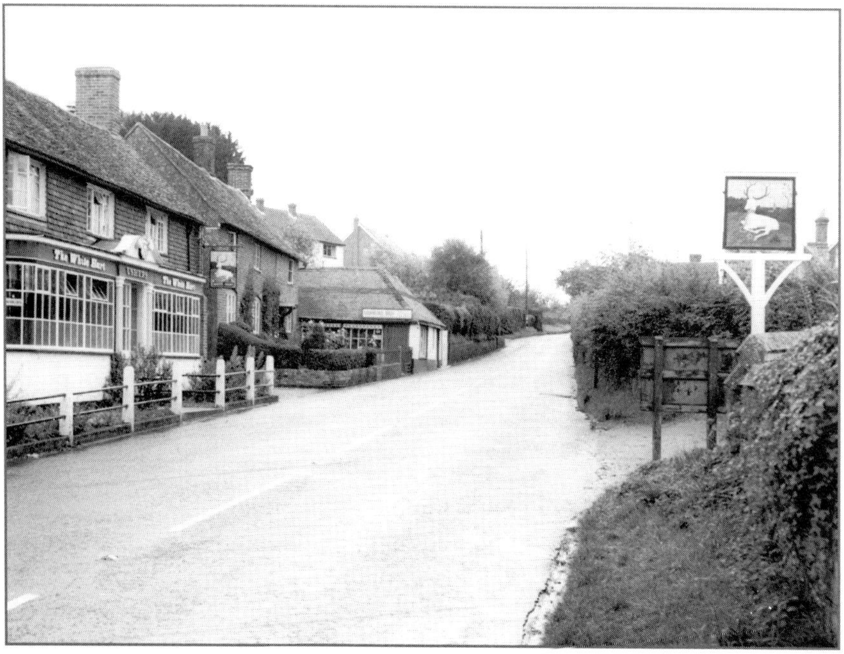

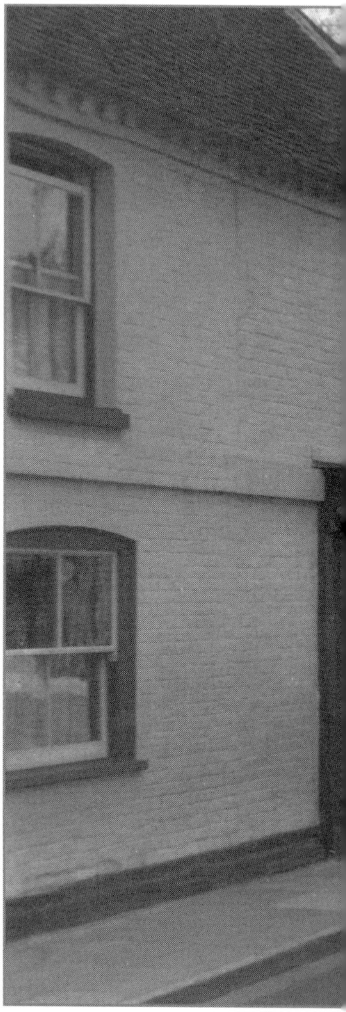

▲ **Wilton, North Street c1950** W166008

Wilton was once the capital of Saxon Wessex, where King Alfred had a residence and founded a priory. Note the International Stores beneath the awning on the left opposite the Six Bells pub (still serving) on the right.

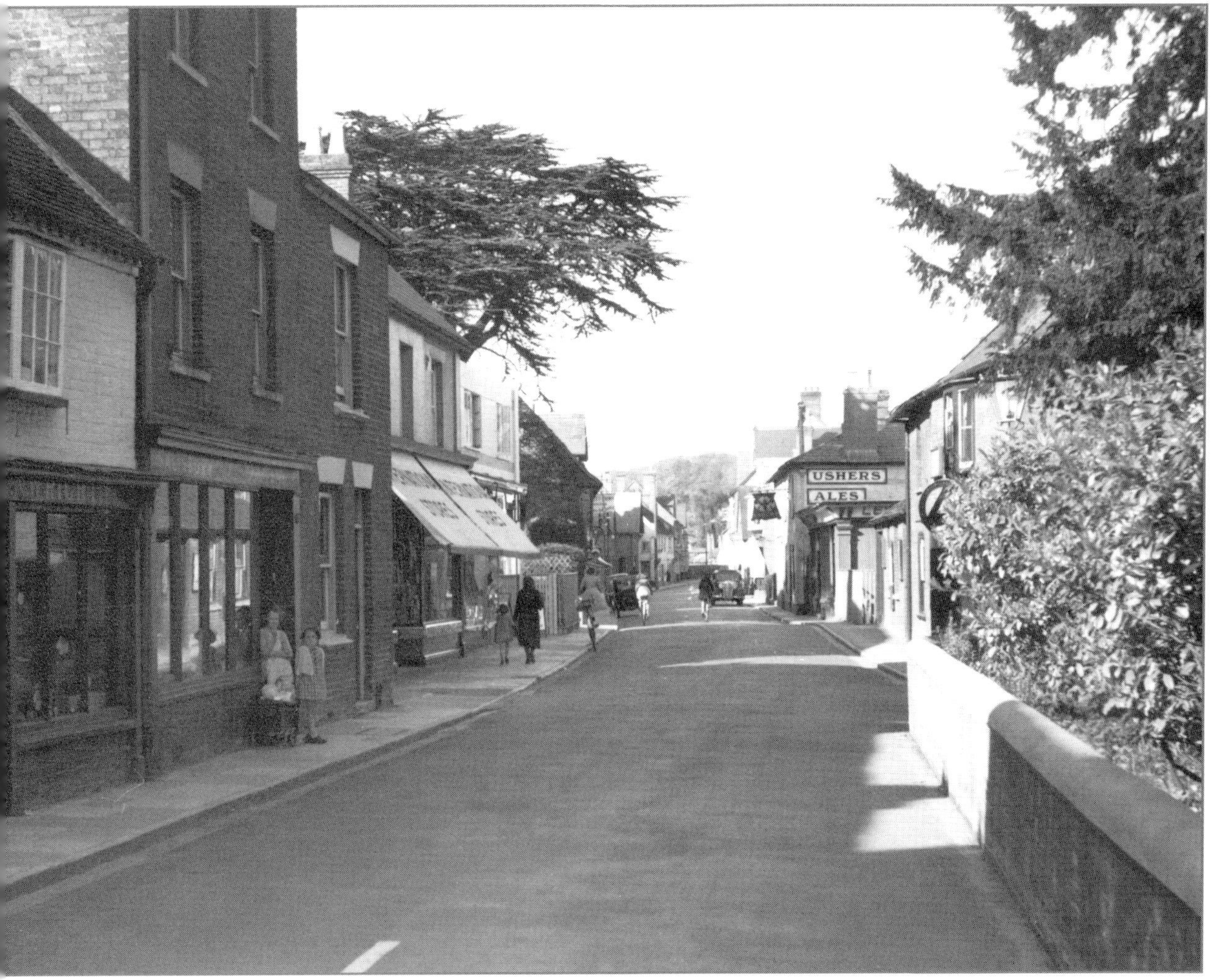

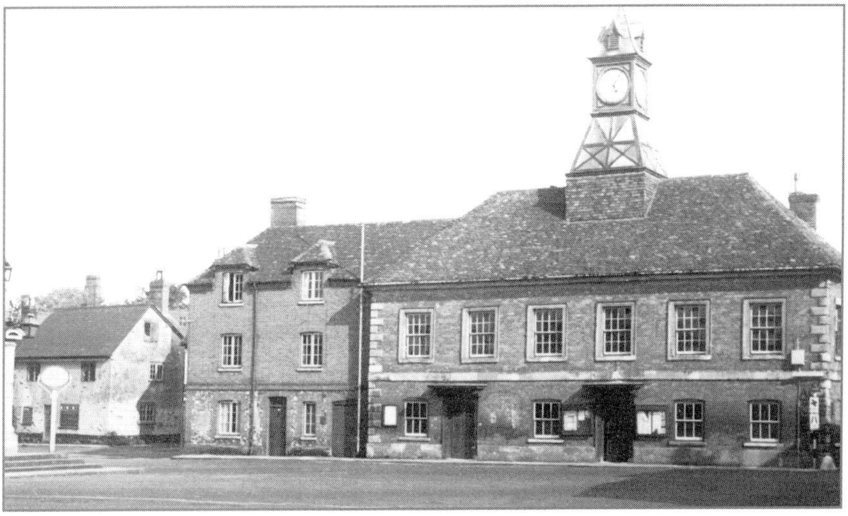

◄ Wilton, The Town Hall from West Street c1950

W166020

This building dates from 1738; it is no longer a town hall, but Wilton Baptist Church. The Royal Wilton carpet factory was granted a royal charter in 1699 by King William III. The town hosted a large weaving industry - the nearby Salisbury Plain was a source of good wool.

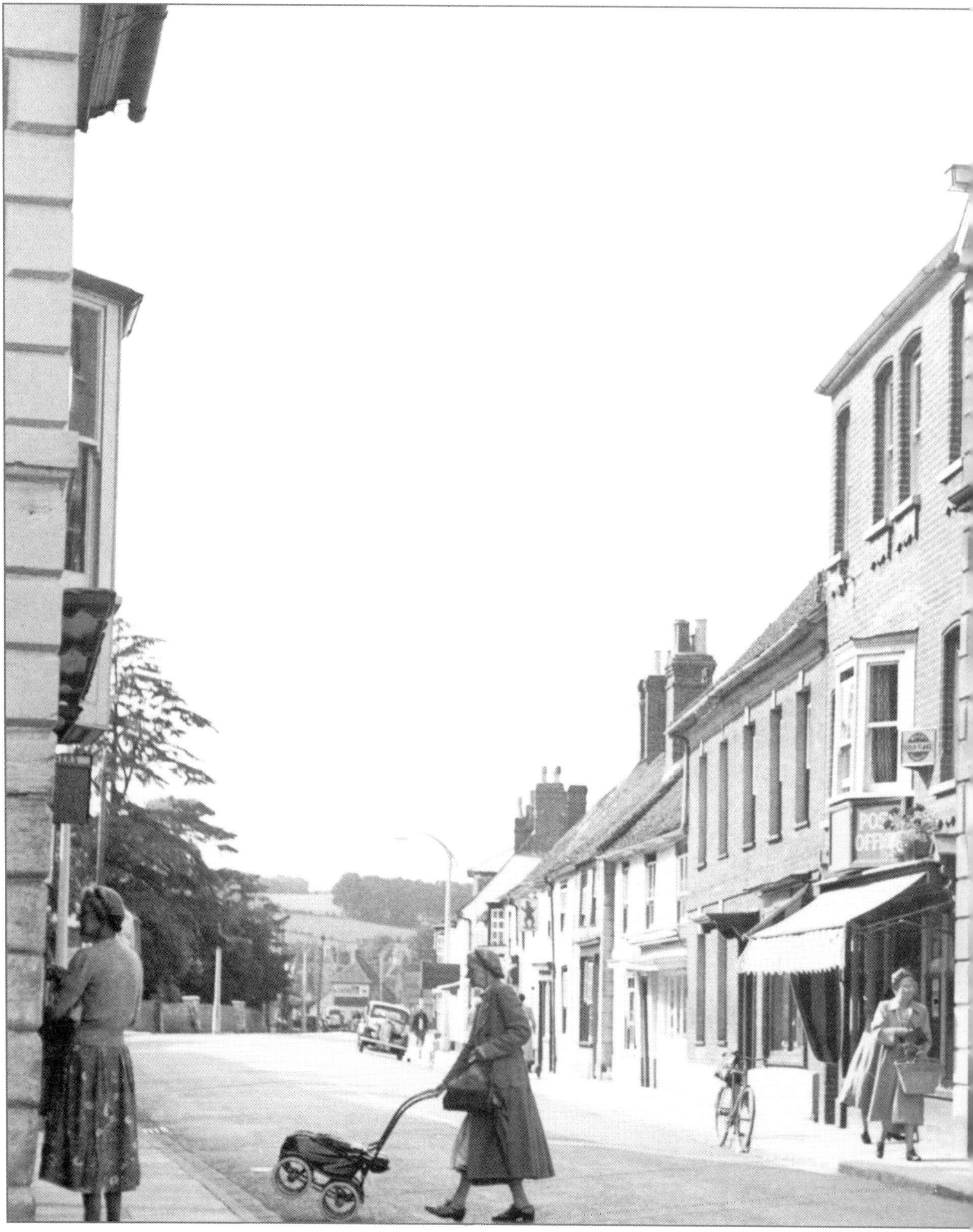

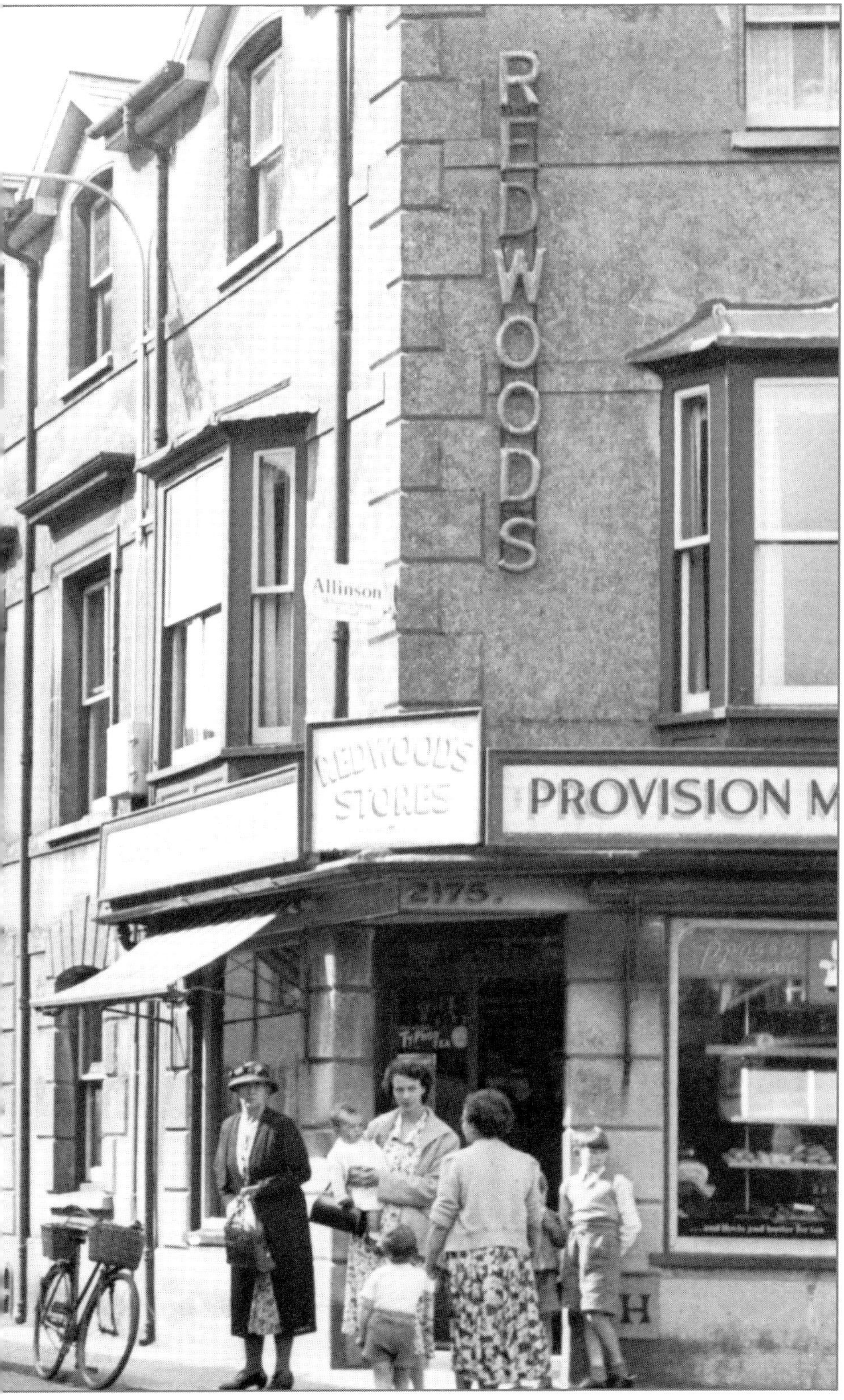

Wilton, West Street c1950 W166027
The town was referred to as Wiltun in 854, so it has changed very little. The town was also once host to an important nunnery, now converted to the stately home of Wilton House. It was from here that the abbess at the time of the Dissolution of the Monasteries retired to Fovant. Note the Post Office on the right.

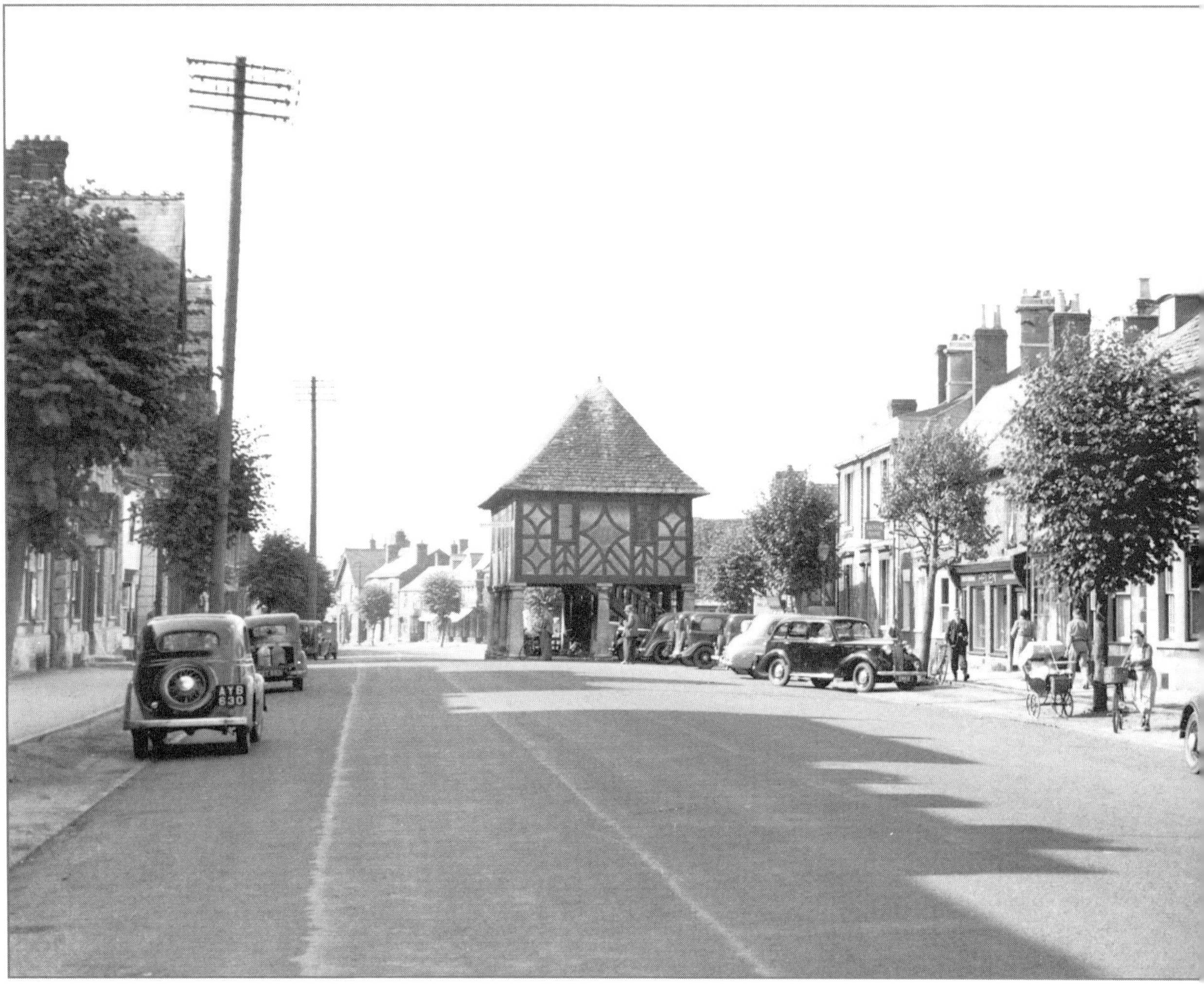

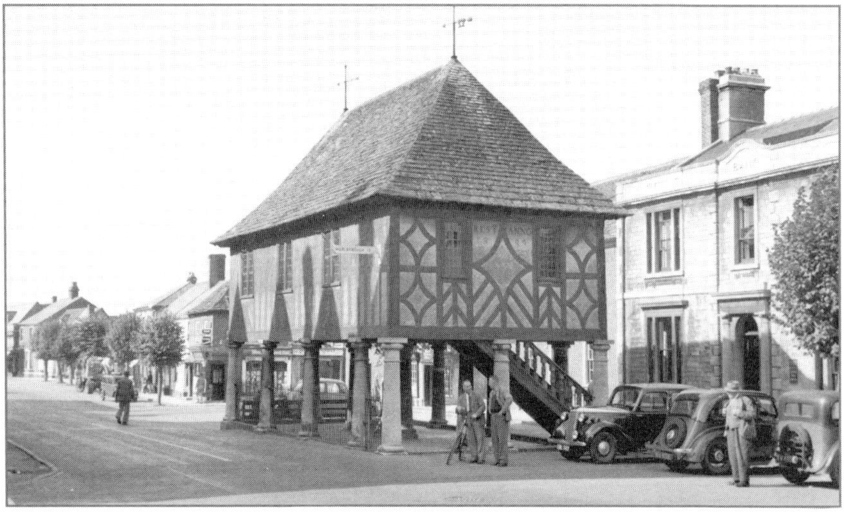

Wootton Bassett
The Town Hall c1950
W171012

Supported on its fifteen Tuscan columns, this curious building now houses a museum of local history. First erected in 1700 by the Earl of Rochester, it was much restored in 1889 by Sir Henry Meux.

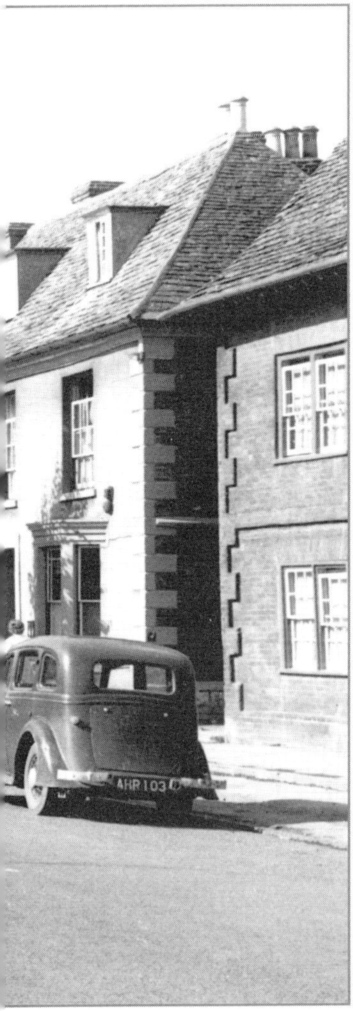

Wootton Bassett High Street c1950

W171011

The village name derives from the Saxon 'wudu' and 'tun'; the name simply means woodland settlement. The Bassett of the name comes from Alan Basset, who held the manor in 1230.

Wootton Rivers The Village c1950

W269002

The village name simply means farmstead by the wood; the Rivers comes from the family name of the lords of the manor in the 13th century. Note the Royal Oak pub on the right.

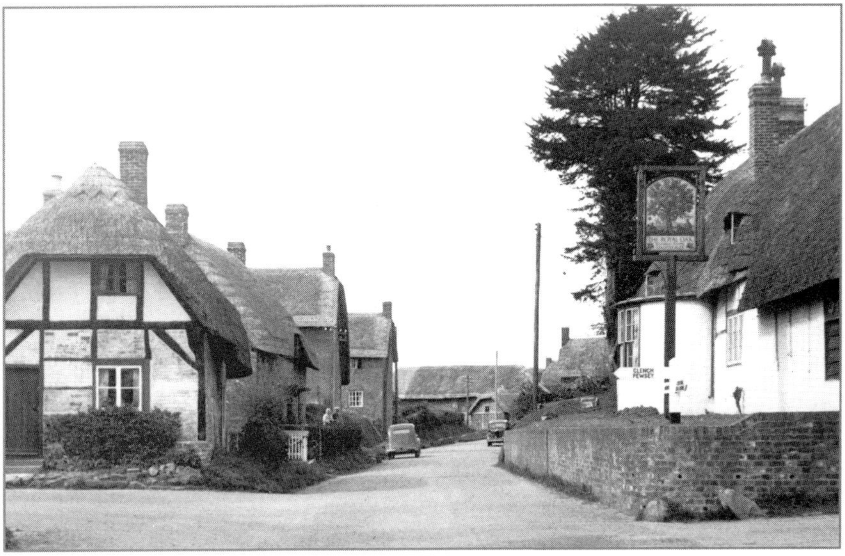

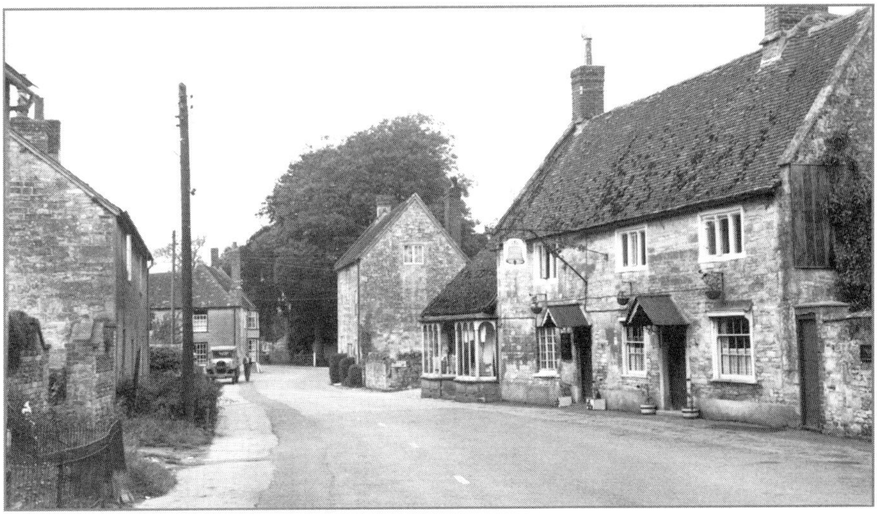

Wylye, The Bell c1950

W270009

The foundations of this pub date from the 14th century. The name of the village simply means the tricky river, one which is liable to flooding.

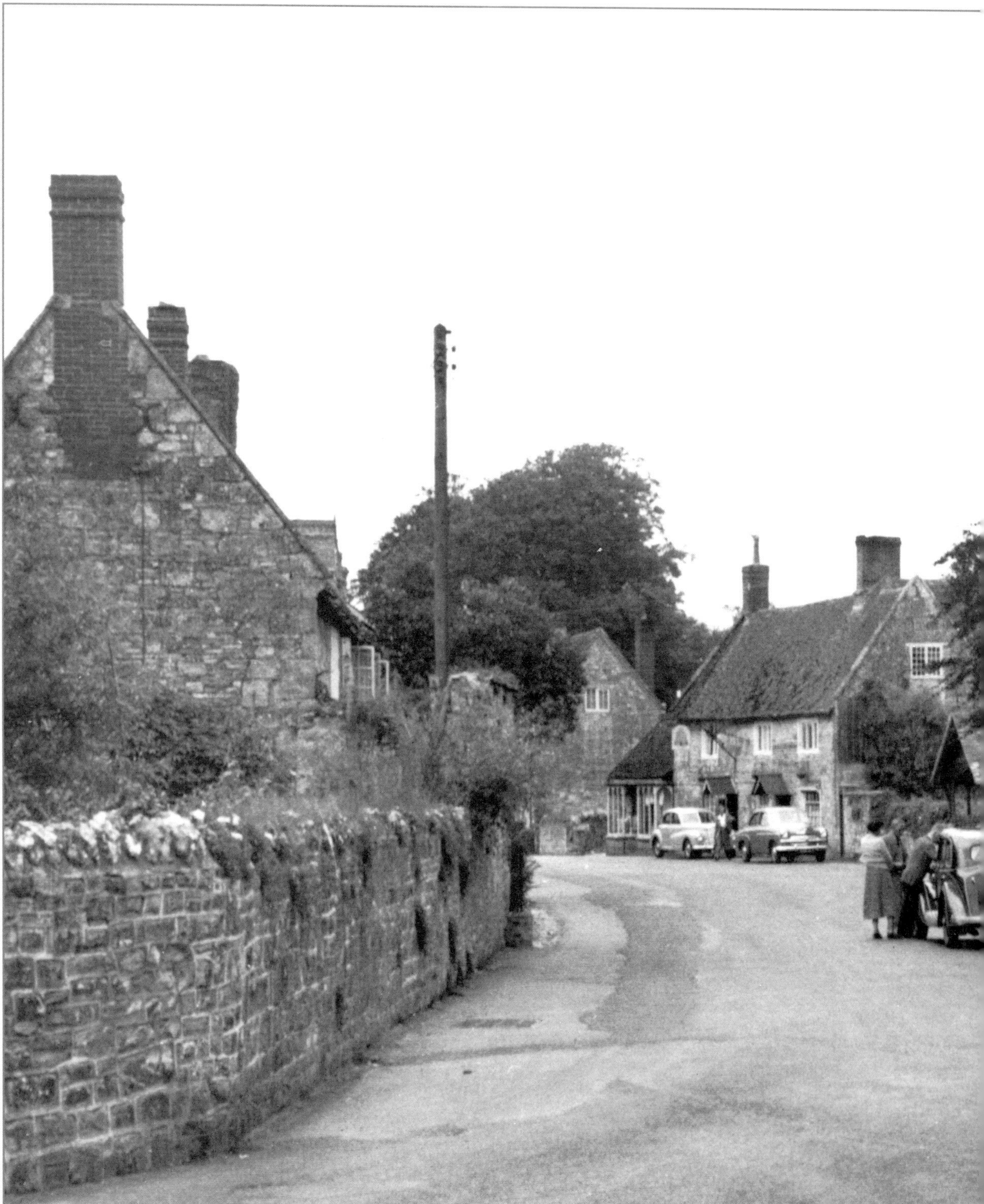

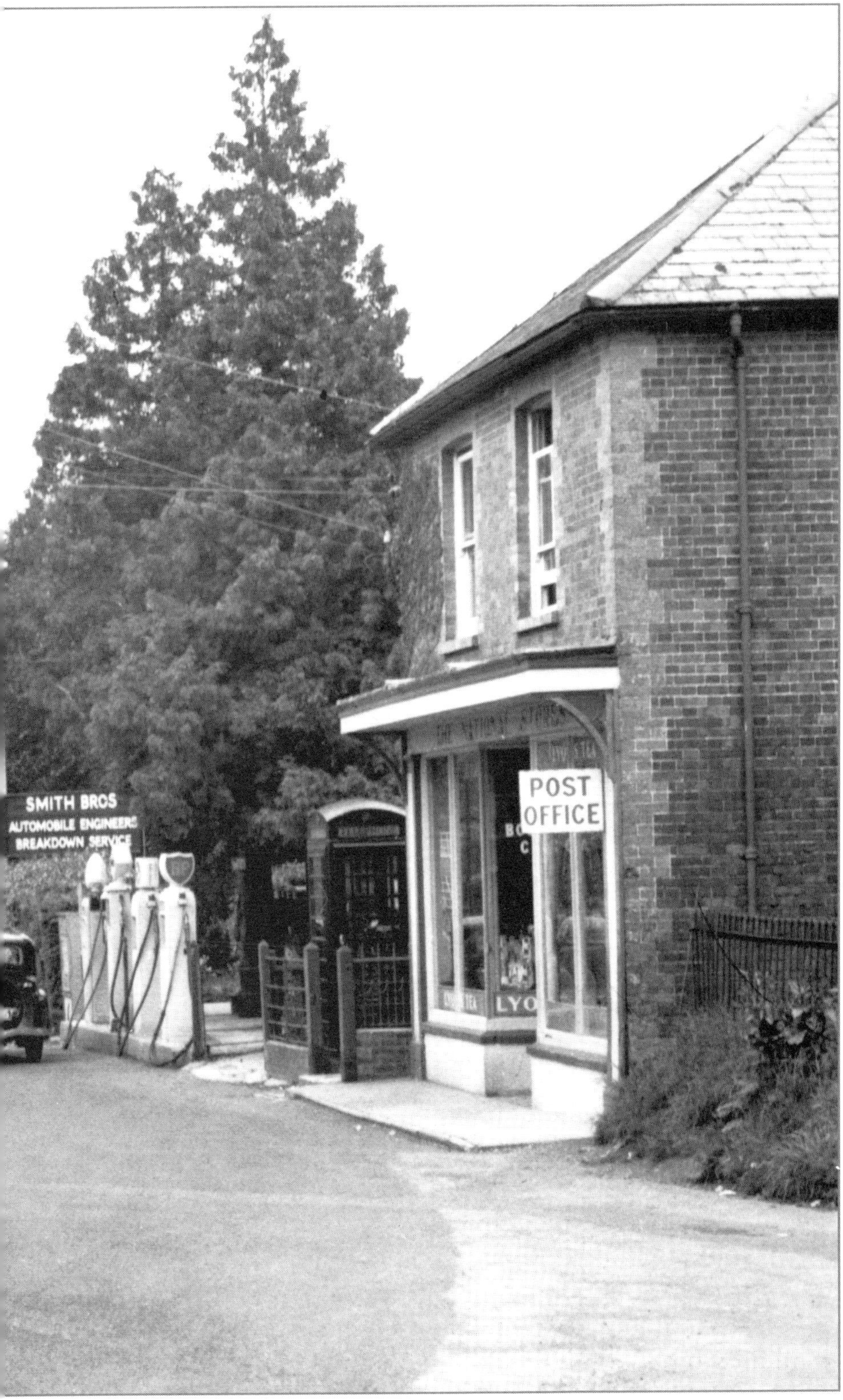

Wylye, The Village c1950 W270005
In the 17th century, the village was credited by John Aubrey with the pioneering of the water-meadow method of farming. Note the Smith Bros sign on the right near the Post Office.

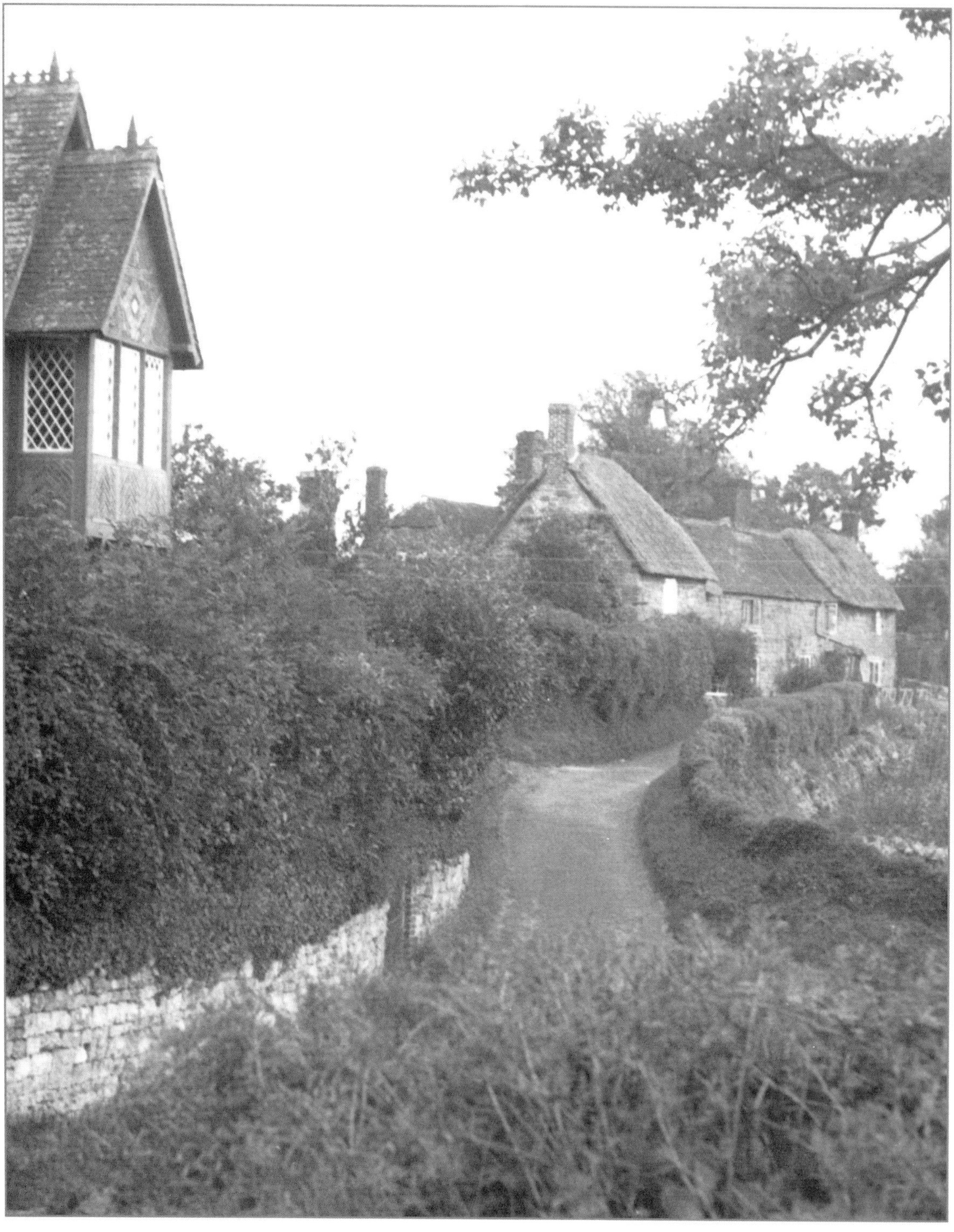

Zeals, The Village c1950 Z3016
Zeals lies on the edge of the ancient forest of Selwood. The name Zeals refers to 'sealas', Saxon for willow tree. In 1655, years after the Civil War was over, Colonel Hugh Grove, a local landowner, joined a Royalist uprising led by Colonel Penruddock. He was executed in Exeter.

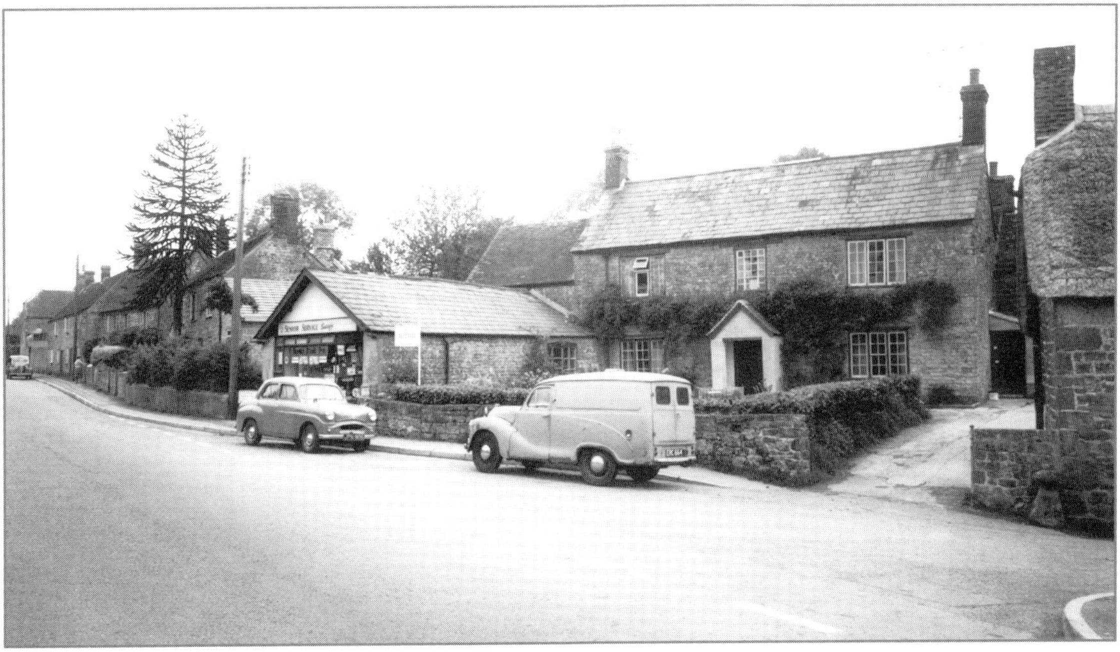

Zeals, The Village c1960 Z3030
The Post Office is now a private residence. The building behind it is also now privately-owned. Fantley Lane, to the right of it, leads past some delightful 17th-century cottages.

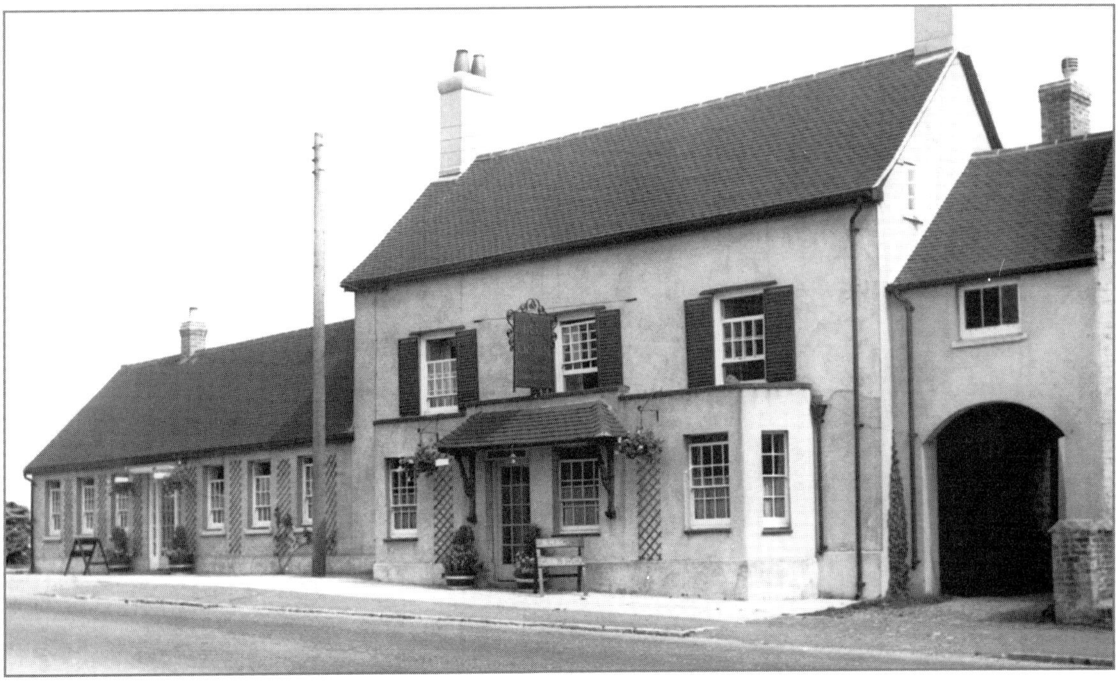

Zeals, The Bell and Crown Inn c1950 Z3006
The pub, on the A303, still exists, and probably benefits from the volume of traffic that makes its way through Zeals on this major trunk road.

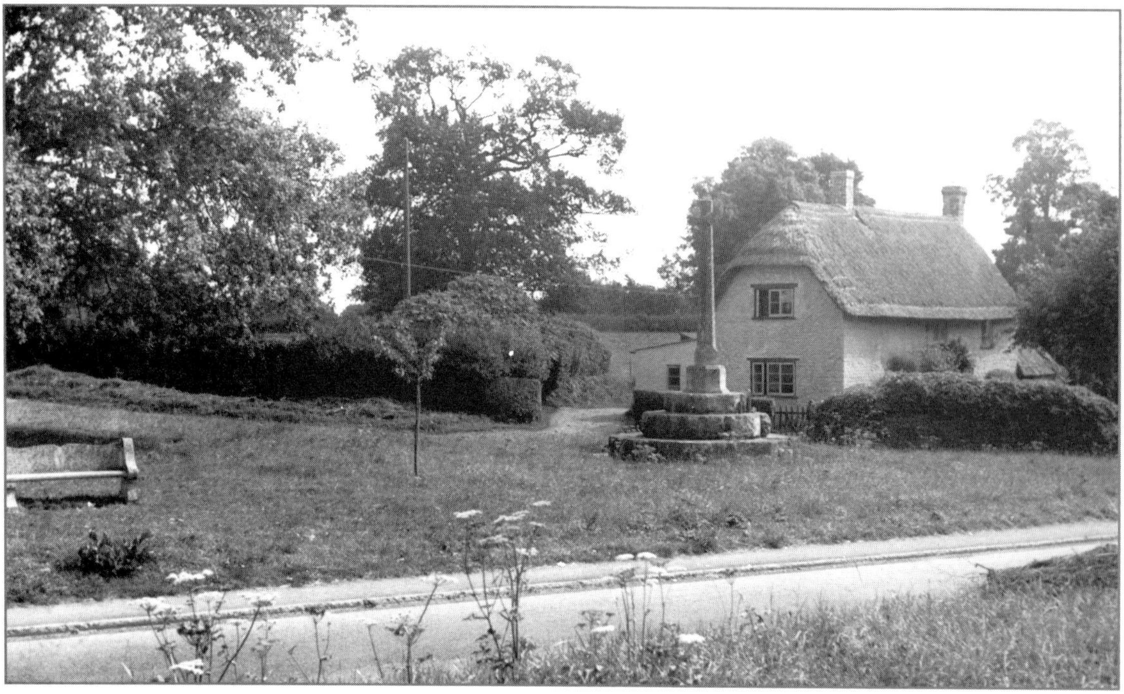

Zeals, The Green c1950 Z3009
The memorial is to the men of the village killed in the two World Wars, and also to 'all patriots'. The nearby bench has been replaced by one inscribed AD MM - the year 2000.

Bibliography

Portrait of Wiltshire by Pamela Street, publisher Hale

The Folklore of Ancient Wiltshire by Katherine Jordan, publisher Wiltshire County Council

The King's England: Wiltshire by Arthur Mee, publisher Hodder & Stoughton

The Wiltshire Village Book by Michael Marshman, publisher Countryside Books

Westbury in Old Photographs by Michael Randall, publisher Alan Sutton

Wiltshire by Ralph Whitlock, publisher Batsford

Wiltshire by Mark Child, publisher Shire Publications Ltd

Wiltshire Place-Names by Martyn Whittock, publisher Countryside Books

Index

Frith Book Co Titles

www.francisfrith.co.uk

The Frith Book Company publishes over 100 new titles each year. A selection of those currently available are listed below. For latest catalogue please contact Frith Book Co.

Town Books 96 pages, approx 100 photos. County and Themed Books 128 pages, approx 150 photos (unless specified). All titles hardback laminated case and jacket except those indicated pb (paperback)

Amersham, Chesham & Rickmansworth (pb)	1-85937-340-2	£9.99
Ancient Monuments & Stone Circles	1-85937-143-4	£17.99
Aylesbury (pb)	1-85937-227-9	£9.99
Bakewell	1-85937-113-2	£12.99
Barnstaple (pb)	1-85937-300-3	£9.99
Bath (pb)	1-85937-419-0	£9.99
Bedford (pb)	1-85937-205-8	£9.99
Berkshire (pb)	1-85937-191-4	£9.99
Berkshire Churches	1-85937-170-1	£17.99
Blackpool (pb)	1-85937-382-8	£9.99
Bognor Regis (pb)	1-85937-431-x	£9.99
Bournemouth	1-85937-067-5	£12.99
Bradford (pb)	1-85937-204-x	£9.99
Brighton & Hove(pb)	1-85937-192-2	£8.99
Bristol (pb)	1-85937-264-3	£9.99
British Life A Century Ago (pb)	1-85937-213-9	£9.99
Buckinghamshire (pb)	1-85937-200-7	£9.99
Camberley (pb)	1-85937-222-8	£9.99
Cambridge (pb)	1-85937-422-0	£9.99
Cambridgeshire (pb)	1-85937-420-4	£9.99
Canals & Waterways (pb)	1-85937-291-0	£9.99
Canterbury Cathedral (pb)	1-85937-179-5	£9.99
Cardiff (pb)	1-85937-093-4	£9.99
Carmarthenshire	1-85937-216-3	£14.99
Chelmsford (pb)	1-85937-310-0	£9.99
Cheltenham (pb)	1-85937-095-0	£9.99
Cheshire (pb)	1-85937-271-6	£9.99
Chester	1-85937-090-x	£12.99
Chesterfield	1-85937-378-x	£9.99
Chichester (pb)	1-85937-228-7	£9.99
Colchester (pb)	1-85937-188-4	£8.99
Cornish Coast	1-85937-163-9	£14.99
Cornwall (pb)	1-85937-229-5	£9.99
Cornwall Living Memories	1-85937-248-1	£14.99
Cotswolds (pb)	1-85937-230-9	£9.99
Cotswolds Living Memories	1-85937-255-4	£14.99
County Durham	1-85937-123-x	£14.99
Croydon Living Memories	1-85937-162-0	£9.99
Cumbria	1-85937-101-9	£14.99
Dartmoor	1-85937-145-0	£14.99
Derby (pb)	1-85937-367-4	£9.99
Derbyshire (pb)	1-85937-196-5	£9.99
Devon (pb)	1-85937-297-x	£9.99
Dorset (pb)	1-85937-269-4	£9.99
Dorset Churches	1-85937-172-8	£17.99
Dorset Coast (pb)	1-85937-299-6	£9.99
Dorset Living Memories	1-85937-210-4	£14.99
Down the Severn	1-85937-118-3	£14.99
Down the Thames (pb)	1-85937-278-3	£9.99
Down the Trent	1-85937-311-9	£14.99
Dublin (pb)	1-85937-231-7	£9.99
East Anglia (pb)	1-85937-265-1	£9.99
East London	1-85937-080-2	£14.99
East Sussex	1-85937-130-2	£14.99
Eastbourne	1-85937-061-6	£12.99
Edinburgh (pb)	1-85937-193-0	£8.99
England in the 1880s	1-85937-331-3	£17.99
English Castles (pb)	1-85937-434-4	£9.99
English Country Houses	1-85937-161-2	£17.99
Essex (pb)	1-85937-270-8	£9.99
Exeter	1-85937-126-4	£12.99
Exmoor	1-85937-132-9	£14.99
Falmouth	1-85937-066-7	£12.99
Folkestone (pb)	1-85937-124-8	£9.99
Glasgow (pb)	1-85937-190-6	£9.99
Gloucestershire	1-85937-102-7	£14.99
Great Yarmouth (pb)	1-85937-426-3	£9.99
Greater Manchester (pb)	1-85937-266-x	£9.99
Guildford (pb)	1-85937-410-7	£9.99
Hampshire (pb)	1-85937-279-1	£9.99
Hampshire Churches (pb)	1-85937-207-4	£9.99
Harrogate	1-85937-423-9	£9.99
Hastings & Bexhill (pb)	1-85937-131-0	£9.99
Heart of Lancashire (pb)	1-85937-197-3	£9.99
Helston (pb)	1-85937-214-7	£9.99
Hereford (pb)	1-85937-175-2	£9.99
Herefordshire	1-85937-174-4	£14.99
Hertfordshire (pb)	1-85937-247-3	£9.99
Horsham (pb)	1-85937-432-8	£9.99
Humberside	1-85937-215-5	£14.99
Hythe, Romney Marsh & Ashford	1-85937-256-2	£9.99

Available from your local bookshop or from the publisher

Frith Book Co Titles (continued)

Ipswich (pb)	1-85937-424-7	£9.99
Ireland (pb)	1-85937-181-7	£9.99
Isle of Man (pb)	1-85937-268-6	£9.99
Isles of Scilly	1-85937-136-1	£14.99
Isle of Wight (pb)	1-85937-429-8	£9.99
Isle of Wight Living Memories	1-85937-304-6	£14.99
Kent (pb)	1-85937-189-2	£9.99
Kent Living Memories	1-85937-125-6	£14.99
Lake District (pb)	1-85937-275-9	£9.99
Lancaster, Morecambe & Heysham (pb)	1-85937-233-3	£9.99
Leeds (pb)	1-85937-202-3	£9.99
Leicester	1-85937-073-x	£12.99
Leicestershire (pb)	1-85937-185-x	£9.99
Lincolnshire (pb)	1-85937-433-6	£9.99
Liverpool & Merseyside (pb)	1-85937-234-1	£9.99
London (pb)	1-85937-183-3	£9.99
Ludlow (pb)	1-85937-176-0	£9.99
Luton (pb)	1-85937-235-x	£9.99
Maidstone	1-85937-056-x	£14.99
Manchester (pb)	1-85937-198-1	£9.99
Middlesex	1-85937-158-2	£14.99
New Forest	1-85937-128-0	£14.99
Newark (pb)	1-85937-366-6	£9.99
Newport, Wales (pb)	1-85937-258-9	£9.99
Newquay (pb)	1-85937-421-2	£9.99
Norfolk (pb)	1-85937-195-7	£9.99
Norfolk Living Memories	1-85937-217-1	£14.99
Northamptonshire	1-85937-150-7	£14.99
Northumberland Tyne & Wear (pb)	1-85937-281-3	£9.99
North Devon Coast	1-85937-146-9	£14.99
North Devon Living Memories	1-85937-261-9	£14.99
North London	1-85937-206-6	£14.99
North Wales (pb)	1-85937-298-8	£9.99
North Yorkshire (pb)	1-85937-236-8	£9.99
Norwich (pb)	1-85937-194-9	£8.99
Nottingham (pb)	1-85937-324-0	£9.99
Nottinghamshire (pb)	1-85937-187-6	£9.99
Oxford (pb)	1-85937-411-5	£9.99
Oxfordshire (pb)	1-85937-430-1	£9.99
Peak District (pb)	1-85937-280-5	£9.99
Penzance	1-85937-069-1	£12.99
Peterborough (pb)	1-85937-219-8	£9.99
Piers	1-85937-237-6	£17.99
Plymouth	1-85937-119-1	£12.99
Poole & Sandbanks (pb)	1-85937-251-1	£9.99
Preston (pb)	1-85937-212-0	£9.99
Reading (pb)	1-85937-238-4	£9.99
Romford (pb)	1-85937-319-4	£9.99
Salisbury (pb)	1-85937-239-2	£9.99
Scarborough (pb)	1-85937-379-8	£9.99
St Albans (pb)	1-85937-341-0	£9.99
St Ives (pb)	1-85937415-8	£9.99
Scotland (pb)	1-85937-182-5	£9.99
Scottish Castles (pb)	1-85937-323-2	£9.99
Sevenoaks & Tunbridge	1-85937-057-8	£12.99
Sheffield, South Yorks (pb)	1-85937-267-8	£9.99
Shrewsbury (pb)	1-85937-325-9	£9.99
Shropshire (pb)	1-85937-326-7	£9.99
Somerset	1-85937-153-1	£14.99
South Devon Coast	1-85937-107-8	£14.99
South Devon Living Memories	1-85937-168-x	£14.99
South Hams	1-85937-220-1	£14.99
Southampton (pb)	1-85937-427-1	£9.99
Southport (pb)	1-85937-425-5	£9.99
Staffordshire	1-85937-047-0	£12.99
Stratford upon Avon	1-85937-098-5	£12.99
Suffolk (pb)	1-85937-221-x	£9.99
Suffolk Coast	1-85937-259-7	£14.99
Surrey (pb)	1-85937-240-6	£9.99
Sussex (pb)	1-85937-184-1	£9.99
Swansea (pb)	1-85937-167-1	£9.99
Tees Valley & Cleveland	1-85937-211-2	£14.99
Thanet (pb)	1-85937-116-7	£9.99
Tiverton (pb)	1-85937-178-7	£9.99
Torbay	1-85937-063-2	£12.99
Truro	1-85937-147-7	£12.99
Victorian and Edwardian Cornwall	1-85937-252-x	£14.99
Victorian & Edwardian Devon	1-85937-253-8	£14.99
Victorian & Edwardian Kent	1-85937-149-3	£14.99
Vic & Ed Maritime Album	1-85937-144-2	£17.99
Victorian and Edwardian Sussex	1-85937-157-4	£14.99
Victorian & Edwardian Yorkshire	1-85937-154-x	£14.99
Victorian Seaside	1-85937-159-0	£17.99
Villages of Devon (pb)	1-85937-293-7	£9.99
Villages of Kent (pb)	1-85937-294-5	£9.99
Villages of Sussex (pb)	1-85937-295-3	£9.99
Warwickshire (pb)	1-85937-203-1	£9.99
Welsh Castles (pb)	1-85937-322-4	£9.99
West Midlands (pb)	1-85937-289-9	£9.99
West Sussex	1-85937-148-5	£14.99
West Yorkshire (pb)	1-85937-201-5	£9.99
Weymouth (pb)	1-85937-209-0	£9.99
Wiltshire (pb)	1-85937-277-5	£9.99
Wiltshire Churches (pb)	1-85937-171-x	£9.99
Wiltshire Living Memories	1-85937-245-7	£14.99
Winchester (pb)	1-85937-428-x	£9.99
Windmills & Watermills	1-85937-242-2	£17.99
Worcester (pb)	1-85937-165-5	£9.99
Worcestershire	1-85937-152-3	£14.99
York (pb)	1-85937-199-x	£9.99
Yorkshire (pb)	1-85937-186-8	£9.99
Yorkshire Living Memories	1-85937-166-3	£14.99

See Frith books on the internet www.francisfrith.co.uk

FRITH PRODUCTS & SERVICES

Francis Frith would doubtless be pleased to know that the pioneering publishing venture he started in 1860 still continues today. A hundred and forty years later, The Francis Frith Collection continues in the same innovative tradition and is now one of the foremost publishers of vintage photographs in the world. Some of the current activities include:

Interior Decoration

Today Frith's photographs can be seen framed and as giant wall murals in thousands of pubs, restaurants, hotels, banks, retail stores and other public buildings throughout the country. In every case they enhance the unique local atmosphere of the places they depict and provide reminders of gentler days in an increasingly busy and frenetic world.

Product Promotions

Frith products are used by many major companies to promote the sales of their own products or to reinforce their own history and heritage. Frith promotions have been used by Hovis bread, Courage beers, Scots Porage Oats, Colman's mustard, Cadbury's foods, Mellow Birds coffee, Dunhill pipe tobacco, Guinness, and Bulmer's Cider.

Genealogy and Family History

As the interest in family history and roots grows world-wide, more and more people are turning to Frith's photographs of Great Britain for images of the towns, villages and streets where their ancestors lived; and, of course, photographs of the churches and chapels where their ancestors were christened, married and buried are an essential part of every genealogy tree and family album.

Frith Products

All Frith photographs are available Framed or just as Mounted Prints and Posters (size 23 x 16 inches). These may be ordered from the address below. From time to time other products - Address Books, Calendars, Table Mats, etc - are available.

The Internet

Already twenty thousand Frith photographs can be viewed and purchased on the internet through the Frith websites and a myriad of partner sites.

For more detailed information on Frith companies and products, look at these sites:

www.francisfrith.co.uk
www.francisfrith.com
(for North American visitors)

See the complete list of Frith Books at:
www.francisfrith.co.uk

This web site is regularly updated with the latest list of publications from the Frith Book Company. If you wish to buy books relating to another part of the country that your local bookshop does not stock, you may purchase on-line.

For further information, trade, or author enquiries please contact us at the address below:

The Francis Frith Collection, Frith's Barn, Teffont, Salisbury, Wiltshire, England SP3 5QP.
Tel: +44 (0)1722 716 376 Fax: +44 (0)1722 716 881 Email: sales@francisfrith.co.uk

See Frith books on the internet www.francisfrith.co.uk

To receive your FREE Mounted Print

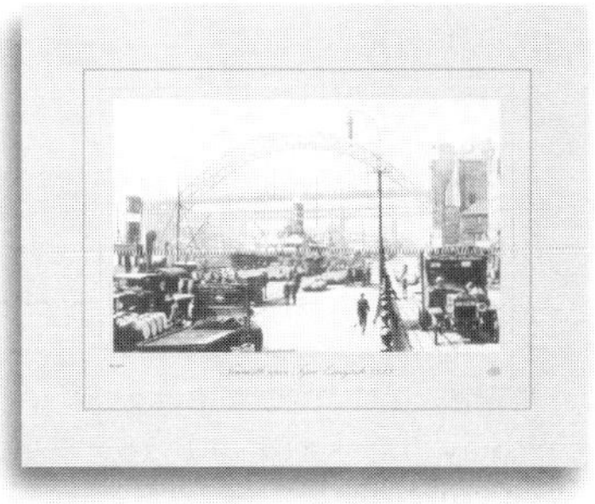

Mounted Print
Overall size 14 x 11 inches

Cut out this Voucher and return it with your remittance for £1.95 to cover postage and handling, to UK addresses. For overseas addresses please include £4.00 post and handling.
Choose any photograph included in this book. Your SEPIA print will be A4 in size, and mounted in a cream mount with burgundy rule line, overall size 14 x 11 inches.

Order additional Mounted Prints at HALF PRICE (only £7.49 each*)
If there are further pictures you would like to order, possibly as gifts for friends and family, purchase them at half price (no additional postage and handling required).

Have your Mounted Prints framed*
For an additional £14.95 per print you can have your chosen Mounted Print framed in an elegant polished wood and gilt moulding, overall size 16 x 13 inches (no additional postage and handling required).

*** IMPORTANT!**
These special prices are only available if ordered using the original voucher on this page (no copies permitted) and at the same time as your free Mounted Print, for delivery to the same address

Frith Collectors' Guild

From time to time we publish a magazine of news and stories about Frith photographs and further special offers of Frith products. If you would like 12 months FREE membership, please return this form.

Send completed forms to:
The Francis Frith Collection, Frith's Barn, Teffont, Salisbury, Wiltshire SP3 5QP

Voucher for **FREE** and Reduced Price Frith Prints

Picture no.	Page number	Qty	Mounted @ £7.49	Framed + £14.95	Total Cost
		1	**Free of charge***	£	£
			£7.49	£	£
			£7.49	£	£
			£7.49	£	£
			£7.49	£	£
			£7.49	£	£

Please allow 28 days for delivery — *** Post & handling** **£1.95**

Book Title .... **Total Order Cost** **£**

Please do not photocopy this voucher. Only the original is valid, so please cut it out and return it to us.

I enclose a cheque / postal order for £ ....
made payable to 'The Francis Frith Collection'
OR please debit my Mastercard / Visa / Switch / Amex card
(credit cards please on all overseas orders)

Number ....

Issue No (Switch only) .... Valid from (Amex/Switch) ....

Expires .... Signature ....

Name Mr/Mrs/Ms ....

Address ....

....

....

.... Postcode ....

Daytime Tel No .... Valid to 31/12/02

The Francis Frith Collectors' Guild

Please enrol me as a member for 12 months free of charge.

Name Mr/Mrs/Ms ....

Address ....

....

....

.... Postcode ....

Free Print - see overleaf

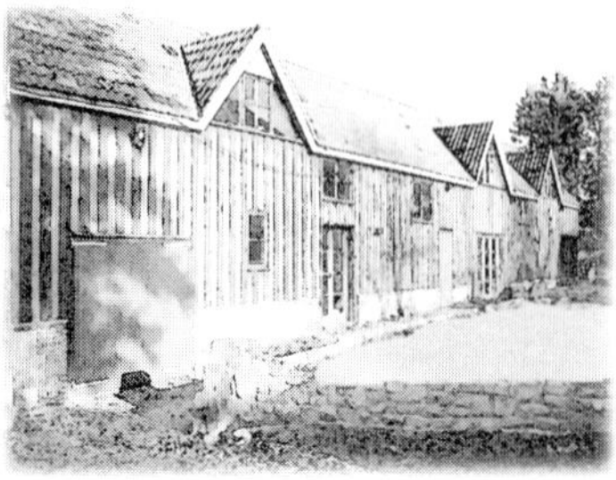

Would you like to find out more about Francis Frith?

We have recently recruited some entertaining speakers who are happy to visit local groups, clubs and societies to give an illustrated talk documenting Frith's travels and photographs. If you are a member of such a group and are interested in hosting a presentation, we would love to hear from you.

Our speakers bring with them a small selection of our local town and county books, together with sample prints. They are happy to take orders. A small proportion of the order value is donated to the group who have hosted the presentation. The talks are therefore an excellent way of fundraising for small groups and societies.

Can you help us with information about any of the Frith photographs in this book?

We are gradually compiling an historical record for each of the photographs in the Frith archive. It is always fascinating to find out the names of the people shown in the pictures, as well as insights into the shops, buildings and other features depicted.

If you recognize anyone in the photographs in this book, or if you have information not already included in the author's caption, do let us know. We would love to hear from you, and will try to publish it in future books or articles.

Our production team

Frith books are produced by a small dedicated team at offices in the converted Grade II listed 18th-century barn at Teffont near Salisbury, illustrated above. Most have worked with the Frith Collection for many years. All have in common one quality: they have a passion for the Frith Collection. The team is constantly expanding, but currently includes:

Jason Buck, John Buck, Douglas Burns, Heather Crisp, Isobel Hall, Rob Hames, Hazel Heaton, Peter Horne, James Kinnear, Tina Leary, Hannah Marsh, Eliza Sackett, Terence Sackett, Sandra Sanger, Shelley Tolcher, Susanna Walker, Clive Wathen and Jenny Wathen.